National Geographic

Essential Visual History of World Mythology

National Geographic

Essential Visual History of World Mythology

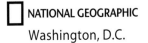
NATIONAL GEOGRAPHIC
Washington, D.C.

The Greek Olympians fighting for supremacy against the Titans, who they eventually replace.

Hierarchy of the
Ancient Near Eastern
gods, see p. 31

Table of Contents

Thoth invents hieroglyphics, see p. 99

Apollo and Daphne, see p. 133

Persephone and the pomegranate seed, see p. 154

Ovid's Metamorphoses,
see p. 212

The Fenrir wolf and the battle of Ragnarok, see p. 235

An avatar of Vishnu, see p. 313

Nüwa creates people and animals, see p. 335

Fukurokuju, one of the seven
gods of luck, see p. 365

The Aztec creator god Quetzalcóatl,
see pp. 390–391

Birth of the Yoruban trickster god Eshu, see p. 447

Uluru, also known as Ayers Rock, see pp. 466–467

Elements of the Book

The bold text states the title of the chapter.

Titles of the spreads are indicated here.

■ Athena was the goddess of arts, crafts, war, and wisdom

■ She invented the plow, rake, bridle, chariot, pot, and flute

■ She taught the Greeks mathematics, as well as how to weave, spin, and cook

■ She was often depicted in full armor

Athena

Athena, also known as Minerva in the Roman tradition, was the goddess of war, wisdom, and the arts. Athena's parents were Zeus, the god who ruled heaven, and Metis, the Titan who governed intelligence.

Athena was often accompanied by an owl, as depicted on this Athenian coin

She was referred to as the Virgin goddess—Athena Parthenos—by the Greeks. True to this, she never had any love affairs, unlike most of the other Olympic gods and goddesses. She was named the patron goddess of many Greek cities including, most famously, Athens and Sparta. The artistic depictions of her in this role often show her bearing full military arms.

However, she was not only a warrior. She was also the patron of craftsmen and artists. As a friend of the demi-god Prometheus, she gladly shared her wisdom and intelligence with humankind.

The Cult of Athena

As goddess of war, Athena Promachos was associated with defense rather than attack. The Greeks built her shrines on top of their citadels so that she might defend their cities against invaders. The Greeks also built her shrines on the prows of their triremes so that she might protect their ships in battle. As Athena was also the goddess of wisdom and the arts, philosophers, historians, teachers, sculptors, weavers, and potters also built her shrines within their homes.

◆ Worship of Isis, p. 79

The **main text** features the given god or myth and identifies its proper cultural and mythological context.

Key facts give the significant attributes and functions of the god or goddess.

Special topic boxes highlight a specific religious or cultural aspect.

Page references to related topics in the book are given at the bottom of the page.

Picture related text that describes a selected narrative or myth. Not a description of the photo itself.

Athena and Arachne When the mortal woman Arachne, a famous weaver, challenged Athena to a contest (**1**), the goddess could not refuse. She wove a tapestry showing her competition against Poseidon at Athens, while Arachne wove a tapestry showing Zeus's 21 infidelities. Outraged by the subject of Arachne's tapestry, Athena destroyed Arachne's work. Later, when Arachne realized her arrogance, she hung herself, but Athena took pity on her. She brought her back to life as a spider.

Competition With Poseidon Over Attica When people moved to Attica, the sea god Poseidon and Athena competed for the new city. First, Poseidon plunged his trident into the ground and a river began to flow, giving the people easy access to the sea. Then, Athena offered the people a domesticated olive tree (**3**), giving the people an endless supply of wood, oil, and food. Seeing the value of the second gift, the people named their city Athens for their new patron.

Numbered picture references within the text match each image with its context.

Athena and Medusa One day Poseidon chased a beautiful young girl named Medusa into one of Athena's temples. Catching the girl under the goddess's statue on the altar, he raped her. Furious about what hap- / pened in her temple, Athena transformed Medusa into a hideous, green gorgon with snakes for hair (**2**). Afterward, all humans who met the gaze of Medusa were turned to stone until she was slain by Perseus.

Figures and Stories Relevant to Athena

Zeus, see pp. 120–123

Competition With Hera and Aphrodite, see Aphrodite, pp. 42–143

The Apostles, see pp. 442–447

Perseus, pp. 442–447

The Trojan War, see pp. 186–187

Framed boxes refer to stories and figures surrounding the given person or theme.

Ancient Near Eastern Mythology

One of the city gates of Babylon was consecrated to the goddess Ishtar

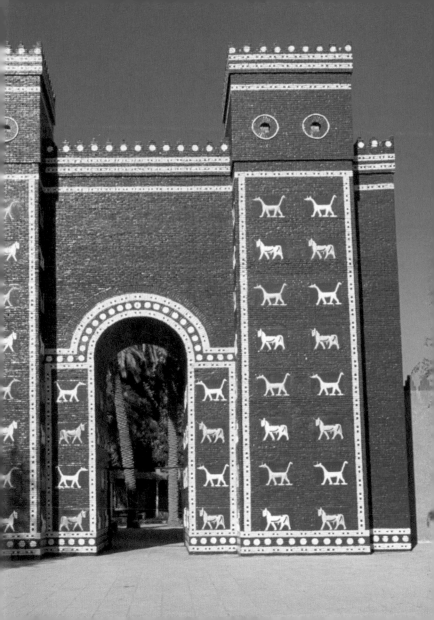

Ancient Near Eastern Mythology

The ancient Near East was the site of the earliest high civilization: Mesopotamia. A rich legacy of texts, addressing all aspects of human life, has survived from this cultural center. Quantum leaps in cultural history took place here, including the invention of writing and the wheel. Thus, in many respects this region can be viewed as the cradle of future cultures, both Eastern and Western.

The cultures of the ancient Near East are considered to include all civilizations that used the cuneiform writing system (**1**), as well as a few other forms of writing, such as Luwian hieroglyphs and astroglyphs, or star pictographs. The most widely used ancient Near Eastern languages were Sumerian, Babylonian-Assyrian, also known as Akkadian, and Hittite. Other languages with more limited reach included Hurritic and Ugaritic. Written sources from these cultures have been found from Turkey (**3**, Hattusa in Central Asia) in the north to the Levant in the southwest and Iraq in the east.

The texts surviving from this period reflect many diverse areas of human endeavor. Documents concerned with daily affairs include administrative and economic texts, such as certificates and notices; legal documents, such as laws and treaties; letters and inscriptions; and scientific records, such as glossaries and medicinal potions. Works of cultural creativity have been preserved in the form of myths, epics, hymns, lamentations, prayers, rituals, elegies, love songs, debates, satires, sayings, fables, riddles, and texts from the ancient educational system, and narratives and dialogues aimed at passing on wisdom to the next generation.

Due to its natural borders, the nearby Egyptian civilization was relatively stable, experienced minimal foreign influence and relatively few wars, and remained monolingual over a substantial part of its history. On the other hand, ancient Mesopotamia was geographically more open, developing into an ethnically heterogeneous state with a multilingual culture. Although continually plagued with wars and unrest, it also repeatedly succeeded in integrating diverse external influences.

This phenomenon is also reflected in the areas of religion and mythology. The worship of a large number of different gods was typical among the diverse cultures of the ancient Near East (**2**, Sumerian religious statuette). By the middle of the third millennium B.C., catalogues of Mesopotamian gods contained hundreds of systematically organized names. While the main gods of different ethnic groups were often similar, the worship of other divinities, even across cultural borders, was an accepted practice. The same god could also be depicted and experienced in quite different ways: as a human-like

3

figure, a symbol, a plant or animal (e.g., wheat or a lion), a heavenly body (e.g., the moon), or a powerful natural phenomenon (e.g., a storm). It was also believed that the gods could appear to human beings in dreams and even carry them off to heaven or the underworld.

Early writers worked conscientiously to record their knowledge about the world in encyclopedia-like collections. The first explicit theological documents arose as part of this effort. These consisted of lists and charts of the gods, which people had attempted to place in a logical order. These texts in particular give modern observers—despite their separation from the chroniclers by up to 5,000 years—detailed impressions of the ideas held by people of those times. The sphere of the gods was considered to be organized in the same hierarchical structures as the human world. Thus, there were high rulers among the gods, responsible for a city-state or an entire country, as well as subordinate gods, who functioned as ministers, officials, or messengers. Ruling deities were supported by family members and court officials, including such diverse personnel as barbers and sweepers. Human rulers were seen as mere representatives of the true, divine sovereign. The gods who ruled cities and states were usually conceived of as male. There were exceptions, however, such as Inana (**4**, ancient Babylonian vase), who was revered as the ruling

goddess of several cities.

Along with the great power attributed to the gods, people believed themselves to be vulnerable to demonic beings, who were viewed as occupying an intermediate zone between humans and the gods. In addition, the dead were believed to hold power over the life and death of people on earth.

The great themes of human existence have remained constant over the millennia: love and hate; birth, illness, and death; rulers and subjects; order and chaos; and war and peace. While some people today seek support in chatrooms and self-help books, the people of the ancient world looked to stories for guidance and inspiration. Myths, such as those passed down in great detail from ancient Mesopotamia, addressed the fundamental questions of life. The

earliest myths are dated from the third millennium B.C. (**5**, Sumerian hero with six locks of hair, 2500 B.C.), while others date to the second and first millennium B.C. The material they report, however, is often much older, since myths were typically handed down orally for centuries before people attempted to set them down in writing. For example, the earliest known clay tablets recording the story of King Etana, who was said to be carried into heaven by an eagle, date from the 18th century B.C. However, surviving artwork depicting motifs from this story prove that the tale was well-known in the 24th century B.C.

Most of the scribes who recorded myths and other literary works went unnamed, and thus remain hidden from us by the mists of time. The earliest exception dates back to the 23rd century B.C. Several texts in the Sumerian language give the name of their author as Enheduana, which might be translated as "adornment of (the god of) heaven." From these texts and other historical sources, it becomes clear that this earliest author of world literature was a woman of royal descent—a high priestess who held the most important religious office of her time.

- Divine entities were present at the beginning of creation

- The first gods were usually heaven and earth or primordial water

- Some myths claim that the world was created when heaven separated from earth

- In other myths, the world was created when heaven and earth united

- In a Babylonian myth, the universe came into being when freshwater mixed together with saltwater

The Creation of the Universe

Rather than an impersonal creation through matter, gods form the center of all Sumerian and Akkadian creation myths. These supernatural entities were either imagined as the universe, consisting of heaven and earth, or as primordial waters. The creation process, through which the very first entities gave rise to new beings, was said to have taken place in one of two ways: either the first entities separated from each other or united with each other.

Indeed, an early Sumerian myth explains that heaven and earth were once one great whole before the god Enlil separated them from each other. In another version, heaven and earth came together to produce the rest of the world. Sometimes Enlil and a mother goddess were personified as heaven and earth. In the Babylonian creation epic, the masculine subterranean freshwater (**1**, Euphrates River) joined with the feminine saltwater, which was described as an enormous monster. As other gods emerged from their union, one of these gods created the world from the saltwater monster's body.

Enki Produces the Necessities of Life for Humankind In the earliest Sumerian myths from the first half of the third millennium B.C., An and Enlil appear as the gods that bring the universe into being. In a myth from 1800 B.C., the freshwater god Enki, together with an entire line of goddesses, produced the basic components of the world (**2**, Babylonian worldview). First, Enki united with Ninhursaga (**3**), the "lady of the highlands," who

then gave birth nine days later to the goddess Ninnisig, "lady of the green plants." When Enki first saw the beautiful Ninnisig, he immediately wanted to kiss and sleep with her. This union created the goddess Ninkura, the "lady of the mountains." In turn, Ninkura's union with Enki produced Uttu, the goddess of wool and weaving. The active role played by the freshwater god demonstrates the importance of freshwater to human life: in the highlands it helped plants grow and flourish, and was also necessary to support livestock.

Figures and Stories Relevant to the Creation of the Universe

An and Enlil, Creator Gods, see pp. 30–31

The Creation of Humanity, see pp. 22–23

Enki, Creator God, see pp. 32–33

The Tooth Worm At the beginning, An, god of the sky, created heaven. Then heaven created earth, earth created rivers, rivers created canals, canals created mud, and mud created the worm. When the worm asked Ea, the god of wisdom, what kind of food he was allowed to eat, Ea answered: "Figs, apricots, and apples." However, as the worm preferred to nibble on the teeth and gums of people, an appeal was made to Ea to destroy the worm, as it did not have the permission to delight in eating human gums. Thus, the myth was not only about the pulling of diseased teeth (**4**, ritual at bedside), but also about giving hope to the sick and assisting the healing process.

Creation Through Water: pp. 71, 380 | **Creation Through a Body:** pp. 27, 229, 288, 331, 380

The Creation of Humanity

According to the ancient myths of the Near East, the first people were either born or formed by hand. Two deities were responsible for creating humankind: a mother goddess known by a variety of names and Enki, the god of freshwater and of practical inventions.

Terracotta figurine in a birthing position

- The mother goddess was variously called Mami ("mama"), Nintur ("lady who is the birthing hut"), or Ninhursaga ("lady of the highlands")

- The mother goddesses created humankind by giving birth to primordial people

- The freshwater god Enki, who was also called Ea, shaped people by mixing clay and a liquid

- People were made of two different substances, "earthly" clay and the blood of a god

- People took on divine characteristics, such as the ability to plan and to reason

Most often, these myths combine the birth and the shaping of the first people into one story. Stories that mention the mother goddess highlight her pregnancy, which lasted only nine days instead of nine months, and the birth itself. In contrast, myths about a more artistic creation have Enki forming people from clay as if he were making a pot. The difference was that the clay was mixed with an extraordinary liquid. Several myths name the liquid used in creation as the blood of a slaughtered deity. Sometimes Enki added divine spittle into the raw clay mixture. Often, the reason given for creating humankind was to provide workers so that the younger generation of gods could be relieved of the hard work of digging canals.

Creation in the Bible and the Atramchasis Myth

Both ancient Near Eastern and biblical gods were said to have formed people from two substances, one of which was clay. In the Babylonian Atramchasis myth, the divine substance was the blood of a god who had the gift of understanding. According to the Bible, in Genesis 2, God breathed life into the first person, which represented endowing him with a divine spirit. While both creation traditions portray hard work as the lot of humanity, it was seen as a punishment in the Bible and as a task in Mesopotamia.

▶▶ **Creation of People With Clay:** pp. 100, 166 | **Zulu—People From Reeds:** p. 444

When the Gods Were Human
The Babylonian Atramchasis myth opens with the words *"inuma ilu awilu"* ("when the gods were human"). The myth is about the gods (**1**, Sumerian cuneiform writing) and humans: their creation, their duties, and their relationship to one another. Even the language indicates the belief that something of the gods (*ilu*) was also present in humans (*aw-ilu*). People were made of clay mixed with the blood of a rebellious god of knowledge. In this way, humans were said to share the gift of divine understanding and received something immortal, a spirit.

Enki and Ninmah Enki and the mother goddesses worked together, but sometimes there were conflicts. In one argument over humans (**2**), Enki wanted to prove to Ninmah that he could assign each person a proper place, even if Ninmah had endowed that person with shortcomings. Enki was successful; he even gave people with disabilities a certain task.

People Who Grew Like Plants In a Sumerian hymn of praise to the axe, the most powerful god Enlil separated heaven from earth. At the "place where living flesh grows," the first people sprang from the soil like plants (**3**), and Enlil was pleased. When the other gods saw the newly sprouted people, they prayed to Enlil, full of admiration, in order to make humanity provide for them and cater to their needs. The mother goddess Ninmena, the "lady of the crown," created rulers thus order was brought to humanity. She also made it possible for human beings to procreate.

Divine Bringers of Culture

To the people of the ancient Near East, the world was a gift from the gods. These divine gods were even credited with cultural advancements, such as the development of agriculture and animal husbandry as well as the creation of sophisticated urban culture. Myths show that irrigation technology was seen as a tremendous accomplishment. Digging canals meant breaking through into the underworld—a dangerous adventure undertook by Ninlil, goddess of the city of Nippur. Many gods were credited with the development of agriculture, especially Ninurta, god of agriculture, who taught about crop production. The shepherd god Dumuzi taught about animal husbandry and Ninkasi how to brew beer.

■ Various myths suggested that cultural accomplishments were gifts from the gods

■ Ninlil gave birth to the god of canal construction

■ Ninazu and Ninmada brought barley to Sumer

■ Ninurta was the god of agriculture; Dumuzi was the god of animal husbandry

■ The gods Enlil and Nisaba invented oral poetry and literature

Ancient Syrian statue of a water goddess

Ninurta's Instructions Regarding Crops When faced with questions about irrigating the land, protecting the fields (**1**) from flooding, and finding the constellation of stars indicating favorable conditions for planting, the Sumerians were given answers from Ninurta, who even recommended a ritual for doing away with mice.

▶▶ **Teachers of Agriculture:** pp. 130, 335 | **Bringers of Culture:** pp. 32, 41, 166, 442

(2)

**Figures and Stories
Relevant to
Divine Bringers of Culture**

The Creation of Humanity,
Hymn of Praise to the Axe, see
pp. 22–23

The Underworld, Constructing Canals, see
pp. 44–45

Canal Construction The goddess Ninlil set out to accomplish an extremely dangerous task of building irrigation works. During the construction, she had to rely on the cooperation of the terrible powers of the underworld, as she had to intrude on their territory in order to dig the canals. Ninlil left her city (**3**, fortress surrounded by canals) and set out for the underworld. There she made a pact with the various gods of the underworld, sleeping with them until she conceived and gave birth to the god of canal construction. Afterward nothing could stand in the way of building canals (**2**, opening of a canal on the Tigris).

Barley and Beer The basic food staple in Sumer and Babylonia was grain, especially barley, which could be grown easily (**5**). This grain was used to make bread and beer, the national drink (**4**, beer mug). Over 60 different types of beer were brewed. Beer production was controlled by the goddess Ninkasi. Barley was also seen as a divine gift. Earlier, people had eaten grass like sheep, but An allowed barley to be taken out of heaven. Yet Enlil took it and held it at the foot of a mountain. The sun god Utu helped the divine brothers Ninazu and Ninmada bring it to Sumer.

(5)

■ Aggressive, heroic gods—such as Ninurta, Marduk, and Assur—saved the world from monsters made of stone and water and predatory beasts

■ The hard-working younger gods rebelled against the privileged, older gods

■ The younger gods caused such an uproar that the older gods wanted to destroy them

■ With the help of the heavenly bull, Inana was as mighty as her father

The Battle of the Gods

The victory stele of Eannatum of Lagash

In one poem, the poet Enheduana sang about the goddess Inana: "It shall be known that your sight inspires terror, that you inflict this terror upon your enemies, that you completely obliterate those who rebel, that you even consume their corpses like an animal."

Daily life in Mesopotamia was everything but harmonious. Various conflicts were reflected in mythology (**1**, Standard of Ur, war panel). The younger gods threatened the old gods, the primordial gods planned to destroy the younger gods, and Inana wanted to challenge her father's position on the throne. She defiantly took the heavenly bull from An, god of the sky, to use as a weapon. Monsters threatened the world, but savior gods, such as Ninurta and Marduk, destroyed them.

⏩ **Fighting Between the Gods:** pp. 117, 118, 238, 245, 458

The Gods Rebel The overworked gods had had enough and they decided to storm the residence of Enlil, the king of the gods. First, they destroyed their tools and burned their spades and the baskets they carried on their backs. Then they marched to Enlil's house and surrounded it. Overwhelmed, the ruler called on An and Ea, other high gods, to help. As the striking gods continued to shout out their demands (**2**), An and Ea gave Enlil advice. Enlil just wanted to crawl away and hide in An's sky, but Ea, the god of wisdom, had a better idea: the gods should be relieved of the burden of work and a new being could be created to take it over. Thus, humanity was created to shoulder the burden.

> ### Figures and Stories Relevant to the Battle of the Gods
>
> The Creation of Humanity, see pp. 22–23
>
> Enlil, Creator God, see pp. 30–31
>
> Inana, Goddess of the City, see pp. 38–39
>
> Marduk, God of the Nation, see pp. 42–43

Marduk Saves the Gods The Babylonian goddess Tiamat and her husband Apsu could not bear the uproar caused by the younger gods and planned to destroy them. When Ea killed Apsu during the battle, Tiamat, an enormous water snake, sought revenge. Marduk was selected to fight her (**3**), and he won. He cut her body in two to form heaven and earth.

The Monster Killer Enlil's oldest son Ninurta, the god of rainstorms, was often drawn into battle. In one story, he pursued Anzu, the lion-headed eagle (**4**) who had stolen Enlil's tablet of destiny. Whoever possessed this one tablet could rule the world. After slaying a series of monsters, Ninurta regained the tablet. Another myth had him battling Asag, a demon from the mountains, who threatened the world with an army of stones. After his victory, Ninurta

collected the water and kept it in the mountains, allowing it to flow down to the plains little by little. In doing so, he created the basis for agriculture.

Heroes Fighting Against Monsters: pp. 181, 165, 251, 315, 361
Creation Through a Body: pp. 20, 229, 288, 331, 380

The Flood

The flood is the subject of a variety of Sumerian, Babylonian, and Hebrew myths. The storyline is always the same, but the details vary. The gods (or a sole God) decided to destroy all of humankind by flooding the entire earth (**3**). Only one person, who the gods protected, was able to save his family and animals. In the Bible, this was Noah, whose ark was supposed to have landed on Mount Ararat (**1**). In the Sumerian myth, this hero was Ziusudra ("a life of long days") and the Babylonians called him Atramchasis ("amazingly clever"). In the *Epic of Gilgamesh*, the gods gave the hero Utnapishtim ("I have found life") eternal life.

While the uninhibited procreation of people, as well as the uproar they caused, brought about the flood in the Mesopotamian myth, in the Bible, the commission of sins was said to have provoked God's anger, causing him to destroy humankind in a flood so as to wash away their sins.

(1)

The *Epic of Gilgamesh*
George Smith, an assistant professor at the British Museum, worked on deciphering a cuneiform tablet (**2**) found in the ruins of Nineveh. In 1872 he discovered fragments of a flood story similar to that in the Bible written on the tablet. Between 1873 and 1874 he traveled to Nineveh and found more pieces of the tablet. Today this tablet is known as the eleventh tablet of the *Epic* of *Gilgamesh*. In an attempt to escape death, King Gilgamesh fled to the end of the world. There he met Utnapishtim, who had survived the flood. When the god Enlil noticed that he was still alive, he was angry. But the other gods were relieved and decreed that such a catastrophe should never happen again.

(2)

» **Great Floods:** pp. 32, 335, 401, 411, 445

3

An and Enlil

■ For a long time, An and Enlil were seen as the highest gods of the Mesopotamian pantheon

■ They were the creators of the universe

■ An translates directly as "sky" and Enlil possibly means "god of the gods"

■ Both were considered prototypes of human rulers

■ An and Enlil's most important places of worship were the cities of Uruk and Nippur

For many centuries, the gods An and Enlil had the highest status among the gods of Mesopotamia. They played a central role in the Mesopotamian cosmology, beginning with creation myths where the god of sky An separated from the goddess of the earth. Together they created the world and its gods. Enlil (**1**, Nippur, sacred city of Enlil) was referred to as the creator of the gods or as the separator of heaven and earth.

While An is clearly translated as "sky," the translation of Enlil remains unclear. Possible meanings include "lord wind," "lord who is a spirit," or also the "god of gods."

An and Enlil both presided over the assembly of gods and decided on the future of the world and humans, either alone or with the assembly. Humans, however, could try to influence their fate. The power of An and Enlil's decisions ensured law and order. Therefore, they were also the most important figures in the constitution of Mesopotamian rulers.

⟩⟩ **Gods as Law Givers:** pp. 40, 178

Order of the Gods The world of the gods was structured according to a strict hierarchy, which can be seen in documents from the second half of the second millennium B.C. (**2**). They list the specific symbols of the gods: the gods of the stars are shown on top, the terrestrial gods in the middle, and the powers of the underworld at the bottom. As far back as the third millennium B.C., there were books similar to encyclopedias that listed the names of all the gods. Each high god was assigned a family with a wife and children, as well as a heavenly household with ministers, scribes, messengers, and even bakers, cupbearers, hairdressers, and groundskeepers. An was always preeminent on these lists of gods.

Audience With the Gods A high god could only be visited when a certain etiquette was observed, just like an audience with a ruler (**3**, Xerxes I) would require. First, one had to register with the gatekeeper. With a little bit of luck and the help of a mediating personal guardian god, one would be allowed to proceed. Before presenting the matter of the visit, one had to prostrate oneself before the god sitting on his throne. A gift for the god (as well as ruler) was a must in order to appease him so that he would be compelled to help (**4**, audience at the court of a ruler from 21st century B.C.).

Figures and Stories Relevant to An and Enlil

Creation of the Universe, An and Enlil as Creator Gods, see pp. 20–21

Marduk and Assur, Later Replaced An and Enlil as High Gods, see pp. 42–43

Nanna, Enlil's Son, see pp. 36–37

⏵⏵ Hierarchy of the Gods: pp. 70, 72, 308

Enki

■ In Sumerian artifacts, Enki was actually written "Enkig" and most likely means "lord kindness" and not, as scholars previously thought, "lord earth"

■ His Akkadian name was Ea (originally Hayya), which means "life"

■ Enki was the god of freshwater, wisdom, and craftsmanship, and the art of conjuration

■ His symbols included the goat and fish, which were later combined into one creature

■ Enki's main city of worship was Eridu, an ancient Sumerian city located in present-day Iraq

In Sumerian mythology, Enki appears as the last resort when everything else seems hopeless. The god of freshwater was believed to have

Half-goat, half-fish creatures, Enki's symbols, on a freshwater tank

provided Dilmun (today's Bahrain Island) with access to freshwater. He was also credited as having filled the Tigris River with streams of water. The life-giving water—said to be his sperm—produced new generations of gods and ensured the development of the cosmos (**1**). Through the cleansing power of water, Enki freed humanity from evil. He was considered a powerful specialist of rituals and the lord of the art of conjuration.

Enki was shrewd, wise, inventive, cunning, and full of ideas. He was also the father of craftsmanship. Like a potter, he created humans with the help of the mother goddesses. Once, Enki even had to be rescued by a mother goddess when he was impregnated by his own sperm. Because he lacked a womb, she saved him by stopping the delivery. This pregnancy was said to have resulted in the birth of various medicinal plants.

⏵ **Bringers of Culture:** pp. 24, 41, 166, 442 | **Great Floods:** pp. 28, 335, 401, 411, 445

Enki Organizes the World

Enki was ordered by the highest god Enlil to assign certain responsibilities and cities to the other gods. But before doing that, he decided to give the country Sumer, the city of Ur, the Persian Gulf, the Indus Valley, and the nomads of Mesopotamia a good fate. He filled the Tigris River with water and made the soil fertile (**2**). Then he assigned roles to various gods, which resulted in gods of the canals and thunderstorms, barley, bread-making, architecture, and so on.

Inana Takes Enki's ME

The gods of the various city-states enjoyed visiting each other. Celebrations during these visits were often exuberant, such as when the goddess of love and sexual desire, Inana, visited Enki in Eridu. They both drank so much beer that Enki lay drunk under the table. Seeing an op-portunity, Inana persuaded him to give her the 50 ME, the heavenly powers necessary to rule over urban culture (**3**, King Gudea of Lagash), priesthoods, crafts, war, peace, and other things. Before Enki had a chance to sober up, she had taken the ME into her city, Uruk.

A Friend to Humanity

When all the other gods wanted to destroy humankind through a massive flood, Enki helped humanity escape the impending disaster. To ensure their survival, Enki warned a man named Ziusudra by whispering to him through the reeds (**4**) that he had to build a boat large enough for the animals and his family. The sage Adapa was another protégé of Enki. Under the god's supervision, he invented the sail boat. Enki also gave humanity rites, such as a priest's vestments and anointment. Many accounts say that people received medical help from Enki, who gave them healing ointments.

Figures and Stories Relevant to Enki

The Creation of People, Enki as Creator God, see pp. 22–23

Inana, Stole Enki's ME, see pp. 38–39

The Great Flood, see pp. 28–29

The Tower of Babel

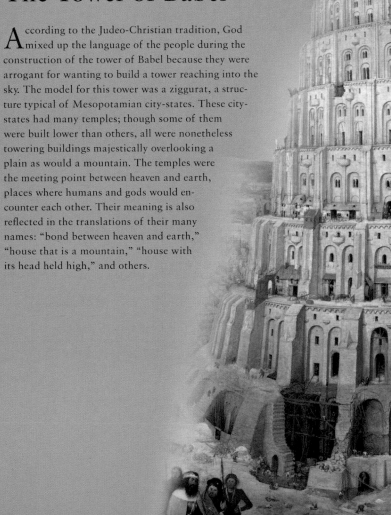

According to the Judeo-Christian tradition, God mixed up the language of the people during the construction of the tower of Babel because they were arrogant for wanting to build a tower reaching into the sky. The model for this tower was a ziggurat, a structure typical of Mesopotamian city-states. These city-states had many temples; though some of them were built lower than others, all were nonetheless towering buildings majestically overlooking a plain as would a mountain. The temples were the meeting point between heaven and earth, places where humans and gods would encounter each other. Their meaning is also reflected in the translations of their many names: "bond between heaven and earth," "house that is a mountain," "house with its head held high," and others.

Nanna

The high god Enlil, together with Ninlil, created Nanna, the god of the city of Ur. There are many connections in this myth made between Ninlil, goddess of the city of Nippur, and Enlil, her consort. For example, it states that Enlil appeared to Ninlil as various forms of the gods of the underworld, and with their union, they created different gods. When the city of Ur (**1**, Zikkurat) became the capital of Sumer in the 21st century B.C., Nanna was honored in this myth as the firstborn of Enlil and Ninlil.

Because Nanna, god of the moon, was Enlil's firstborn son, he had high stature among the gods. Nanna was considered to be the father of the celestial deities Inana (Venus) and Utu (sun). As father he was believed to be supreme. The three deities were seen as particularly important in assisting with the pleas and needs of humans, and thanks were given to them for their guidance.

There were many different symbols for Nanna; for example, a boat or the horns of a bull for him as a crescent moon, or a ripe piece of fruit resembling the full moon.

■ The Sumerian names of the moon god were Nanna and Dilimbabbar, "he who resplendently hurries there alone"

■ In Akkadian, Nanna was called Suen or Sin

■ Nanna's symbols were the crescent moon, the bull, and the number 30, representing the number of days in a month

■ Many well-known rulers bore the name Nanna in their names, e.g., Naram-Sin, "favorite of Sin"

■ His main city of worship was Ur

①

City God of Ur Nanna was the god of the city of Ur. He controlled Ur, which by the third century B.C. was already a thriving city. The earliest known high priestesses performed their duties there. When Ur became the capital of a large empire in the 21st century B.C., Nanna maintained a high place among the gods for governing the city perfectly. State enterprises registered each arrival and exit from the city, down to the last cattle carcass. Large scale cattle breeding was necessary so that sacrificial offerings could be made to Nanna (**2**, left, on the crescent moon).

The Shapes of Nanna
The best known symbol for Nanna was the crescent moon, upon which he was depicted standing. This symbol was often mounted on a pole and taken on military campaigns as a sign that Nanna was present. As the crescent was reminiscent of bull's horns, the bull became a particularly popular representative of Nanna (**4**), who was seen as the bull who grazed his herd, the stars, at night. The full moon was often depicted as fruit.

Nanna—Giver of Time The new day began with the appearance of the moon (**3**). Nanna's symbolic number, 30, stood for the 30 days of the month. These were divided by feast days for the new moon, half moon, and black moon.

> ### Figures and Stories Relevant to Nanna
>
> Enlil, Nanna's Father, see pp. 30–31
> Inana, Nanna's Daughter, see pp. 38–39
> Naram-Sin, Named After Nanna, see pp. 48–49
> Utu, Nanna's Son, see pp. 40–41

■ Her Akkadian name, Ishtar, became the word for "goddess"
■ Inana was the goddess of love and war
■ In Sumerian, Inana means "lady of the heavens"
■ Her main city of worship was Akkad

Inana/Ishtar

Inana, goddess of the celestial body of Venus, is the best known goddess in ancient Near Eastern mythology, and one of the most ambiguous. She stood for opposing ideals, like love and fertility, and war and annihilation. Some texts describe how these opposites worked in unison; for instance, Inana waged war against the enemies of the beloved ruler to whom she had promised good governance through the ritual of the holy marriage. Many myths speak of her deeds. She stole the temple of the celestial deity An, and the divine powers, or ME, of the god of freshwater, Enki. She brutally subjugated the gods who did not submit to her. She traveled fearlessly through the underworld, was killed and then brought back to life. One myth states that she handed over her lover to the underworld, while in another she searched desperately for him. Her symbolic animal was the lion (**1**).

» **Terrifying Goddesses:** pp. 93, 265, 300

Inana in the Underworld

Inana journeyed into the realm of the dead elaborately adorned with her ME. Her intention might have been to overthrow the queen of the underworld, but she failed. At every door to the underworld, a piece of her adornment was taken, and she eventually was naked and stripped of her powers. Eventually she was killed and turned into a rotting lump of flesh. After three days, beings which had been created especially to rescue her managed to restore her using an elixir of life. The myth has several meanings, one of which is an attempt to explain the temporary invisibility of the celestial body of Venus. Another might be the extraordinary power of Inana's servants (**2**), as well as the significance of certain constellations.

The Author Enheduana

Little is known about the people who wrote myths and other texts about gods. The earliest exception is from the 23rd century B.C. when the king's daughter, Enheduana (**3**, in the middle), became the world's earliest known author. Although she was a high priestess of the moon god Nanna, she ended up offering her services to Inana, and thus honed her skills as a theologist. When she was threatened with death, she tried to persuade Inana to help her through her writing so as to act out against her enemies on her behalf. Her song was a testimony to maintaining hope in seemingly hopeless situations, and centuries later it was still taught in schools.

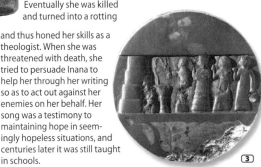

Holy Marriage

Myths about Inana and her lover Dumuzi (or Tammuz), god of vegetation, form the background behind the holy marriage (**4**) ritual that took place between Inana and the king. In the myth, Inana elects the king as her husband and gives him her blessing. However, it has been speculated that Inana may have been represented in this ritual by a priestess or the queen. It is more plausible that contact with the goddess was made only through her statue, her celestial body, or while in a trance.

Figures and Stories Relevant to Inana

The Battle of the Gods, Inana Competes With Nanna, see pp. 26–27

Enki, Inana Gets Heavenly Powers, see p. 33

Nanna, Inana's Father, see pp. 36–37

Naram-Sin, Inana Protects Him, see pp. 48–49

The Underworld, Inana Traveled There, see pp. 44–45

Utu, Inana's Brother, see pp. 40–41

Journeys in the Underworld: pp. 41, 159, 353, 407 | **Holy Marriage:** p. 127

■ Utu can mean either "light" or "day" in Sumerian

■ His Akkadian name, Shamash, is related to *schamschu*, "sun"

■ Utu was the son of Nanna and brother of Inana

■ As god of the sun, Utu brought light, but was also responsible for justice

■ He led the living into the realm of the dead

■ His main cities of worship were Larsa and Sippar

■ He was often depicted enthroned with a staff and a ring

Utu/Shamash

The sun god Utu brought light, and with this illumination was able to see clearly. This made him the ideal guardian and protector of equality and justice. The ancient relationship between sunlight and justice can also be found in the Bible, as the "sun of justice" (Malachi 3:20).

Every morning Utu made his way through the mountains in eastern Mesopotamia, where the gatekeeper gods opened the gates for him. After he had shone for the living during the day, he took the opposite route from west to east, which brought him through the regions of the underworld. Utu was the judge of both the living and the dead.

The famous ruler of Babylon, Hammurapi, depicted Utu as the guardian of law and order on a pillar that contained his code of law. In a region in which constant warfare was the order of the day, the desire for peace and stability was as strong as the longing for light in seemingly threatening darkness.

Hammurapi law code pillar

Shamash and Hammurapi's Pillar

The pillar bearing Hammurapi's code of law, one of the very first, names Shamash as the "great judge of heaven and earth" from whom the king is "bestowed the right and given the task" to protect and serve the weak. To prove that he had fulfilled his duty, Hammurapi portrays himself as a herdsman who allows the people to camp on his green meadow. This image shows how Shamash hands over a measuring stick and rope, the symbols of authority, to Hammurapi, who respectfully stands before him. In this pillar, the temple serves as a throne for the god, and his feet rest on the mountains.

≫ **Gods as Law Givers:** pp. 30, 178

Utu Passes Through the Realm of the Dead Celestial gods were seen as something similar to human rulers. It was said that Utu (**1**, with gate keepers), after finishing the daily tasks along his heavenly route, returned to his chambers to rest with his wife Ningal. There are several myths that claim that Utu continued his

journey through the cosmos, traveling into the night. He went through a large tunnel from the west back to the east, crossing through the regions of the underworld, in a difficult and dangerous journey. Utu brought light to the dead in the underworld, and presided over legal cases. On his way, he brought the dead to the underworld, and took spirits back with him to the world. When he arrived at the end of the tunnel, Utu used his saw to get back up out of the mountains, and with his emergence, the sun rose (**2**) again.

Legal Texts Dating from the 18th century B.C., Hammurapi's code of law is part of a long tradition. In the 21st century B.C. the codex of the Sumerian ruler, Urnamma, was established. In all, there are two Sumerian and four Akkadian jury laws known today. Even older than these are the reform texts of the 25th-century B.C. ruler, Urukagina, which attempted to reverse the privileges of the ruler for the good of the temple (**3**).

Utu as Gilgamesh's Helper In the tales about King Gilgamesh, Utu is depicted as his protector. When Gilgamesh wanted to travel to the mountains to cut down cedars, the god sent with him seven local warriors who knew the place well. In the *Epic of Gilgamesh*, the goddess Ninsun (**4**), mother of the hero, complains that the sun god is responsible for the restless heart of her son, which drives him to dangerous adventures.

Figures and Stories Relevant to Utu

Inana, Utu's Sister, see pp. 38–39

Nanna, Utu's Father, see pp. 36–37

The Underworld, Utu Brought the Dead Here, see pp. 44–45

Marduk and Assur

The history of the gods Marduk and Assur charts their steep ascent from relatively unimportant local gods into the great national gods of Babylon and Assyria that they later became. Prior to the 18th century B.C., when King Hammurapi made Babylon the center of a great empire, the city and its god Marduk were only important regionally. However, under Hammurapi Marduk's influence grew, as did the state cult and the number of individuals who paid him worship. A great number of hymns and prayers were sung in praise of Marduk.

Something similar happened during the second millennium B.C. with the god Assur in Assyria (**1**, Assyrian King Assurnasirpal II). Both Marduk and Assur took over the position formerly held by the god Enlil, and the myths associated with him were transferred to them accordingly. In the world creation epic *Enuma elish,* Marduk and Assur interchangeably take over the role of the warring god Ninurta, and saved the universe from destruction by the dragon Tiamat. This quest was played out by cult members every year during New Year festivities.

■ The name Marduk translates as "calf of Utu (the sun god)"

■ He was considered the son of the god Enki

■ The cult of Marduk centered on Babylon

■ Assur had the same name as the city in which he was worshiped

■ Both gods were initially regional gods before later becoming state gods

■ Both gods were to protect the king's sovereignty

Figures and Stories Relevant to Marduk and Assur

An and Enlil, Enlil Was Replaced by Marduk and Assur, see pp. 30–31
The Battle of the Gods, Marduk Saves the Younger Gods Against the Older Gods, see pp. 26–27

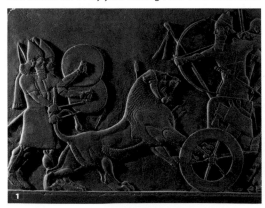

The 50 Names of Marduk

After Marduk (**3**, his symbol, the dragon) saved the gods from Tiamat, he was given the highest position among them. The 50 most important gods gave him their powers by assigning one of their names to him.

Lord of Assyria

As Assur's name was identical with that of his city, it is likely that at first a place near the city was initially worshiped as holy. In contrast to other gods who had many temples, Assur had a temple only in his city (**4**, relief of a god found there). His rise to preeminence was theologically explained by his association with the primordial god Anshar. It was believed that Anshar had existed prior to heaven and earth, and he was called the source of all things.

The New Year Festival

The best loved festival in Mesopotamia lasted 11 days. People carrying their idols from neighboring states arrived, and after many preparations, the gathered crowd confirmed the rule of the highest god Marduk (or Assur) and acknowledged the king as his representative. Alongside this, these gods ensured a good destiny for the capital and the country. On the eighth day, a large procession (**2**) left the temple area and carried a statue of Marduk into the city and throughout the surrounding countryside. It was probably the only time in the year that the populace saw their god Marduk's victory over the dragon Tiamat was reenacted in rituals in which the king played the role of the god and had to participate in various challenges. These celebrations would continue for three more days outside the city.

■ The rulers of the underworld were the goddess Ereshkigal ("lady of the great place") and the god Nergal

■ The dead could affect the fate of the living

■ Spirits and demons could haunt the living

■ Among the best known demons were Lamashtu, who caused puerperal (childbirth) fever, and Pazuzu, a wind demon

The Underworld

The underworld is usually presented as dark, dusty, and inhospitable in most ancient Near Eastern mythology. It was the realm of the underworld gods, Nergal and Ereshkigal, and of various demons and spirits. The fate of the dead in the underworld was dependent upon their earthly life. After his death, Enkidu reported to his friend

Genie performing a protective magical gesture

Gilgamesh that someone who had no children would, as a result, starve in the afterlife. The more sons one had, the more one would have to eat and drink. These beliefs shaped people's behavior in life. Faring particularly well in the underworld, still-born babies were allowed to play on the tables of the gods and received honeyed treats to eat.

The Death Dream of Enkidu
What happened in dreams was considered very real for the Mesopotamians. It was in a dream that Enkidu, the companion of Gilgamesh (**1**), was seized by a heinous demon and brutally carried off to the underworld. Terrified, Gilgamesh refused to help him. It was after this dream, that Enkidu lost all hope of recovering when he fell ill, and died.

①

Evil Spirits and Demons

Anyone seized by a demon would become ill and die. The terrible demon Lamashtu (**3**) primarily targeted pregnant women and babies. First, she offered them her breast like a caring nurse only to then snatch them into the underworld a moment later. Another demon, Pazuzu (**2**), had the power to expel the evil Lamashtu, so people often wore Pazuzu amulets for protection. Spirits were also to be feared. The ghosts of people who had not been properly buried, and who did not have enough to eat in the afterlife, could not rest and they haunted, tortured, and injured the living. Many rituals grew as a result of these beliefs in demons and spirits. But the dead, particularly members of one's own family, could also be merciful judges and intercessors when a living person faced judgment. The dead also passed on their knowledge of the future to the living.

Death of a Royal Household

The excavation of a cemetery in Ur from the early 25th century B.C. revealed what was considered to be a unique find: an entire royal household, including wagons, animals, and treasures of gold (**4**) and lapis lazuli, buried alongside their ruler. Amazingly, not so long ago a Sumerian text describing just such a scene was discovered: *Gilgamesh's Death* tells the story of Gilgamesh who, in a dream, was called to a gathering of the gods. There he learned that the sky god had decreed his death, even though Gilgamesh was the son of a goddess. But the god of wisdom, Enki, told Gilgamesh a way to obtain a particularly good position in the realm of the dead. To become a ruler in the afterlife, Gilgamesh should build a burial palace under the Euphrates River. So Gilgamesh diverted the river, built a stone house, and moved into the palace with his favorite wives, concubines, children, servants, and many treasures to give to the gods of the underworld. The river was then returned to its natural course.

Figures and Stories Relevant to the Underworld

Divine Bringers of Culture, Ninlil in the Underworld, see pp. 24–25

Inana, see pp. 46–47

Utu, Judge of the Dead, see pp. 40–41

The Epic of Gilgamesh

The *Epic of Gilgamesh* is renowned as being one of the oldest known literary works. The earliest tablets of the Babylonian version are thought to have been written at the beginning of the second millennium B.C. Its about 3,600 lines of verse were written on 11 tablets. The epic tells the story of Gilgamesh's quest for eternal life (**1**, depicted on cylinder seals). In the first section, Gilgamesh attempts to perform heroic deeds in order to win undying fame for his name (**3**, as a lion slayer, 12th century). His friend Enkidu accompanied him in these famous adventures. The second part of the epic, after the death of Enkidu, revolves around the basic physical survival of the hero.

Alone during this part of the journey, Gilgamesh searches for a way to overcome the obstacle of death. His journey took him through the Tunnel of the Sun and the Water of Death, and on to Utnapishtim, hero of the flood, who told Gilgamesh where to find the herb of life. He found the herb, but it was stolen and eaten by a serpent, and thus his search for eternal life failed. All that remains of Gilgamesh's fame today is the wall built by him around his city, Uruk.

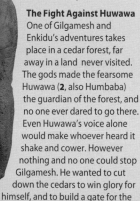

The Fight Against Huwawa

One of Gilgamesh and Enkidu's adventures takes place in a cedar forest, far away in a land never visited. The gods made the fearsome Huwawa (**2**, also Humbaba) the guardian of the forest, and no one ever dared to go there. Even Huwawa's voice alone would make whoever heard it shake and cower. However nothing and no one could stop Gilgamesh. He wanted to cut down the cedars to win glory for himself, and to build a gate for the temple of the goddess Enlil in Nippur. After Gilgamesh receiving the promise of protection from the sun god Shamash, Gilgamesh, accompanied by Enkidu and several men from the city, headed for the forest. There, he successfully tricked Huwawa, taking away his seven *auras*. Afterward Gilgamesh (some versions say Enkidu) killed Huwawa and became the first to ever cut down a sacred cedar tree. But Gilgamesh paid dearly for his daring, as his beloved friend Enkidu died from this sacrilege of cutting down the sacred trees.

②

3

Naram-Sin

Naram-Sin was the grandson of the celebrated Sargon of Akkad, who founded the first great empire of the ancient Near East. During his reign, Naram-Sin found himself facing violent resistance. The situation became dangerous when cities to the south and north of his land combined their forces against him. Because of this, he was forced to fight in nine battles in just one year. He claimed that he was aided by the love of his personal protection goddess, Inana. To aid him, the high priestess Enheduana, his aunt, was praying for Inana to destroy the opposition.

When he won, the citizens of Akkad prayed to the gods to make Naram-Sin their patron deity. He was worshiped in a temple. While previous rulers often identified themselves as children of the gods, the actual deification of the sovereign himself was first found here with Naram-Sin.

■ Naram-Sin was the emperor of Akkad, grandson of the empire's founder Sargon of Akkad

■ Naram-Sin means "favorite of Sin"

■ He bore the title "king of the four quarters of the world"

■ Naram-Sin was deified as a god after he prevailed over a great coalition of enemies; he became the protector god of his capital, Akkad

■ On the Naram-Sin stele he is seen wearing a crown of horns

The Naram-Sin Stele

Battles for the continuation and expansion of his empire brought Naram-Sin as far as the Mediterranean Sea. In the northeast, he came against a mountain tribe, the Lullubi. A six-foot-high, artfully crafted stele made of sandstone (ca 2230 B.C.) describes his victory. He is seen as a majestic ruler rising over the world of man and beyond into the world of gods. Beneath him, his soldiers are seen marching. Undoubtedly it is an attempt to liken the ascension into the steep mountainous territory to Akkad's ascension to power. The stele shows three scenes: in the first, the opposing leader has his hands raised, begging for mercy. Next, he is shown with a spear in his neck and finally, in the center of the stele, he can be seen falling headfirst into the abyss. In the mid-12th century, the stele was stolen by the Elamites and taken from Babylon to Susa.

» **Divine Rulers:** pp. 84, 201, 220, 336, 368

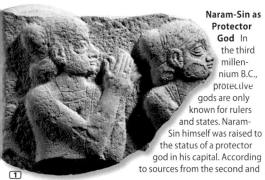

Naram-Sin as Protector God In the third millennium B.C., protective gods are only known for rulers and states. Naram-Sin himself was raised to the status of a protector god in his capital. According to sources from the second and first millenniums B.C., every person had two protective gods, who created a sort of parental pair. In rituals, a person would add their father's and their protective god's (**1**, praying woman from Lagash) name to their own. If the gods were benevolent toward humanity, all was well. If not, the gods would leave them, and they would face sickness, poverty, and social isolation.

The Curse of Akkad The fall of the great Akkadian Empire was explained by a myth, a lamentation known as *The Curse of Akkad* (**2**). Within the poem, Naram-Sin (**3**) was described as an unholy ruler. He only worshiped and loved the goddess Inana, which angered the other high gods. These gods, along with Inana, took away their protection. Because he had no permission to renovate the temple of Enlil, he plundered and destroyed it. Because of this, Enlil sent hosts of barbarian enemies to attack Naram-Sin, leaving the land devastated. In order to calm Enlil down, the other gods cursed the city of Akkad: it would forever remain in ruins.

Figures and Stories Relevant to Naram-Sin

An and Enlil, Enlil Was Naram-Sin's Enemy, see pp. 30–31

Inana, Naram-Sin's Protector Goddess, see pp. 38–39

Nanna, Naram-Sin's Namesake, see pp. 36–37

Teshub and Kumarbi

As in the entire ancient Near East, the Hittites believed the world was created by the gods. Already during antiquity, the people spoke of the thousand gods of the Hittite Empire (**1**). The weather god Teshub was adored in the Hittite Empire, which spanned from Anatolia to Syria and Mesopotamia, as the supreme god. He had particular significance in agriculture, and was worshiped as the protector of the cosmic order and of the kingship. Frequently, he was seen on a bull or in a carriage pulled by bulls.

Aside from Teshub, it is possible to distinguish countless gods of nature: of rivers, springs, mountains, stones, and trees. The gods and their myths indicate that the Hittites were influenced by many foreign cultures, such as Mesopotamia, the Hurrites, and the region of Syria. Conversely, the Hittite mythology influenced the Greeks, which is why Hesiod's *Theogony* resembles the myths of Kumarbi. Furthermore, the Greek tale of Jason's hunt for the golden fleece shows influence from the myths of the Anatolian god Telipinu.

■ Teshub was the supreme god of thunderstorms in the Hittite pantheon

■ Kumarbi, the father of the gods, was a grain deity

■ The Hittites also worshiped countless nature gods

■ Kumarbi gave rise to Teshub, who became his successor

■ Teshub's symbol was the lightning bolt; he was frequently depicted together with bulls

▶▶ **Jason and the Argonauts:** p. 182 | **Castration of Uranus:** p. 115 | **Battles Against Serpents:** pp. 291, 233

Teshub Battles Against the Serpent Illuyanka

Teshub (**3**) and the serpent Illuyanka (**2**) both fought against and complemented each other. Both represented a part of the year: the serpent for the winter time; the weather god for the time of crops. One version of the myth reported that the serpent nearly vanquished the

weather god, but then Teshub received help from humanity and the gods. The great goddess of the land arranged a magnificent feast, during which Illuyanka and her kin drank so much that one man was able to capture the serpents and release the weather god. This man wished to be thanked for his help by being granted a night to sleep with the goddess. When he wanted to return to his family,

she killed him. In another version, Illuyanka stole Teshub's eyes and heart. His son succeeded in getting both back for his father, so that he could defeat the serpent.

Figures and Stories Relevant to Teshub and Kumarbi

An and Enlil, An as Kumbari's Predecessor, see pp. 30–31

Inana, Holy Marriage, see pp. 38–39

The Search for Telipinu

Telipinu, the god of vegetation, went missing. The gods, large and small, searched for him, but the results were fruitless. Finally a bee (**4**) found the sleeping god and woke him up by stinging him. After Telipinu's anger had ceased, a bag made of sheepskin (reminiscent of the story of Jason and the golden fleece) was hung in an oak tree. Within the bag, there were blessings for the new year for fertility, long life, and offspring.

Kumarbi and An The Babylonian, Hittite, and Greek mythologies contained generations of gods, developing from and replacing each other. At the center of the Hittite myth, the grain god Kumarbi castrated his predecessor, An. Afterward Kumarbi carried An's sperm, which created many things like the Tigris River (**5**) and Teshub. Eventually, Teshub came to remove Kumarbi from power.

El and Baal

■ El, "god," was the king god of Ugarit and father of the gods and people

■ Baal, "lord," was a god of weather and agriculture, and ruler of the earth

■ The cult of El was primarily observed in Ugarit

■ Baal was worshiped from Ugarit to Egypt; he was especially worshiped during the first millennium in Byblos, Sidon, Tyre, and Carthage

■ A bull was the symbol of Baal; he was often pictured with a thunderbolt

■ Several conceptions of the biblical God correspond to characteristics of El and Baal

El and Baal were gods of Ugarit, a city-state on the coast of the Mediterranean Sea. The city reached its prime during the second half of the second millennium B.C. Standing at the head of the pantheon, El acted as the king of the gods and as the creator of

El and a worshiper, Syrian relief, 13th century B.C.

both gods and people. He gave blessings and endowed people with offspring. His importance was apparent through his numerous appearances in sacrificial lists, and as a part of people's names.

Baal also appeared in people's names during the third millennium B.C. in Mesopotamia and Ebla. As a weather god, he was a cloud rider, exhibiting his power over thunder and lightning. He ruled over the earth as a king. His cult reached to Egypt and was also supported by many kings in Israel. Yahwe, the Judeo God, shares traits with El and Baal. In the Phoenician-Punic religion, the adoration of Baal maintained itself, while El became much less important.

The Golden Calf Baal was also worshiped in Israel. In Jerusalem, there was even a temple dedicated to him. Psalm 29, a song of praise to Yahwe in a thunderstorm, likely goes back to the hymns of Baal. In the narrative of the Israelites' escape from Egypt, found in the book of Exodus, the adoration of a golden calf is denounced. The people danced wildly and lustfully around this idol (**1**). Thus, it could have been referring to an orgiastic cult of Baal in his guise of a bull. In biblical texts, his worship was strongly punished and condemned.

①

>> **Resurrection of Osiris:** p. 77

Baal and Mot Once Baal found himself in a fight against Mot, the god of death and infertility. He was defeated and had to descend into the abyss of monsters, the land of the dead. Baal's lover, the warlike Anat, challenged Mot to

a new battle. When she succeeded and killed Mot, Baal (**2**) was free to return from the underworld. He brought his dead ancestors with him so that

they could partake in a feast. The myth has different interpretations: Baal's death and resurrection reflect the annual cycle of vegetation between continuous crops and yield. Yet elements of the king and ancestor cults are seen here that also assume a connection with the New Year festival.

Palace Building for Baal El had asserted that a palace be built for his son Yamm, the sea god. However, Baal ended up with the palace when he conquered the threatening sea god in battle. He threw a feast to celebrate his new role as ruler

of the sea. But later, Baal wanted renovations to the palace (**3**). His lover, Anat, approached the god king El with the request. Because of her menacing threats to destroy him, El eventually ap-

proved the reconstruction. In another variant of the myth, Baal and Anat called on El's wive, and she advocated the reconstruction. Thus, the holy master builder Kothar-wa-Khasis was called from Crete and Memphis to build the palace out of silver and gold.

From Baal to Beelzebub

At various points in the Bible, Baal and his cult are mentioned negatively. In the second book of Kings, a god named Baal Zebub was said to be the patron of the city of Ekron. In the Gospels, Jesus was said to have used the power of Beelzebub to expel demons. Both names are defamations of the name "Baal the prince" or "Baal the destroyer."

Figures and Stories Relevant to El and Baal

Inana, Parallels to the Myths of Baal and Mot, see pp. 38–39

Marduk and Assur, New Year Festival, see pp. 42–43

Nanna, Moon God Related to Bulls, see pp. 36–37

Teshub and Kumarbi, Teshub Similar to Baal, see pp. 50–51

Ahura Mazda

Ahura Mazda ("omniscient ruler") was the most powerful god in the ancient Iranian pantheon. The closer the religion of ancient Iran moved toward monotheism, the more Ahura Mazda was described as possessing characteristics of an omnipotent, all-encompassing god. Because of his identification with the sun and as the god of light, Ahura Mazda's symbols are the winged sun (**1**) and fire, a purifying element. He created the universe with his thoughts.

The reforms encouraged by his prophet, Zoroaster (ca 650–553 B.C.), changed him from a personal god into a representation of the principles of creativity and goodness. He also upheld a just world order, and was a world ruler who was willing to stand in judgment over the deeds of humankind. Ahura Mazda was also the father of the "twin spirits" Spenta Mainyu ("good spirit") and Angra Mainyu ("destructive spirit"), who determined what happened in the world. At the end of time, Ahura Mazda was identified as an aspect of Spenta Mainyu, who was to emerge victorious to lead the world and humanity to redemption.

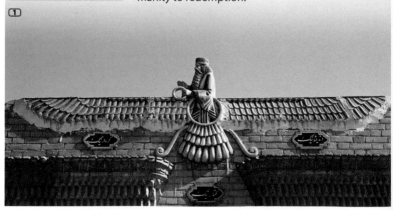

①

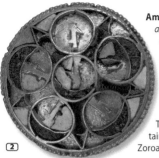

(2)

Amesha Spenta The six *amesha spenta* (**2**, "beneficent immortals") were originally autonomous Iranian deities. Later, they became companions of Ahura Mazda, who also helped him to keep order in the world. They each embodied certain principles important to Zoroastrianism: Khshathra Vairya ("power"), good governance; Haurvatat ("purification"), integrity and health; Armaiti ("compliant disposition"), devotion and love; Ameretat ("immortality"), life force; Vohu Manah ("righteous thinking"), purity of spirit; and Asha Vahishta ("right order"), clarity and truth.

Figures and Stories Relevant to Ahura Mazda

Mithra, Ahura Mazda's Helper, see pp. 58–59

Ormazd and Ahriman, Ahriman Was Ahura Mazda's Adversary; Ormazd Was Identified With Ahura Mazda, see pp. 56–57

Saoshyans Saoshyans ("one who brings benefit") is the central messianic figure in the ancient Iranian religion. It was said that "the spirited one" will conquer death and will restore life at the end of time. He will shake the dead until they wake so as to attend the divine final judgment. He embodies righteousness and truth. The teachings say either that Saoshyans will be conceived miraculously from the preserved seed of Zoroaster (**3**), or that the prophet himself will return at the end of the world as Saoshyans.

3

Fire Altars

Like the Vedic religion, which was a precursor of Hinduism, the ancient Iranian religion has been linked with a fire cult. In the days of the ancient Persian empire, the burning sacrificial fire was ignited on a stone altar "in the face of the sun" (Ahura Mazda) and tended by fire priests. The fire served as a symbol of cultic purification. It also represented the relationship between the original purity of the beginning and of the end time that was still to come. The fire temple or altar in Naqsh-i-Rustam (left), located in Fars province, Iran, was likely a major center of worship for the Iranian fire cult.

▶▶ **Fire Cult:** p. 282

Ormazd and Ahriman

The Persian religion demonstrated dualism, which was best exemplified by the teachings of the twin spirits Ormazd and Ahriman. According to these teachings, everything that happens is determined by the struggle between the principles of light and darkness, which both complement and antagonize each other. During the Sassanid period (A.D. 200–700), attempts were made to harmonize these principles with each other by regarding both as the sons of the god of time Zurvan: the "bright and sweet smelling" Ormazd embodied the principle of goodness and the "dark, foul smelling" Ahriman, the principle of evil. As he had wanted a son, Zurvan had made a sacrifice, but he had doubts of it working. Ormazd, who was often compared to Ahura Mazda (**1**), arose from the sacrifice, while Ahriman was produced by Zurvan's doubt.

■ In the ancient Persian religion, the twins Ormazd and Ahriman embody goodness and evil

■ Dualism is an important principle in Zoroaster's teachings; it was said to determine everything that happens in the world

■ In the teachings of Zurvanism, Ormazd and Ahriman are seen as the sons of the god of time

■ The Parsis in India are the modern believers of the Zoroastrian teachings

■ The purifying fire in the Parsi temples is supposed to provide protection from Ahriman and evil

Figures and Stories Relevant to Ormazd and Ahriman

Ahura Mazda, Ahriman Was His Adversary; Ormazd Was Often Identified With Him, see pp. 54–55

Mithra, Incorporates Aspects of Ahriman, see pp. 58–59

The Lion-Headed Mithra Aspects of both of the opposing powers were later combined in the lion-headed god Mithra (**2**). He also obtained a new significance as an aeon, or power, in that he was associated with the limitlessness of time that goes on and on, epoch after epoch, and creates as well as destroys. The snakes that wind around his body symbolize the path of the sun; the four signs of the zodiac on his chest and thighs represent the two solstices and the two equinoxes. His scepter and keys also refer to the power of the sun.

» Dualism: pp. 332, 384

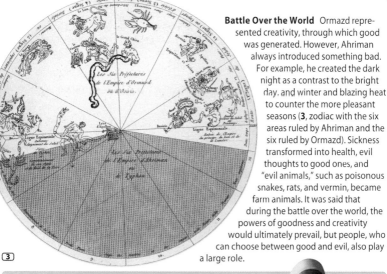

Battle Over the World Ormazd represented creativity, through which good was generated. However, Ahriman always introduced something bad. For example, he created the dark night as a contrast to the bright day, and winter and blazing heat to counter the more pleasant seasons (**3**, zodiac with the six areas ruled by Ahriman and the six ruled by Ormazd). Sickness transformed into health, evil thoughts to good ones, and "evil animals," such as poisonous snakes, rats, and vermin, became farm animals. It was said that during the battle over the world, the powers of goodness and creativity would ultimately prevail, but people, who can choose between good and evil, also play a large role.

3

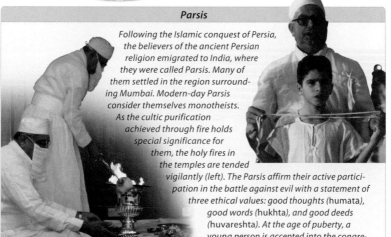

Parsis

Following the Islamic conquest of Persia, the believers of the ancient Persian religion emigrated to India, where they were called Parsis. Many of them settled in the region surrounding Mumbai. Modern-day Parsis consider themselves monotheists. As the cultic purification achieved through fire holds special significance for them, the holy fires in the temples are tended vigilantly (left). The Parsis affirm their active participation in the battle against evil with a statement of three ethical values: good thoughts (humata), good words (hukhta), and good deeds (huvareshta). At the age of puberty, a young person is accepted into the congregation of the righteous in a ritual that involves putting on a white shirt and tying a sacred cord around the waist (right).

Mithra

■ The ancient Persian god Mithra is related to the Indian god Mitra; the Romans knew and worshiped him as Mithras

■ Mithra, whose name means "contract," was the god of justice and of honoring contracts

■ As a god of light, he was a messianic figure

■ From about A.D. 100, he was also worshiped in Rome

■ His attributes were a torch, in reference to his function as the bringer of light, and a weapon (a spear, dagger, or axe), with which he killed the bull

In the ancient Iranian pantheon, Mithra, analogous to the ancient Indian god Mitra, was the god of contracts and friendship, but he was also worshiped as the god of light and of the sun. He played an important role in the rituals of male societies in Persia. Later, Roman soldiers took up the practices of this cult. The ethical principles he stood for include justice, virtue, and honoring contracts. He made sure that order was kept in the universe and in the passing of the seasons and days. In his original depiction, he was riding in a chariot pulled by white steeds, so the Greeks identified him as their sun god, Helios. Mithra also carried a silver spear. He was also regarded as one of Ahura's helpers at the final judgment when Ahura measured the deeds of humankind.

Killing the Primeval Bull Mithra's most important act was killing the primeval bull. He knelt down on the bull, grabbed it by the nostrils with his left hand, and wrenched its head up (**1**). With his right hand he thrust his dagger into the bull's throat. This act symbolized the rebirth of all living things because new life arose out of the bull's blood and semen that poured onto the ground. It also symbolized the taming and domination of wild, natural powers by the orderly rule imposed by humans.

>> **Eastern Gods and Cults in Rome:** p. 222 | **Mitra:** p. 294

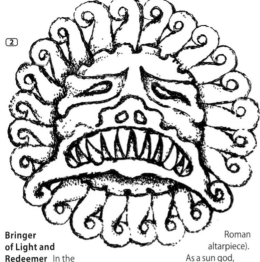

Bringer of Light and Redeemer

In the Avesta, a sacred book of Zoroastrianism, it is said that Ahura Mazda created and instructed Mithra, thus he should be worshiped as though he were the powerful god himself. From the start, Mithra was known as the god of light and the sun, and was depicted either as the sun (**2**) or surrounded by rays of light (**3**, Roman altarpiece).

As a sun god, Mithra was also a giver of life, and, by the time of the Parthians (247 B.C.–A.D. 226), he was transformed into a savior, depicted as a youth with a Phrygian helmet, tunic, and cape covered with zodiac signs. He was also brought into the Roman pantheon as a savior and redeemer. The goal of Mithra's believers was personal salvation. Representations of the Mithraic mysteries include a depiction of a banquet attended by the sun god Sol and Mithras.

Figures and Stories Relevant to Mithra

Ahura Mazda, Mithra Was One of Ahura Mazda's Helpers, see pp. 54–55

Ormazd and Ahriman, Mithra United Both Principles in One, see pp. 56–57

The Roman Mithras Cult

Mithras, who was supposedly born in a rocky cave, was worshiped in underground sanctuaries, called the Mithraea (left). Only men could participate in the mysteries, which were kept strictly secret. Believers had to go through various rites of initiation. Roman soldiers, who became familiar with this cult in Asia Minor, brought it back with them to Europe. In the third century, Mithras was linked with the Roman state sun god Sol Invictus ("unconquerable sun"). For a long time, the worship accorded to this god was more powerful than Christianity.

Egyptian Mythology

Pharaoh Tutankhamun is embraced by Osiris

Egyptian Mythology

With its annual floods and silt-rich soil, the Nile River Valley was the seat of one of the earliest civilizations. The two kingdoms of Upper (south) and Lower (north) Egypt rivaled against one another until they were unified under Narmer (**1**, Narmer stele) in around 3050 B.C. Centralizing the kingdom strengthened the developing pharaoh cult that lasted into the later dynasties.

Alongside the expansion of their political structure, the ancient Egyptians created an astounding religion that included a staggeringly complex pantheon of more than one thousand gods and goddesses. Most of these deities have survived as little more than names, but others are known through the images that depict them, the hymns that praise them, the magic spells that invoke them, and the tales that narrate their myths.

Egyptian gods, like the gods of any other culture, served the purposes of the people who worshiped them, reflecting their needs, desires, and concerns. Some pertained to fertility, agriculture, and animal husbandry, which provided the staples of life. Others served the political needs of the state, invoked to protect Egypt's borders or the person of the pharaoh, or facilitated the promise of an eternal afterlife. Most often, one deity served many purposes, which might overlap with those of another god. Even the singular act of creation was attributed to different gods, as each major cult center had its own unique theory of genesis. While today this might seem to be a breeding ground for theological confusion, for the Egyptians this multiplicity—and redundancy—of divinities produced a layering of meaning. It attempted to express their perception of the subtlety and complexity of the world around them. By the late fourth millennium B.C., precursors of gods that became famous later had made their appearance in Egyptian art, in the forms of figurines carved of stone or ivory, or modeled in clay. Always keen observers of the natural world, the Egyptians embodied the divine in animals before adapting the human body as an expression of the sacred. Although such forms, often combining human and animal features, might seem primitive, they were not intended to be taken literally. A god's power might be manifest in a sacred animal, such as the Apis bull of Osiris, or in a cult image made of gold and precious stones, but neither the animal nor the statue was the god. These things were merely concrete expressions of more complex meanings. Gods (**2**, Anubis and Horus, for example, who are depicted on this wall mural with Ramses I) were described as "mysterious," their true natures lying beyond human understanding. However, the Egyptian gods still suffered from human frailties. They could be greedy, lustful, or physically weak. They could grow old and they could die. Yet this did not stop them from pervading and controlling every aspect of the Egyptians' world.

The Egyptians envisioned that they lived in a universe centered on the Nile River, which flowed across not a globe but a flat earth. Above the earth stretched the watery realm of the sky, while below lay the underworld. Surrounding this created world were the waters that existed before creation, a primordial state personified by Nun, the father of the gods. The geography of the earth, sky, and underworld were known, but not even the gods knew the limitless, lightless, and motionless expanse of Nun. The Egyptians saw much of the universe in dualities, composed of pairs of either opposite or complementary elements. This concept of duality was best exemplifed in mythology by the gods Seth and Horus, who battled over the rule of earth. While Seth was the protector of Upper Egypt, including the desert areas and nomadic tribes (**3**, tribesmen in the Sahara), Horus was the protector of Lower Egypt, which saw greater urban development and held the pharaonic cult. Thus, both gods personified chaos—Seth and the deserts—and order—Horus and the pharaoh.

From the unification of Narmer, Egyptian society was highly stratified, with the pharaoh at the peak, interceding between his subjects and the gods. Next followed a bureaucracy that included nobles and other officials (**4**, figure of a scribe) who occupied administrative positions of varying degrees of importance, including the priesthood.

3

Beyond the government was the overwhelming majority of the Egyptian population. They eked out livings as farmers, fishermen, craftsmen, and laborers. With a centralized government, the pharaoh could mobilize these peasants on a scale previously unimaginable. With the labor of thousands at their disposal, the rulers of the Old Kingdom (ca 2687–2191 B.C.) commissioned enormous funerary stone monuments, the pyramids, that even today symbolize the apex of Egyptian civilization. Pharaohs of this period also dedicated temples to the gods throughout the country.

Late in the Old Kingdom, temples received grants of land to provide resources, including peasant labor, to support their upkeep. With such wealth, which had formerly belonged to the pharaoh, more power came into the hands of the priesthood and nobility. This relatively small, though important, shift in the balance of power scarcely mattered in the daily lives of most Egyptians. However, the period (ca 2190–2061 B.C.) following the Old Kingdom loosened the pharaoh's grasp on another important aspect of Egyptian culture that did have an impact on their afterlife: Other social classes now adopted funerary spells formerly reserved for pharaohs. Now all Egyptians could aspire to participate in the myth of Osiris, god of death.

Other changes also lay in store. By about 2061 B.C., a dynasty from the Upper Egyptian city of Thebes ruled the whole of Egypt. The falcon-headed war god of Thebes, Montu, became an important national god. However, soon another god venerated at Thebes, Amun, eclipsed him in importance. When yet another Theban dynasty freed Egypt from a humiliating century of rule by the foreign Hyksos (ca 1664–1555 B.C.), Amun's place at the pinnacle of the Egyptian pantheon was secured. As these few examples demonstrate, the prominence of individual gods—as well as how they were perceived and portrayed—was, like the fortunes of pharaohs, shaped by the flow of 3,000 years of pharaonic history.

The pharaoh had to continually defend his position as the "son of the gods" against the priesthood, especially the mighty Amun priests of Thebes. This gave the drafting of cosmologies (the gods and their families)—such as the Ennead of Heliopolis or the Ogdoad of Hermopolis—and the cults of the various gods large influence. Many changes in the importance of individual gods, especially the Aten cult of Pharaoh Akhenaten, are seen as a direct result of the power struggles between the pharaoh and the priesthood.

Throughout ancient Egyptian history, the official religion remained focused on the temples (**5**, Ramesseum temple in Thebes). Within them, reliefs and statuary portrayed the pharaoh presenting offerings to the gods because the pharaoh was the sole intermediary between humanity and the divine. In reality, the temples were staffed by an extensive priesthood, which—acting explicitly on behalf of the pharaoh—cared for the cult images, attended to the daily rituals, and oversaw the workshops, farms, fleets of boats, and other holdings of the temple.

5

Within each sanctuary stood a statue (the *ka*, or "double") of the god, made of precious materials such as gold and lapis lazuli. The Egyptians believed that their gods, although divine, required care like any living creature. Providing for these needs formed the basis for the daily ritual. Each day, priests unsealed the sanctuary door and left a meal within the shrine, which was then shut and sealed until the next morning. Renewing the god's offerings pleased the deity, who was expected to express satisfaction by maintaining cosmic order. These were private rituals, witnessed only by the priests. Periodically, the statue was removed from its sanctuary and carried in a festive procession.

The bureaucracy did not sever the relationship between ordinary Egyptians and their gods. Although they did not participate in the daily ritual within the temple, men and women had themselves depicted honoring the gods. They left votive offerings at the temples. Ranging from clay figurines, which could be purchased from temple workshops, to flowers, these were given in hopes of some divine favor, such as a child, good health, or success in a lawsuit. Some priests, acting as magicians, performed rituals for individuals. Physicians were also priests, and magic was an important element of the medical arts of ancient Egypt. Whether performed for official or personal purposes, these rituals commonly reflected some aspect of the myths of the gods whose powers they sought to invoke. When the cult statue was refreshed each day, it was placed on sand symbolizing the first land that

emerged from the primordial waters of Nun in the moment of creation. Water poured over a statue of the child god Horus became a cure for snakebites because Horus's mother Isis had protected him from the dangers of the swamps. In funerals, female mourners accompanied the body as the goddesses Isis and Nephthys, who lamented the murdered god Osiris.

For the ancient Egyptians, mythology was not merely a collection of stories about the gods. Mythology was an active force in their daily lives.

The Great Mystery of the Pyramids

The pyramids in Egypt that served as tombs for the ancient Egyptian pharaohs have come to represent an entire culture today. Contemplating the immense amount of labor and resources involved in these constructions always leaves one wondering the same question: why? The form of the pyramid suggests the primordial mound of land that rose from the primeval waters during the process of creation. A temple complex dedicated to the deceased pharaoh surrounded each pyramid, for at his death he became a deity, joining the gods Osiris and Re. Carefully aligned to the north, the pyramid and its temple facilitated the royal soul's journey to the sky to join the "imperishable stars," as the Egyptians called the circumpolar stars.

» **The Step Pyramids of Pre-Columbian Cultures:** p. 398

Heliopolitan and Hermopolitan Theogonies

■ The chief deity of Heliopolis was Atum; he created himself from Nun, the primordial waters that existed before creation

■ Atum was the head of the Heliopolitan family of gods

■ The Ogdoad of Hermopolis was argued to be the oldest of the theogonies

■ Thoth, the main god of Hermopolis, was symbolized as a baboon or an ibis

In early Egypt, each city had its own separate gods. As a theological step toward unifying the kingdom, priests created theogonies—stories about the gods' births and the creation of the world. By showing the gods as being connected through a hierarchical family structure, it also ranked the importance of the city. The two most well-known theogonies are the Ennead of Heliopolis and the Ogdoad of Hermopolis. Re-Atum (**1**, seated on a cow with Ptah) was the main god of Heliopolis. From him, the rest of the Ennead (family of nine gods) came into existence. Hermopolis, located between Thebes and Memphis, worshiped Thoth, the god of wisdom. In Hermopolis, he gave life to the Ogdoad (family of eight gods), who created the world.

The different theogonies are important for understanding the power dynamics of ancient Egypt. For example, when the pharaohs ruled from Heliopolis during the Old Kingdom, the Ennead became dominant in Egypt. The pharaohs called themselves the "son of Re," legitimizing their rule. Heliopolis was later replaced by Thebes in the Middle Kingdom.

⏩ **Hierarchy of the Gods:** pp. 31, 72, 308

Heliopolis—Nun and the Birth of Atum

Nun (**2**, his arms outstretched to support the rising sun) was the personification of the inert, lightless, watery abyss that existed before creation. Atum created himself by emerging from Nun's waters as a mound of earth. From this earth, he arose again as Re-Atum, the sun. The place where the first sun rays shone, the sacred benben mound, was housed in the temple of Re. Although Atum—the first god who sprang from Nun—was self-created, Nun was honored in Heliopolis as "father of the gods." The next gods to be born were also not really "procreated." The god-pair Shu and Tefnut (**3**) were sneezed or spat into existence, or developed as a product of Atum's masturbation. Shu was

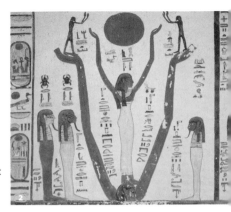

the dry air between earth and sky, through which sunshine reached the world. His garments were the

3

"wind of life." Second-born Tefnut, a lioness goddess, was moist air. One day when Shu and Tefnut got lost in the primeval waters, Atum sent out his eye to find them. Once reunited with his offspring, he shed joyful tears that became humankind. Together, Shu and Tefnut produced the sky goddess Nut and the earth god Geb. From them the remaining gods of the Ennead were created: Isis, Nephthys, Osiris, and Seth.

Hermopolis—Thoth and Creation of the World Before the existence of time, Thoth (**4**), who gave birth to himself out of speech, created the world with the Ogdoad, or four god-pairs: Nun and Naunet; Huh and Hauhet; Kuk and Kauket; and Amun and Amaunet. Each pair represented a primordial element: water, boundlessness, darkness, and air, respectively. When they collided, a mound of earth emerged—the city of Hermopolis, "the island of flames." As a bird, Thoth laid an

egg from which the sun god, Re, was born. As the god of words, Thoth was the heart and tongue of Re. The Hermopolitan version of creation was complementary to other theogonies, and so was maintained. Therefore, as Re was the main god of the Heliopolitan theogony, the inclusion of the sun god Re in the Hermopolitan Ogdoad allowed it to thrive amid the dominance of Heliopolis in the Old Kingdom. Similarly, Amun and Amaunet became the main gods of the Theban theogony, which gained importance during the Middle and Late Kingdoms.

▶▶ **Creation Through Water:** pp. 21, 380

■ Ptah was the chief god of Memphis, the capital of the Lower Kingdom

■ Ptah, the universal creator, thought the cosmos into being

■ He progenerated all the gods

■ In art, he is portrayed as a bearded mummified man, often wearing a skullcap and holding an *ankh* ("life"), a *was* ("power"), and a *djed* ("stability")

Memphite Theogony

The ancient capital of the Lower Kingdom, Memphis was known as Ankh-Tawy, or "that which binds the two lands." It was the religious and administrative center of Egypt during the pre-dynastic period and part of the Old Kingdom.

The theogony of Memphis is found on the Shabaka Stone

The theogony of Memphis was headed by the god Ptah (**1**, on the right), who was believed to have created the universe using his heart and tongue. Together with his wife, Sekhmet, and his son, Nefertem, they formed the main triad of the Memphite theogony. Other gods from neighboring Heliopolis were also assimilated into the Memphite theogony, often as incarnations of Ptah.

As the creation tale can be found inscribed on the Shabaka Stone, which dates from the New Kingdom, the Memphite theogony is one of the first to be text-based, like Jewish and Christian theologies.

1

▷▷ **Hierarchy of the Gods:** pp. 31, 70, 308

Ptah and Sekhmet The divine pair of Memphis was Ptah and his wife Sekhmet (**2**). Because Ptah created the gods through thought and speech—giving each life (ankh) and life force (ka)—he was known as the patron god of craftsmen. He appears as a mummy, wearing a skullcap and grasping a staff with the signs of authority, life, and stability. The lioness goddess Sekhmet, "the powerful one," was a fierce, fire-breathing goddess. Pharaohs claimed her power and protection on the battlefield. Because plagues served as Sekhmet's messengers, there were many strict rituals surrounding her cult to keep her happy.

Figures and Stories Relevant to Memphis
Apis—Holy Black Bull, Manifestation of Ptah, see Animal Gods, p. 105
Atum, Manifestation of Ptah in Heliopolitan Theogony, see pp. 70–71
Destruction of Humanity, Hathor Becomes Sekhmet, see Hathor, p. 93
Heliopolitan Theogony, Rival to Memphis, see pp. 70–71
Horus, Falcon God Working With Sokar in Underworld, see pp. 82–83

Sokar The falcon god Sokar (**3**) was the patron of metalworking, which led to his identification with Ptah, another craftsman god. Most important, Sokar was a deity of the cemetery. His main function was the purifying of the dead. When a dead pharaoh was reborn among the gods by hatching from an egg, Sokar cracked the shell with a harpoon. Then another falcon god, Horus, carried the dead aloft in Sokar's boat to judgment. In the underworld, Sokar ruled over the desert through which the sun god, Re, passed in the fourth and fifth hours of the night.

Nefertem
Although Sekhmet was a fierce goddess, she also had a maternal aspect. Her son with Ptah was Nefertem, the god of the lotus. He represented the blue lotus that sprouted from the primordial waters during creation; from the lotus's petals emerged the sun. Nefertem became a deity of perfume (**4**, women squeezing flowers). Worshiped at Memphis, he often appears as a man with a lotus blossom on his head or as a child seated on a lotus.

⏩ **Lotus Flower in India—Lakshmi and the Lotus Flower:** p. 299

Geb and Nut

Part of the Ennead of Heliopolis, Geb and Nut were the offspring of Shu and Tefnut, the first divine

Nut swimming with a lotus flower

pair created by Atum. Geb was the god of the earth. Images of Geb depict him as a man lying on his side, beneath the outstretched body of his sister-wife, Nut, the sky. Geb could also be identified with the divine goose that laid the egg from which the sun hatched. Geb's body was the land, making him responsible for earthquakes, but also soil and moisture, which made him a god of fertility. Plants sprout from his body. Geb reigned over the earth and appointed his son, Osiris, to succeed him.

The mother of Geb's children was Nut, the sky goddess. Her star-spangled body (**1**, Nut spanning over Geb, depicted lying on his side) made up the expansive vault of the sky, and she might have originally been a goddess of the Milky Way. As the celestial cow, she carried the aging sun god Re into the sky when he abandoned the earth. The sun was also said to be a child of Nut. Each evening she swallowed him. He passed through her body to be reborn from her every morning.

■ Geb was the god of the earth; Nut was the sky goddess

■ Geb's body is used to represent the earth, the mountains, vegetation, and the fertile valley of the Nile

■ Nut, often represented as covered with stars, swallowed the sun and stars and gave birth to them every morning

■ Geb and Nut were passionate lovers, separated in the day by their mother—the air goddess Shu—and together by night

■ The glyph used for Geb means goose and he is often represented as a black goose; black symbolizing fertile soils

Primordial Pairs: pp. 114, 352, 446

Role in the Underworld
Because she was symbolized by a coffin, Nut often appears on coffin lids (**2**), stretching protectively over the mummy. She is often depicted emerging from a sycamore fig tree to offer food and water to the dead upon their arrival. As the goddess who repeatedly gives birth to the sun, she figured prominently in the symbolism of resurrection. Geb was seen as the grave, from which the dead hoped to escape.

Nut Gives Birth to the Gods
Once, Re forbade Nut (**3**) from giving birth during the 360 days of the year. Thoth, who was in love with Nut, gambled with the moon to win enough light to create five more days. During this between-year time,

Nut gave birth. A voice announced that the firstborn, Osiris, would be a great king. Rhea delivered Horus next, followed by Seth, who actually tore himself from the womb. The goddesses Isis and Nephthys emerged last.

Figures and Stories Relevant to Geb and Nut

Osiris, Isis, and Seth, Geb and Nut's Children, see pp. 76–81

Shu and Tefnut, Geb and Nut's Parents, see pp. 70–71

Mummification: pp. 94, 416

Osiris

Osiris was a major god in Egypt mythology, as lord of the underworld and promiser of eternal life. He was most important for his death and later resurrection. Perhaps originally a god of vegetation, he was the first-born son of Geb and Nut. He was often paired with his sister and wife, the goddess Isis.

■ Osiris ruled the underworld and was the god of vegetation

■ He was depicted as a mummified king, wearing the white crown of Upper Egypt

■ His skin was either black—the color of decay or fertile earth—or green—the color of renewal and abundance; he carried the crook and flail

After having inherited the earthly throne of Geb, Osiris was said to have civilized Egypt and then went out to do the same to the rest of the world. When Osiris was murdered by his envious brother Seth, the magic of Isis, Anubis, and other gods revived him. However, Osiris took his place as lord of the underworld, so that his posthumously conceived son, Horus, could inherit the throne of the living.

Osiris wearing the white crown of Upper Egypt

Because of this story, the pharaoh was said to become Osiris upon his death, as portrayed in various funerary depictions. Eventually, common people, if they were mummified, also claimed to become Osiris when they died. This identification with the god who overcame death promised perpetual life and rebirth.

The Crook and Flail

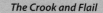

Depictions of Osiris often show him grasping two scepters—a short shepherd's crook and a flail with three strands of beads. These two objects were part of the regalia of Andjety, another god identified with the dead pharaoh. In the Old Kingdom, the Egyptians merged Andjety's appearance and identity with Osiris. The living pharaoh also carried the crook and flail as symbols of sovereignty over Egypt, because humanity was considered the "flock of the god."

Lord of the Underworld

After his murder and resurrection, Osiris did not return to the throne he had occupied as a living king. Instead, he bequeathed the role to his son Horus and remained in the underworld as ruler and judge of the dead. When Seth contested Horus's authority to rule, Osiris replied that if anyone disagreed with his decision, he would dispatch the spirits of the underworld. Osiris's ability to command these spirits made him a powerful deity. His threat was so horrible that none of the gods, except Seth, dared defy Osiris's will. Mortals likewise had to fear Osiris as a judge. He oversaw the proceedings in which Anubis weighed the heart of the deceased against *maat* ("truth") to determine the soul's ultimate fate. It was this role that earned Osiris the title of the lord of truth, and his throne (**1**, the dead standing before the enthroned Osiris in the underworld) stood atop a mound in the form of one of the hieroglyphs used to write the word *maat*.

Dismemberment and Resurrection of Osiris

After murdering Osiris, Seth butchered the body (**3**) and scattered the pieces throughout Egypt. Isis gathered them all except Osiris's penis, which had been eaten by three fish (**2**, the oxyrhynchus, one of the three fish). Fashioning a new organ, she brought Osiris's corpse back to Egypt from Byblos. Anubis and other gods helped Isis bind up the corpse as a mummy, which she and her sister Nephthys magically restored to life. As Osiris overcame this mutilation, mortals too were given hope of everlasting life. The act of dismemberment, which is not present in earlier sources, was a particularly strong violence. Thus, Osiris's ability to overcome it became an important part of the god's myth.

▶▶ **Resurrection of Baal—Baal and Mot:** p. 53

Isis

Isis was the greatest of the Egyptian goddesses. Daughter of Geb and Nut, she was the wife of her brother Osiris and gave birth to their son Horus. Ever faithful to her murdered husband, she restored Osiris to life with her immense knowledge of magic. Then, she served as Horus's tireless advocate when Seth, the god of chaos, challenged Horus's right to become king. In this role, she guarded the pharaoh, whom she was said to nurse as her own son.

A powerful goddess, Isis was identified with the Eye of Re, the sun god. As mourning goddesses or guardians of the dead, she and her sister Nephthys often took the form of kites, a species of scavenging birds of prey. The Egyptians identified Isis with the star Sirius, which appeared at about the same time as the flooding of the Nile.

Her protective, nourishing role made her an immensely popular deity among the populace. Curiously, she never had a centralized cult, and did not have her own major temple until about 380 B.C.

- Isis was also named Weret-Hekau, "great of magic"
- She was a protective mother goddess
- She was often depicted as a woman with a throne on her head or headdress
- She is often wearing a sun disk and has cattle horns on her head in Egyptian art
- She was identified with the dog-star Sirius

Isis as Ruler of All Lands Isis's worship spread from Egypt. At Byblos, in Syria, she was identified with Astarte. The Greeks and Romans adopted her worship and spread it throughout western Asia, North Africa (**1**, temple in Libya), and Europe. She was the focus of one of the mystery religions of antiquity, a rival to Christianity. Late hymns to Isis portray her as a universal goddess of countless names. She was ruler of all lands and giver of laws, languages, and agriculture. She separated earth from sky and good from evil, and could conquer fate itself.

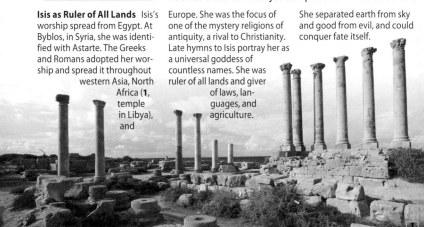

➤➤ **Eastern Gods and Cults in Rome:** p. 220

Secret Name of Re
As the gods were not immortal, they grew old. When Re, the sun god, became elderly, he was so feeble that spittle dribbled from his mouth. Despite his infirmity, he still possessed great powers. Isis wanted to learn Re's secret name, which would increase her own magic. She took

some dirt onto which Re's spittle had dropped and formed a snake. This snake bit Re, who cried out in pain. When he asked Isis to find the antidote against the venom, she agreed, but only if he told her his secret name. Re resisted until his suffering was unbearable. He revealed his name, and Isis became Weret-Hekau ("great of magic") (**2**, sorceress).

Isis Finds Osiris's Body
Osiris's coffin floated from Egypt to Byblos, where it grew into a tree that the pharaoh used in his palace. To bring Osiris back to life, Isis disguised herself as a nurse to the pharaoh's youngest son. She burned away the boy's mortal parts, intending to make him immortal, but the queen snatched him away. Isis revealed herself and demanded the timber with Osiris. Isis returned to Egypt with Osiris's corpse (**3**, Isis and Nephthys grieving) and the other prince.

Gods of the Canopic Jars

Four goddesses were paired with the sons of Horus to protect the organs. The vessels in which the preserved organs were stored were called canopic jars. Isis and Imsety guarded the liver; Nephthys and baboon god Hapy protected the lungs; war goddess Neith and jackal-headed Duamutef guarded the stomach; and scorpion goddess Serket and falcon-headed Qebehsenuef guarded the intestines.

Spells to protect against Seth engraved on a tablet

Seth

Seth, god of chaos and violence, was first a god of the desert and storms, the unruly forces of nature. By extension he became lord of all foreign countries beyond the fertile lands and orderly society of Egypt. Beginning sometime after the eighth century B.C., Seth became a god of evil, a deity to revile rather than worship.

As a son of Geb, Seth attempted to claim his father's throne by murdering his brother Osiris and depriving Osiris's son Horus of his birthright. Seth and Horus competing over the throne can be seen as symbolizing the competition between Upper and Lower Egypt. Horus's eventual victory over Seth meant the reunification of the land (**1**, Seth and Horus depicting the unification of Egypt).

The Hyksos, a Semitic tribe who conquered Egypt around the 17th century B.C., identified Seth with their god Baal. Thus, the Semitic war goddesses Astarte and Anat were said to be Seth's wives.

■ Seth, also known as Set, was the god of violence and strength; he embodied chaos

■ He was also a god of storms and the desert, which explains why he was associated with Upper Egypt

■ He was often depicted as a tall beast—perhaps a jackal or donkey—with a long muzzle

Figures and Stories Relevant to Seth

Geb and Nut, Seth's Father and Mother, see pp. 74–75

Heliopolitan Theogony, Seth as God of the Ennead, see pp. 70–71

Horus, Seth's Nephew, see pp. 82–83

Isis, Seth's Sister, see pp. 78–79

Osiris, Seth's Brother, see pp. 76–77

Thoth, Born Out of Seth's Head, see pp. 98–99

①

▶▶ **Baal:** p. 52

Isis Tricks Seth After his death, Osiris abdicated the thone of Geb to rule the under-world. His and Isis's son Horus was named as his successor. This initiated a feud between Horus and Osiris's brother Seth over the rule of Egypt. Seth insisted that his claim was more legitimate than Horus's, and appealed to the court of gods, which was headed by the sun god Re. While the process

dragged on, a beautiful woman approached Seth and appealed for his aid. Her late husband's brother was laying claim to her cattle, although her son was still alive. Hoping to gain the woman's favor, Seth said that the cattle should go to the son. When the woman turned out to be Isis (**2**) in disguise, the court of gods laughed at Seth for judging in Horus's favor.

Rape of Horus The day before the gods were to judge Horus and Seth (**3**), Seth invited Horus to his house and raped him. However, Seth did not realize that Horus had caught Seth's semen in his palm. When Horus went home to Isis, she cut off his hand, throwing it into water. After replacing his hand, she took some of Horus's semen and went to Seth's garden to speak with his

gardener. After learning that Seth only ate lettuce, Isis placed Horus's semen on the lettuce leaves. The following day Seth had his breakfast and went to the court. When he claimed to have raped Horus, the god Thoth summoned

Seth's semen from Horus's body to prove it, but the semen emerged from the water. When Thoth summoned Horus's semen, it emerged from Seth's head as a sun disk (**3**, the symbol of Horus).

The Warrior Seth's role was not defined by his chaotic aspect. He was also a god of great physical strength. Some pharaohs called themselves the "beloved of Seth" or compared their strength to his, for ex-ample, Thutmose III had himself depicted being taught to shoot a bow by the god. When the argument between Seth and Horus ended with Seth's defeat, Re appointed the god to serve him in the sun boat. Each night while traveling through the un-derworld, Seth fought the great serpent Apep (**4**).

Horus

■ Horus was known in various forms, such as Horakhety, a fusion with the sun god Re and Harmakhet, god of the dawn and the morning sun

■ As god of the sky, he was the patron of the sun and moon

■ He appeared as a boy, a falcon, or a sphinx

■ Because of his association with the pharaoh, Horus was symbolized by the sun disk

One of the most ancient of the Egyptian gods, Horus (**1**, on the left, leading Pharaoh Ramses I and Atum) was worshiped throughout Egypt in various forms. These forms often placed him in two distinct roles: as a sky god and as the pharaoh's protector.

Originally, Horus appears to have been associated with the sky, with the sun as his right eye and the moon as his left. His associa-tion with the pharaoh began

Horus as a sky god often wears a sun disk on his head

when he was incorporated into the myth of Osiris, as Osiris's son. In his battles against his uncle, Seth, to succeed Osiris to the throne, Horus acts as the pro-totype of the legitimate ruler. Ultimately, Seth's attempts to exploit Horus's weaknesses failed.

Horus is portrayed both as a boy and as an adult. In his youth, he is often seen as a boy sucking his finger, seated on the lap of his mother, Isis. The mature Horus appears as a falcon, hovering protec-tively over the pharaoh.

Figures and Stories Relevant to Horus

Birth of Horus Osiris impregnated Isis as a lightning flash while she was sleeping. When she awoke, she joyfully told the other gods that she was pregnant with the child who would inherit the throne. Atum warned her to be careful, or else Seth would discover the pregnancy and cause a miscarriage. So Isis hid in the marshes and gave birth to Horus (**2**, Isis feeding Horus).

Victory Over Seth After Seth killed Osiris, Isis presented Horus as his father's heir. However, Seth protested that he was better fit to rule than a young boy. The gods sent a letter to Neith, the war goddess, who decided Horus was the heir, but Re-

The Eye of Horus As a falcon god, Horus's eye was depicted as a human eye with the markings of a falcon (**3**), or the *Wadjet*, "sound one." In their battles for Osiris's throne, Seth grievously wounded Horus's eye, which was said to be the moon and thus explains its dim light versus the sun. In return, Horus mutilated Seth's testicles. Thoth restored Horus's eye to completeness by applying a salve. Because the sick hoped also to be made whole again, the Eye of Horus was often invoked in

Horakhety, the sun god, favored Seth. Arguments continued for years. Between trials at court, Horus and Seth fought and tried to outwit one another (**4**, Horus riding Seth). Finally, the gods asked Osiris to judge. Osiris decided in favor of his son and threatened to unleash the forces of the underworld if his decision was challenged. Seth demanded one more contest

Thutmose IV and the Sphinx During the reign of Amenhotep II, Prince Thutmose went hunting. At noon he lay down to nap in the shadow of the Sphinx (**5**). The god Haremakhet (an earlier form of Horus) appeared to him in a dream, announcing: "I am your father." If the prince cleared

medical spells. Wadjet amulets were considered powerful. Depictions of the Eye of Horus are often found within tombs to assist in the process of rebirth.

but the gods awarded Osiris's throne to Horus.

the sand away from the Sphinx's body, Haremakhet would make him king. Thutmose awoke and went straight to the temple where he made offerings to the god. He ordered the colossal statue to be freed from the sand. Upon his father's death, the prince, who was not his father's first-born, succeeded Amenhotep II to the throne as Thutmose IV.

Deified Rulers and Other Mortals

Egyptian pharaohs used their relationship with the gods to legitimize their rule. They commissioned shrines and temples dedicated to images of themselves. The Great Sphinx, a portrait of the sun god in the form of a man-headed lion, portrays the pharaoh's face. Government officials were shown prostrated before the pharaoh as if he were a deity. The pharaoh even appears worshiping his own deified image. This pharaoh-as-god often wears the sun disk or the curly horns of Amun, ruler of the gods, as a mark of his divine status.

Although seen as a god in the Old Kingdom, later the living pharaoh was either an earthly vessel harboring divine power or a god's son. Death made rulers into gods (**3**), joining them with Re and Osiris, who could also transform the souls of commoners into powerful spirits called *akhu*.

Imhotep A few private individuals became gods. The most famous was Imhotep (**1**). Also a high priest, he was the architect of the step pyramid for the pharaoh Djoser (ca 2687–2668 B.C.). Long after his death, Imhotep gained a reputation as a sage and physician, and became a saint of scribes. Considered a son of the god Ptah, he was deified during the Late Period (724–33 B.C.). The Greeks identified Imhotep with their god Asclepius.

The Pharaoh's Life After Death Upon his death, the pharaoh united with Osiris to continue his existence as a sovereign in the underworld. Architectural figures often depict the pharaoh in this role (**2**, Pharaoh Sesostris I depicted as Osiris). The pharaoh often appears mummified, wearing Osiris's crown, and holding either ankhs—symbols of life—or the royal crook and flail to his chest.

≫ Divine Rulers: pp. 48, 201, 220, 336, 368

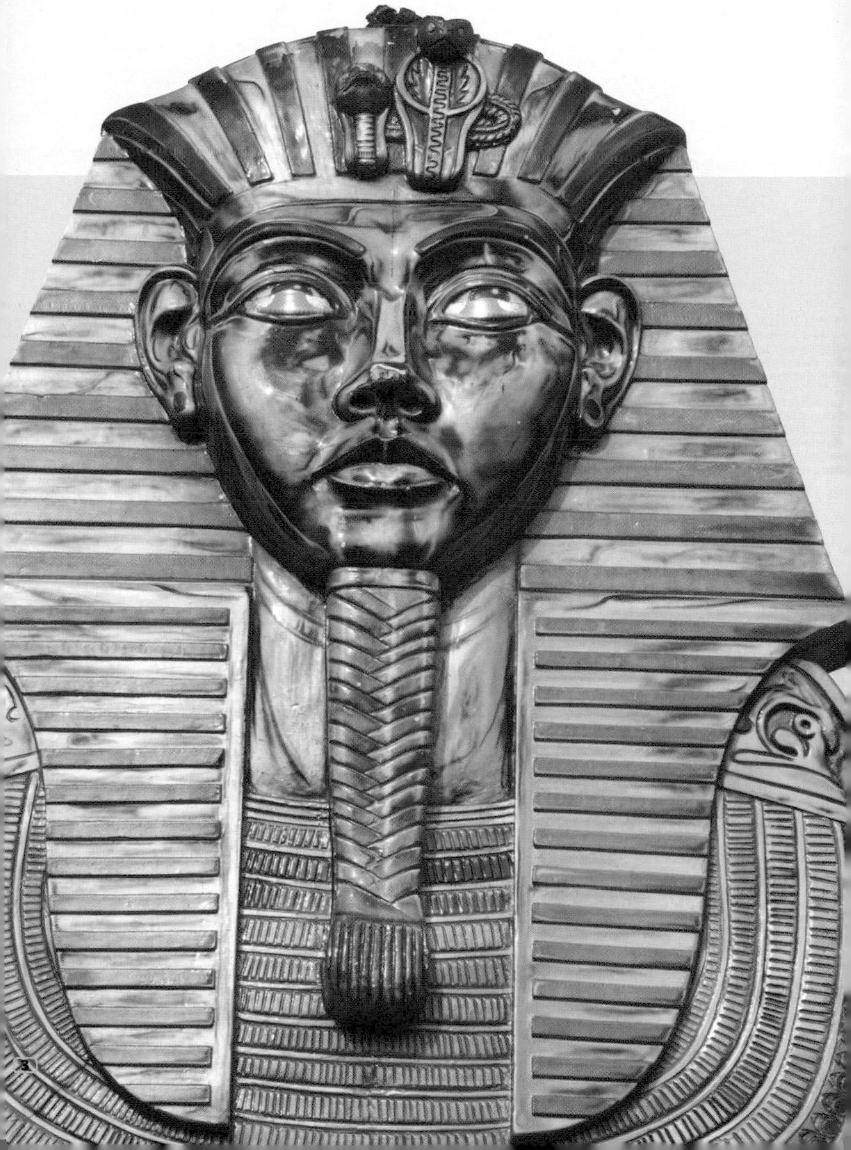

Amun-Re

■ Amun-Re was the combined form of the "hidden" god Amun and the sun god Re

■ This new figure was initially worshiped in Thebes

■ In the New Kingdom he became the main god of Egypt

■ He was celebrated as king of the gods and as the creator god

■ As Re, he journeyed across the sky and underworld causing the sun to rise and set

■ He was usually depicted as a man wearing a tall white crown with feathers

Amun (**1**, temple of Amun in Karnak) appears as one of the Ogdoad, four pairs of male and female gods personifying primordial forces. His name means "hidden" and he was invisible, perhaps originally appearing in Egyptian mythology as a wind god. Even other deities could not perceive his true form.

Amun appears only a few times during the Old Kingdom. Through the course of history he rose in prominence in the city of Thebes until the New Kingdom when he became king of the gods and chief god of Egypt. In Thebes, Amun was combined with the sun god Re—a common occurrence within Egyptian mythology. Thus, the sun (Re) became the visible manifestation of the concealed god (Amun).

Usually, artists showed him as a man with a tall white feathered crown, but sometimes they gave him the head of a curly-horned ram or the form of a ram-headed lion. When he appears with an erect penis, he is Amun Kamutef ("bull of his mother"), emphasizing his role as a god who engendered himself and embodied fertility. The poor also appealed to him for aid because of his power.

① 1

Amun Fathers the Pharaoh
Eager to underscore the legitimacy of her claim to the throne, the female pharaoh Hatshepsut (**2**, pictured with Amun) recorded her conception by Amun. One day, Amun announced to the gods that he would create a daughter to rule Egypt. The mother of this child would be the most beautiful woman in the world, Ahmose, the wife of Thutmose I. Then Thoth announced the child's name: Hatshepsut. That night, Ahmose received a visitor she believed was her husband. As the palace filled with the

perfume of Amun's body, he impregnated Ahmose. Khnum and the goddess Heket gave the baby life, strength, health,

dignity, and unsurpassable beauty. In the presence of the gods, Hatshepsut was embraced by her divine father.

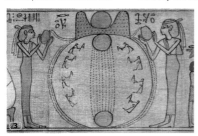

Creation By Amun Several myths explain Amun's role in creation (**3**, depiction of creation). In one, Amun was one of the eight gods existing in the primordial waters. They died after creating the universe, but continued to influence the solar cycle and the Nile flood. Another has Amun thinking himself into existence before making the egg from which he hatched. He also appears as the divine goose that laid the cosmic egg. Unlike gods in all other Egyptian creation myths, Amun remained outside his creation.

Journey of the Day and Night
Each morning, Re started a 12-hour voyage across the sky in the day-boat. At sunset (**4**), he descended in the west. From here, for another 12 hours, he traveled the perilous waters of

the underworld in the night-boat. The monstrous serpent Apep and other forces of chaos attempted to thwart his progress. Aided by other gods, he escaped his foes—and death—to reappear at dawn.

Creation Through a Cosmic Egg: pp. 289, 330, 439, 457

Temple of Luxor

Like the pyramids, Egyptian temples expressed the idea of the primordial mound. A temple like that at Luxor consisted of halls and courts lined by tall columns in the forms of the plants that grew in the marshy land early in the process of creation. The floor rose in height from the temple entrance to the inner sanctuary, where the cult statue of the god was kept, so that symbolically the god stood on the height of the mound. At Luxor Temple—constructed by pharaohs of the 18th and 19th dynasties—Amun-Re and his family were honored. Each year a festive procession brought the cult statues from the nearby Karnak Temple to visit Luxor. The pharaoh took part in these rituals, which reaffirmed him as the son of Amun-Re and rightful ruler of Egypt.

Aten

■ Aten was the sun disk and was associated with the sun god Re

■ Early in the New Kingdom Aten appears in the form of Re-Horakhety, as a falcon-headed man

■ Later, Aten lost all anthropomorphic symbolism, becoming the sun disk symbol, whose life-giving rays extended outward

■ During the reign of Akhenaten, Aten was believed to have initiated all creation

■ He replaced the figure of Amun to become the main god in Egypt until after the pharaoh's death

■ The sun disk of Aten often appears on the gods' crowns

Frequently worn as part of a god's crown, Aten was the sun disk, officially an aspect of Re. During the New Kingdom, the Aten became a distinct sun god. While Pharaoh Thutmose IV honored him, his grandson, Amenhotep IV, went even further. He changed his name to Akhenaten, "effective for Aten," and focused all worship upon the sun disk. He closed the temples to other gods and dismantled the powerful priesthoods of Amun.

The head from a colossal statue of Akhenaten

Early in Akhenaten's reign, Aten acquired the falcon-headed form of Re-Horakhety. Later Akhenaten rejected this image in favor of the disk, which reached down to earth in rays (**1**, being received by Akhenaten and his queen, Nefertiti).

The cult of Aten held him as the universal creator. However, only the pharaoh could know Aten. Unlike the other gods' secretive temples, the temples of Aten were roofless, which effectively exposed offering tables to the sun. When the sun set, the earth fell into frightening darkness and the living slept as if dead until the next dawn.

Figures and Stories Relevant to Aten

Amun-Re, Predecessor to Aten as Main God, see pp. 86–87

Hathor, Wearing the Sun Disk, p. 92

Horus, Part of the Synthsesis of Gods, Re-Horakhety, see pp. 82–83

▶▶ **Sun Cult:** p. 414

The City of Amarna When Akhenaten dedicated himself to Aten, he rejected the worship of other deities, especially Amun. So Akhenaten moved the capital away from Amun's temples in Thebes to a virgin plain halfway between Thebes and Memphis. Here he founded a new city, Amarna (**3**), "horizon of Aten," which he dedicated to the god for eternity. Akhenaten's reign is thus known as the Amarna Period, after the modern name for the site.

Assuming Divinity The son of Thutmose IV, Amenhotep III, called himself "the dazzling Aten" and, by claiming to be Atum, Re, and other gods, deified himself. After his death, his son Akhenaten (**2**) fused his worship with that of Aten. Akhenaten and Nefertiti assumed the identities of Atum's offspring.

What's In a Name?

When Akhenaten turned to Aten as his god, he ruthlessly persecuted the god Amun. People named after Amun changed their names. Throughout Egypt, Amun's name and images were hacked out. Some years after Akhenaten's death, when worship of Amun resumed, Akhenaten and those associated with him suffered the same fate. For the Egyptians, to destroy someone's image and name was to destroy their very existence, even in the afterlife.

Hathor

Hathor played many roles, most influenced by her identity as a goddess of fertility. Her name meaning "mansion of Horus," she, as a sky deity, was this god's wife or mother. She was also the wife or daughter of Re and, like several other goddesses, manifested as the fearsome Eye of Re.

Hathor was often depicted as a cow

Love, music, and joy were all under Hathor's patronage. The goddess looked after all aspects of female sexuality, including childbirth, and the fairy godmother-like Seven Hathors forecast a newborn's fate. As mistress of the west, Hathor greeted the soul when it entered the underworld. Hathor was shown as a horned woman wearing the sun disk or as a cow.

■ Hathor was the goddess of love, female sexuality, music, and joy

■ She also acted as the cow goddess of the underworld

■ She was Re's daughter and also the wife of Horus or Re

■ Hathor often appeared as the destructive Eye of Re

Mother of the Pharaoh The pharaoh, as earthly representative of Horus, was called the "son of Hathor." Depictions show the goddess—sometimes as a cow—offering her milk to the pharaoh as a young child (**1**). She also appears in a protective role, striding forward with her chin resting atop the head of the adult king. As Hathor was considered Horus's wife, she was also the wife of the pharaoh. Exemplifying this, when Amenhotep III identified himself with Re, his wife took the role of Hathor.

Destruction of Humanity As Re grew old, he discovered that humanity was plotting against him. He secretly summoned the gods, but the humans learned of the meeting and fled into the desert. Re sent his destructive Eye, as Hathor, after them. Hathor slew the people, becoming the lion goddess Sekhmet (**2**). To keep her from killing everyone, Re had an immense quantity of beer, dyed red, flood the fields. Mistaking it for blood, Hathor drank so much that she could no longer hunt. With Hathor pacified and the rest of humanity saved, Re retired to the sky on the back of Nut.

Figures and Stories Relevant to Hathor

Amun-Re, Hathor Appeared as the Eye of Re, see pp. 86–87	**Animal Gods**, pp. 104–105
Aten, the Sun Disk Worn By Hathor, see pp. 90–91	**Deified Rulers and Other Mortals**, the Relationship of the Pharaoh to the Gods, see pp. 84–85
Bastet—Cats in Ancient Egypt, Related to Hathor in the Form of Sekhmet, see	**Horus**, Hathor's Husband or Son, see pp. 82–83

Lady of Drunkenness
Although the ancient Egyptian wisdom texts warned against the dangers of intoxication, alcohol had its place in their rituals. The goddess Hathor was called the "lady of drunkenness, jubilation, and music," which could be taken to exuberant excess during religious festivals. Some tombs depict scenes of banquets at which the guests are so drunk that they vomit. Even the king danced for Hathor, offering jars of wine made especially for her (**3**, scene of making wine), to keep the goddess happy.

▷▷ **Deities of Wine—Dionysus:** p. 160 | **Terrifying Goddesses:** pp. 38, 265, 300

Anubis

The jackal-headed Anubis was originally the supreme Egyptian funerary god who oversaw the burial of the pharaoh and judged the dead. As the cult of Osiris grew in importance around 2400 B.C., Anubis was incorporated into the Osiris myth. Along with the political and economic exchanges between the Greeks and the Egyptians, their mythologies were transmitted.

The Egyptians proposed various gods as Anubis's parents, among them the goddesses Bastet and Nephthys and the gods Re, Seth, and Osiris. The Greek writer Plutarch relates that Nephthys seduced her brother Osiris, resulting in the birth of Anubis.

As patron of embalmers, Anubis played the same role for royal and common persons. He guided the soul into Osiris's Hall of Two Truths, where he placed the dead person's heart upon a scale to weigh it against maat ("truth"). After Osiris passed judgment, Anubis ushered the righteous toward Osiris for entry into the afterlife. The unrighteous went to the monstrous Eater of the Dead.

■ Anubis was the god of the mummification wrappings and associated with funerary rites

■ He assisted in the judgment of the dead and led the righteous to Osiris

■ He was depicted as a jackal or a man with a jackal's head

■ His black fur represented both death and fertility

The Role of Anubis in Mummification The Pyramid Texts, composed when mummification was in its early stages of development, speak of Anubis washing the entrails of the dead pharaoh (**1**). In the myth of Osiris, Anubis embalmed the murdered god's corpse, an act which was vital for his resurrection. During Egyptian mummification rituals, a priest wore an Anubis mask, thus assuming the god's role. This ceremony was important as the body had to be perfectly preserved in order to be successfully resurrected.

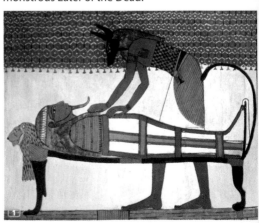

▶▶ **Mummification:** pp. 75, 416

The Book of the Dead

One of the most famous of all the ancient Egyptian funerary writings, the Book of the Dead grew out of the earlier Pyramid Texts and Coffin Texts. Written on papyrus, linen, or tomb walls, it contains spells that the ancient Egyptians believed would permit the deceased to exist safely in the underworld and to "come forth by day" among the living. This gave the texts their ancient name, the Book of Coming Forth by Day.

Figures and Stories Relevant to Anubis

Amun-Re, Anubis's Father, see pp. 86–87

Journey Through the Underworld, see pp. 96–97

Maat, Weighed by Anubis on the Soul Scales, see pp. 102–103

Osiris, Embalmed by Anubis, see pp. 76–77

Anubis as a Jackal The early Egyptians probably saw jackals and wild dogs scavenging in cemeteries and transformed these harmful animals into symbolic protectors of the dead. Thus, Anubis was often depicted as a jackal (**3**), with the black color of his fur representing both death and fertility.

Egyptian Burial Rites The embalming of Osiris by Anubis and his burial by Horus provided the ideal model for Egyptian funerary rituals (**2**). As the Egyptians hoped to live forever after death, just like Osiris, they mimicked the rites and prepared the dead for their judgment by Osiris.

Journey Through the Underworld

Funerary texts, such as the *Book of the Dead*, provided the soul with spells needed in the gloomy underworld of Osiris. Along the way through the underworld, the dead encountered a series of gates or caverns. Only by correctly identifying the guardians, who had names like "Reviler" and "She Who Cuts Repeatedly," could the soul pass through. The dead had to fight crocodiles, snakes, and the dangerous serpent Apep. The sun god Re—temporarily united with Osiris—also risked the underworld's dangers aboard his boat in the company of millions of blessed souls. Just before dawn he brought them to the Field of Rushes, a paradise of waterways, lakes, and fields from which the sun rose each morning and where the dead hoped to dwell. But, like Re, they had to return to the underworld each nightfall to repeat the cycle.

>> Osiris, Lord of the Underworld: p. 76

Thoth

The ibis-headed god known as Thoth (**1**, with Isis on the right), appeared early in Egyptian history as a lunar deity. Responsible for the regular phases of the moon and cycle of the seasons, he became the patron of professions associated with

Thoth was the patron of scribes

learning and recordkeeping. He was also a divine judge and an advocate for Horus and Osiris.

Thoth was often called the son of Re. However, certain texts also relate that he was born out of the head of Seth, who had been tricked into eating some of Horus's semen. In some versions of the theogony of Hermopolis, Thoth was the first god to emerge from the primordial mound. He then created four pairs of god—including Amun—who personified key elemental forces.

■ Thoth was known as Hermes Trismegistos to the Greeks

■ He was the god of writing, knowledge, time, and the moon

■ He appears as a baboon, as an ibis, or as a man with the head of an ibis

①

▶▶ **Hermes:** p.148

Thoth in the Underworld As one of the allies of Osiris, lord of the underworld, Thoth also functioned as an aide for the deceased. Although Anubis was the embalmer, Thoth played a role in making the dead body whole again, by restoring the head and heart. Thoth either flew to the heavens carrying the soul, or guided the dead person through the underworld into the court of Osiris (**2**). Here, Thoth would declare the dead man or woman to be innocent of all wrongdoing. If the dead was righteous, he or she was considered to be "true of voice" and entered the underworld. If not, the soul was doomed to damnation.

Thoth Invents Writing In the myth of Horus and Seth, Thoth was constantly writing (**3**) and delivering letters recording the arguments between the two gods' supporters, so that other deities could settle the matter. As a scribe of the gods, Thoth was viewed by the Egyptians as the inventor of all spoken and written languages. His skills also gave him access to special knowledge beyond the reach of other gods, and he invented the rituals practiced by priests in the temples. Thoth's female counterpart was Seshat. Called Thoth's daughter or his wife, this goddess was responsible for the measurements of all temple foundations and also for recording the years of each pharaoh's reign.

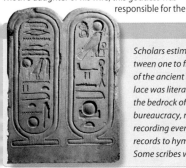

Scribes in Egypt

Scholars estimate that between one to five percent of the ancient Egyptian populace was literate. Scribes were the bedrock of the Egyptian bureaucracy, responsible for recording everything from tax records to hymns to the gods. Some scribes were taught at a House of Life, a sort of college and library associated with each major temple. Student scribes first learned the hieratic, or cursive, script, and were taught mathematics and complex geometry. Most never learned to fluently read the hieroglyphs of Egyptian writing.

Odin—Inventor of the Runes: p. 231

Khnum

Among the oldest gods in the Egyptian pantheon, Khnum appears as a ram or a ram-headed man. His wavy horns are distinct from the curly

Ba amulet: Khnum was the ba of Re

ones of Amun, although Khnum is also depicted sometimes wearing Amun's horns as part of his crown. Considered a god of creation, Khnum built a ladder and boats for the gods. He controlled the Nile floodwaters, believed to originate from a cave near modern Aswan, which laid fresh mud upon the fields each year. The floods were so vital to life that the Egyptians believed Khnum created all living things. Late in antiquity he became a universal creator-god. Khnum's wife was Heket—a frog goddess who assisted childbirths.

As Khnum was also known as the "ba of Re," it is not surprising that images of the solar journey through the underworld sometimes show the sun god, Re, in the form of a man with the head of a wavy-horned sheep.

■ Khnum was a creation god and a god of fertility, believed to be the originator of all life

■ Late in Egyptian history, he was named as the creator of the world

■ He formed gods, people, animals, and plants out of clay on a potter's wheel

■ The annual floods of the Nile River were controlled by Khnum

■ He appeared as a wavy-horned ram or as a man with a ram's head

Figures and Stories Relevant to Khnum

Amun-Re, Khnum's Shared Attributes With Amun-Re, see pp. 86–87

Journey of the Day and Night, Khnum Helped Re on His Solar Journey, see p. 87

Deified Rulers and Other Mortals, the Gods' Relationship to the Pharaoh, see pp. 84–85

Mural painting from the grave of Queen Nefertari showing Khnum leading two other deities; Khnum was believed to control the flooding of Nile and helped Re travel through the underworld every night

The Concept of Soul: Ib, Shut, Ren, Ba, and Ka

For the Egyptians, an individual consisted of several distinct elements. The heart (ib) was the seat of thought. The shut was the shadow. Preservation of a person's name (ren) was necessary for the soul's survival, and the true names of gods, being extremely powerful, were kept hidden. The ba corresponds closely to the modern idea of a soul. The ka, often called the "double," was a complex concept. It was a person's character and life force, and received offerings in the afterlife.

Djoser and the Seven-Year Drought On the island of Sehel, south of Aswan, is a stele text that claims to have been written during the reign of Pharaoh Djoser (2687–2668 B.C.). The inscription actually dates to more than 2,300 years later. This "Famine Stele" (**1**) relates that for seven years the Nile did not overflow its banks, which led to a dreadful famine. As a result, disorder spread throughout the land. The distraught pharaoh went to a priest of Imhotep, who consulted the Scrolls of Re. This priest explained that Khnum controlled the floods from the rock of Elephantine. The following night, Khnum appeared to Djoser in a dream, promising an end to the drought if the pharaoh would grant further concessions to his temple. When Djoser awoke, he eagerly ordered the governor of Aswan to increase the donations to Khnum's temple and to record this miraculous story.

Creation of People and Their Ka With Clay Khnum fashioned the bodies of all living things, earthly and divine. In art, he appears bent over a potter's wheel (**2**), creating the figure of a human child. He made the human form by "knotting" blood to bone, causing hair to grow. Then he built the skull and gave all the internal organs—from heart to bladder—their purposes. In creating the child, the god sometimes pointed with his first two fingers and thumb, a magical protective gesture. Artists also depicted Khnum forming the royal ka, which appears as a double of the young pharaoh. During the conception of the female pharaoh Hatshepsut (ca 1502–1482 B.C.), Amun instructed Khnum to form her body and ka. Khnum gave Hatshepsut the shape of a man, which was considered

more appropriate for her royal role. Khnum also fashioned the bodies of the gods, although the divine flesh was made not of clay but of gold.

Creation of People With Clay: pp. 22, 166

Maat—Universal Order

■ Maat was the goddess of justice and truth, as well as the personification of order

■ As a feather, she was the standard against which the dead were judged

■ She appears as a woman wearing a tall feather in her hair, and sometimes has wings

Maat embodied the Egyptian notion of truth, cosmic order, and justice. She was above all a principle, which was personified as a goddess. People perceived

The Maat feather was placed on the scales to determine a soul's worth

her through the regular cycles of sun and moon, the annual flooding of the Nile, stable government, and social harmony. She was the daughter of the sun god Re and she accompanied him on his sun boat (**1**). Thoth, scribe of the gods, was Maat's husband. Also known as Maati ("two truths"), she originally assessed the pharaoh's worthiness to claim the "throne of Geb," the god of the earth. Rulers showed their legitimacy by presenting Maat to the gods, who consumed her.

①

▶▶ **Universal Principles:** pp. 295, 332, 384, 430

Figures and Stories Relevant to Maat

Amun-Re, Maat's Father, see pp. 86–87

Deified Rulers and Other Mortals, Maat Assessed the Pharaohs, see pp. 84–85

Osiris, Maat in Osiris's Underworld, see pp. 76–77

Thoth, Maat's Husband, see pp. 98–99

Maat Feather on the Scales

Maat became an instrument of judgment for the dead commoners, as well as the pharaoh. If a soul survived the dangers on the path to Osiris's court, he or she entered the Hall of Two Truths. Here the dead underwent their final judgment. The deceased faced the 42 judges, during which a list of transgressions against Maat that he or she did not commit was read out. Then Anubis placed the heart, seat of intelligence, upon one balance pan of a scale (**2**). On the other was either the seated figure of Maat or her feather. Ideally, the soul knew the spells to prevent the heart from testifying against him or her. If the scale balanced, Thoth proclaimed the dead "true of voice" and Osiris welcomed the soul into the underworld.

Abstract Principle Among Beings

Maat was not simply a goddess. As the governing principle and "plan" of the created universe, maat made existence possible. Maat was also something that people, from pharaoh to commoner, did. People performed maat in everyday life through everyday acts. Generosity was maat, along with the proper collection of taxes. However, although founded on maat, the world was imperfect. The rebellion of humanity, which caused Re to withdraw from the earth, was one cause cited for the existence of chaos or evil (isfet) in the world. Isfet was the counterbalance to maat. In order for the world to be stable, isfet and maat must be balanced. However, the Egyptians believed that even if the universe ended, maat, inseparable from the divine creator, would persist.

Animal Gods

Representations of the earliest divinities in the Nile Valley take the forms of animals. The Egyptians honored gods in the shape or with the features of the domestic animals that were the basis of their economy, such as cattle and goats. Behavior, such as baboons barking at sunrise, inspired the forms given to other gods. Dangerous creatures also found their way into the pantheon as the Egyptians turned them into helpful, protective deities. In this way, potentially deadly cobras and scorpions became patrons of the pharaoh and were called on to heal the sick. Unpleasant scavengers, such as vultures and jackals, also acquired helpful roles.

Animal imagery was intended to be symbolic rather than literal. Likewise, the sacred animals honored in the temples were, like the statues in the sanctuary, manifestations of divinity in the world. At the temples, people could purchase mummies—most often not an entire animal but only bits and pieces wrapped up to look complete—to present as either a petition or thanks to a god.

- Animal appearance and behavior inspired Egyptian religious beliefs and symbolism

- Animal cults became important in Egypt and animals on earth were worshiped as manifestations of the gods

- In Memphis, the Apis bull was worshiped as a receptacle for the ba, or soul, of Ptah

- Many animals were mummified; sacred animals were often offered to their respective gods

- Female cats would be offered to Bastet, the goddess of childbirth and fertility

- Flocks of ibises for Thoth and falcons for Horus were reared by the priests in dedicated building complexes

Khepri—The Scarab The lowly dung beetle, or scarab (**1**), occupies a hallowed place in Egyptian mythology. The beetle's habit of rolling a ball of dung along the ground suggested the motion of the sun across the sky. The female scarab lays eggs in dung buried in the ground. From this emerge young scarabs. To the Egyptians, always seeking

symbolism in the natural world, this suggested life reborn from death, eternal renewal, and the sun emerging after the darkness of night. The scarab god Khepri's name means one who "becomes," "develops," or "manifests." Khepri was the sun that arose on the first morning of creation, and thus was a form of the god Re. He appears with the sun disk in the sun

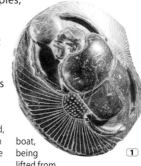

boat, being lifted from the eastern horizon by Nun, god of the primeval waters. Amulets in the form of a scarab were inscribed with a spell that prevented the heart from testifying against the soul when the dead stood before Osiris for judgment.

(1)

▶▶ **Animals in Myth:** pp. 230, 322, 424

Bastet—Cats in Ancient Egypt

Bastet (**2**) first appeared as a lioness who nursed the pharaoh. With the domestication of the cat, this gentler feline became her animal, but she always remained a protective deity. She was also a goddess of fertility, and bronze statuettes often show her surrounded by kittens.

People appealed to her especially at the New Year, when it was hoped she would grant gifts of abundance and protection. While her destructive aspect was the fearsome lioness Sekhmet, Bastet was also related to Hathor, the goddess of love.

2

Nekhbet—The Vulture Goddess

Nekhbet (**3**) was the patron guardian of Upper Egypt. Her name means "she of Nekheb," a town near the ancient capital of Upper Egypt, where her cult originated. Paired with the snake goddess Wadjet ("the green one") of Lower Egypt, she **3** was one of the great protective deities of the pharaoh. These two goddesses appear on the royal crown, and Nekhbet often clasps the hieroglyph for eternity in her claws as she shades the pharaoh with her wings. Royal wives wore golden headdresses in the form of a vulture, the goddess's wings covering the sides of the head and her head poised watchfully on the brow of the queen. Sometimes Nekhbet appears as a snake, wearing the white crown of Upper Egypt. Because she aided in the birth of the pharaoh, the Greeks equated her with their own goddess of childbirth, Fileithyia.

Apis—Holy Black Bull

For more than 3,300 years, from the first dynasty until Roman times, the Egyptians worshiped the Apis bull (**4**). A living embodiment of fertility, the animal was a manifestation of Ptah. Only a single Apis bull was kept at a time, and the cow that gave birth to it was honored as sacred to Isis. Distinctive patterns on its body marked a calf as being the Apis bull. The shape of a vulture appeared on its back and a triangle was visible upon its forehead. Its tail had double hairs, and the image of a scarab could be found on its tongue. When the bull died, the animal became identified with Osiris. Priests mummified the body and gave it an elaborate funeral. The Apis bull was shown carrying the deceased in a coffin to the underworld.

4

Greek
Mythology

Pandora and her box brought evil, but also hope, into the world

Greek Mythology

Greek mythology is the result of a unique process of acculturation that began when Greek-speaking peoples first migrated to the Mediterranean from the Balkans around 2100 B.C. Their language, religion, and culture were very likely rooted in the Indo-European tradition; and, like all nomadic peoples, they were able to adapt their beliefs and way of life to the new environment in which they found themselves.

The "Minoan" Empire of Crete, named after the mythic king Minos, with extensive commercial contacts in Egypt, Asia Minor, and the Balkan Peninsula, offered the Greeks their first introduction to the Mediterranean. The new arrivals on Crete would have witnessed their bull cults and the sport of bull-leaping, where boys vaulted heroically over the horns of charging steers. This spectacle alone could have inspired tales like the legend of Theseus and the Minotaur (**1**). The Greeks also learned about the goddess cults of this great, peaceful island civilization, and as they made contact with other islands and peoples in Crete's sphere of influence, they began to integrate these religious traditions with their own.

The Minoans were non-Greek speakers, but within a few centuries adopted Greek for record-keeping; a hybrid alphabet, known by scholars as Linear B, used Minoan letters to record names and items in this new language. Later, as Greek-speaking peoples established kingdoms on the mainland, the influence of the Minoan civilization waned. In its place a new more aggressive Mycenaean culture developed. Hilltop cities (**2**), palaces, and mausoleums began to rise in the Peloponnese, with high defensive walls built from stones so large that later Greeks believed only giants and gods could have put them there.

①

Around 1200 B.C. the whole eastern Mediterranean was rocked by a series of catastrophes; the port city of Troy in northwest Asia Minor was destroyed in a great fire, and the empires of the Hittites and Phoenicians collapsed with the attack of sea peoples. Even the Greek kingdoms of Mycenae, Argos, and Pyros with their massive stone defenses were ransacked. In the following centuries, known as the Dark Ages, mainland Greek communities became more insular, forming political alliances around smaller population centers that gave rise to the *polis*, or city-state. Seeking new opportunities, many Greeks sailed from the Balkan Peninsula to found colonies along the coasts of Italy, Sicily, Asia Minor, Africa, and the Black Sea, bringing their traditions with them. Because the Greeks were already a dominant force in the Mediterranean before the great collapse, these scattered communities would remain in contact with each other. They were united by a common language, a common religion, and by fading memories of an idyllic age when life was more secure.

When these scattered Greek communities began to stabilize in the ninth and eighth centuries B.C., they still had much in common. In addition to the Olympic games, Hellenic musical contests sprung up and Greek performers met in open competition, lyres and pan-pipes in hand, sharing the stories of their past.

Meanwhile, the Greeks had spread across so much new territory and encountered so many foreign cultures that their religion and worldview became far more nuanced. Through contacts with Phoenician traders, they had even adopted a new writing system—the Greek alphabet (**3**) was originally Phoenician—and they made perhaps their first contact with Assyrian and other Eastern religious traditions. The gods they had brought with them from the Balkans continued to interact with those from the rest of the world. To reconcile all these cults and present the world of the immortals as a unified whole would have presented a tremendous challenge.

Scholars have pointed out the important role that cultural biases played in Greek mythology: the survival of female figurines from archaic times has led many to believe that the earliest cults focused on female fertility, or at least respected the woman's role in childbirth. Myths also reflected the complex realities of the natural and spiritual world as the ancient Greeks saw it. For instance, the identity and position of constellations, so vital to the yearly agricultural cycle, were preserved in some of them. Others recounted, in abstract narrative fashion, historical encounters between rival civilizations. The raw forces of nature, to which all of humankind was subject, were also granted divine status. Mythology, then, spoke to the Greeks' natural and historical experience, but was also framed in part by their cultural and ideological biases.

In its earliest form, Greek religion had a more domestic function, with worship centered around *koans*, simple carved and painted images of the family's guardian spirits. Archaic figurines like these continued to be the focus of civic ritual processions throughout ancient Greece's history. But these humble household rites were comple-

mented by grander, civic ones. Urban festivals featured sacrifices of prized animals from the flocks of the city's most prosperous figures, but these offerings were largely an opportunity for ostentatious display, as well as a chance for the city's poor to get a good meal.

From these largely unknown household gods, the Greek pantheon began to take shape. Because the natural world was believed to be filled with divinity, the Greeks believed there were thousands of gods, all of them with names, natural habitats (such as trees, mountains, and springs),

and more-or-less specific functions. At their head, after generations of internal struggle, were the Olympian gods (**4**, sea god Poseidon), who were perceived as a kind of royal court. Like most royal courts it had more than its share of sex scandals, political intrigues, attempted coups, and acts of vengeance. An interesting point is that the rule of the gods was a monarchy, while the contemporary Greek political system was characterized by competing independent *poleis* ("city-states").

A key part of Greek religion was its reliance on oracular gods. Apollo's temples in Delphi or Delos, and Zeus's in Dodona became the focus of major cult activity, as people from all walks of life consulted the gods on matters past, present, or future. They had all-encompassing authority and power, as members of all Greek colonies asked their advice regarding foundations of cities or wars. Other central temples became the trusted repositories of a city's or a kingdom's most valuable property; these items, in turn, formed the basis for financial exchanges and loans, so that temples often served in effect as sacred banks. The temples reflected their riches in great statues, such as the famous Athena in the Parthenon (**5**), erected for all to see. The statues were housed in open temples, positioned to face the east so that they could exploit the light of the morning sun and create a spectacle god visible for miles around. Prosper-

⑤

ous civic leaders like Pericles in Athens sought to promote themselves and their cities with these great public works projects.

In ancient Greek, *mythos* did not mean "story" so much as it meant a carefully constructed, unified sequence of events or actions. It was the word they used to describe the plot of a story, not the story itself. As these stories were orally transmitted by rhapsodists for centuries, they existed in hundreds of variations. The earliest and main literary sources for Greek myth are the seventh- and eighth-century B.C. epic poems of Homer (the *Iliad* and *Odyssey* about the Trojan War and the adventures of the hero Odysseus) and Hesiod (the *Theogony*, a detailed genealogy of the gods). With these, numerous hymns and odes dedicated to the Olympian gods have survived, providing important background information on myths only hinted at in other sources. Dramatic poets, such as Aeschylus, Sophocles (**6**, performance of *Oedipus*), and Euripides, continued to revise the mythic traditions during Athens' golden age in the fifth century B.C.

While the origins of the Greek theater are found in religious festivals—more precisely the Dionysus cult—the main mission of the dramatic poets was to entertain. They spent much of their careers competing for prizes in contests throughout the Greek-speaking world. To understand the tendency toward anthropomorphism, the portrayal of the gods as human beings, and to appreciate the most shocking aspects of Greek mythology—Zeus's career as a serial rapist, the gods' inherent selfishness and irrationality, not to mention crimes of incest, cannibalism, even the eating of one's own children—it helps to place them in the context of the competitive music and theater scene for which they were made. Audiences and judges demanded vivid stories with bold narrative techniques; the more colorful and memorable the story, the more likely its author would go home crowned with the olive and/or laurel wreath of the champion. Yet, stories about the scandals of the gods served an additional purpose: shedding doubt upon the gods' power and ethical example. This led to the emergence of philosophy as a search for other principles of the world and life, found either in nature or in the mind of humanity.

Musicians, singers, actors, and dancers continued to perform these myths into the Roman era and beyond. However, centuries later, scholars and artists in the Renaissance were fascinated by the literature and visual arts of the Greeks, and thus introduced many topics and plots of their mythology to the modern era.

6

■ Gaia was an ancient earth goddess and a primordial creator of the world

■ Uranus was Gaia's son and husband and a personification of the sky

■ Together they symbolize the ancient Greek concepts of male and female

Gaia and Uranus

Gaia was one of the first gods to emerge from chaos—along with Tartarus ("underworld"), Nyx ("night"), Erebos ("darkness"), and Eros ("universal love")—at the world's creation. Although briefly coupled with Tartarus, Gaia is better known for her union with Uranus, her son. Gaia had Uranus to help her create rivers, seas, and plants.

Gaia and Uranus were the primordial couple of Greek mythology

Together the couple provided homes for mortals and the gods alike. They were also credited with parenting the Cyclopes, massive one-eyed creatures who created thunder and lightning, and the rebellious Hecatoncheires, mighty 100-handed giants with 50 heads. Their most notorious offspring were the Titans, whose rebellious nature led to the first in a series of uprisings among the gods.

Creation of the Earth, Sky, and Underworld Tartarus emerged with Gaia at the creation of the world (**1**). Together with Uranus they encompassed the universe. Uranus was above Gaia, who rested above Tartarus, and supported Oceanus and other waters that were her children. The world's size was so great that if an anvil was dropped from above, it would fall for nine days between heaven and earth, and take another nine days to reach the underworld.

》 Primordial Pairs: pp. 74, 352, 446 | **Castration of An:** p. 51

The Mother of All Gaia had a multitude of offspring (**2**, Hippodameia, Pelops, and Triptolemos). Her powers were so great that she gave birth to the hills and Pontus ("sea"). Because of her children—produced alone and with Uranus—she was revered as the all-producing and all-nourishing mother. Also the source of vapors arising from underground, she was seen as an oracular goddess. Temples honored her powers throughout Greece.

Castration of Uranus When the Cyclopes and Hecatoncheires were first born, Uranus was so offended by their looks and attitudes that he pushed them back into Gaia's body, who doubled in pain. Weary of her burden, Gaia fashioned a sickle of hard flint and urged the six male Titans (also her offspring) to rise up against their father. Her youngest son Cronus agreed. One night, when Uranus came to lie with Gaia, Cronus cut off his father's genitalia (**3**) and threw them into the sea. Uranus's blood was spattered all over the earth and gave birth to the Furies, the Giants armed with spears, and the Meliae of the ash tree.

The Titans

The most powerful of Gaia and Uranus's offspring were the Titans, who became the rulers of the world following their father's castration. The most well-known Titans were six males (Oceanus, Hyperion, Coeus, Crius, Iapetus, and Cronus) and six females (Theia, Rhea, Themis, Mnemosyne, Phoebe, and Thetis). In Greek, "Titan" evokes the image of "strainers" or "strugglers," and thus reflects their desire for power.

■ The first generation of Titans ("strainers") were named after primal ideas, e.g., Coeus, "query"

■ The youngest Titan, Cronus, was king after he overthrew his father, Uranus

■ The Titans symbolized pre-historic disorder to the Greeks

■ Cronus's son, Zeus, represented the birth of order

While most myths center around Cronus and Oceanus ("ocean"), their brothers—Coeus, Crius, Iapetus, and Hyperion—were associated with the four ordinals or pillars of the cosmos (north, south, east, and west). The Titans were also the first generation of gods associated with the realm of ideas: Themis ("custom" or "law") was renowned as a bringer of justice, and Mnemosyne ("memory") had the Muses with her nephew, Zeus. Rhea, Cronus's sister and wife, became the mother of the most important Olympian gods and was instrumental in her husband's overthrow.

Cronus and the Prophecy of His Downfall

As king of the gods, Cronus (**1**) shared his father Uranus's fear of being overthrown. Cronus repeated Uranus's mistake of once again imprisoning the Cyclopes and Hecatoncheires in Tartarus. Seeing this, Uranus and Gaia warned that Cronus would also be brought down by his own son. In fear of this prophecy, Cronus proceeded to devour his first five children, taking them from his wife Rhea as she bore them. Rhea pleaded with Gaia for help, and the two of them plotted against Cronus. When the next child, Zeus, was born they gave Cronus a stone wrapped in diapers instead. Not realizing the trick, he swallowed the stone and in so doing set the stage for his downfall. Later, Zeus forced him to cough up his brothers and sisters.

The War of the Titans After liberating his brothers and sisters—Hestia, Demeter, Hera, Hades, and Poseidon—Zeus led a rebellion against his father with their help. He wanted to take over the rule of the world. For ten years the war raged, until Gaia revealed to Zeus he would win if he liberated the Cyclopes and Hecatoncheires from Tartarus. Once they were freed, the Cyclopes fashioned lightning bolts for Zeus, which became his greatest weapons. The Titan gods were soon defeated (**2**) and sent down to Tartarus, where they remained for eternity, guarded by the Hecatoncheires.

Daughters of Oceanus
The Titan Oceanus (**3**) was said to be a river that circled the entire earth. He was the eldest of Gaia and Uranus's children. Together with his wife Thetys, he produced the 3,000 rivers of the world and 3,000 ocean nymphs, known as the Oceanides.

Punishment of Atlas As the son of the Titan Iapetus, Atlas led the fight of the Titans against Zeus and the Olympians. When the Titans lost, Atlas was condemned to support the heavens on his shoulders for eternity (**4**). The punishment was alleviated only once: Heracles agreed to shoulder the burden for a short time if Atlas went to get him the Hesperides' golden apples. When Atlas returned with the apples, he did not want to take back the burden of carrying the world, but Heracles tricked him into it.

➤➤ **Fighting Between the Gods:** pp. 26, 118, 238, 245, 458

The War of the Giants

When Cronus castrated his father Uranus, the blood that fell upon the earth became the Giants. Seeking revenge for the banning of her children, Gaia united with the Giants against the Olympic gods led by Zeus. The great battle (Gigantomachy) possibly took place on the Phlegraean Fields. There the Giants attacked the Olympians with enormous boulders and torches. Then an oracle said that the Olympians could only win with the help of a mortal human. Gaia started searching for an herb to make her children invulnerable against mortals; however, Zeus stopped her by prohibiting the sun and moon from giving light. Zeus asked the demigod Heracles for help. With Heracles, the Olympians succeeded in beating the Giants. Like the war of the Titans, this fight was interpreted by the Greeks as a symbolic battle between prehistoric disorder, darkness, and chaos, and the new world of order, light, and justice under the Olympians.

The Gigantomachy depicted on a frieze of the Pergamon altar, which was built in the second century B.C. in the ancient Greek city of Pergamon (in modern-day Turkey)

»» Fighting Between the Gods: pp. 26, 117, 238, 245, 458

■ Zeus ("sky") was patriarch of the gods, king of the kings, and denoted power, rulership, and law to the Greeks

■ He was known as Jupiter in Roman mythology

■ When the world was divided into three, Zeus took the sky

■ He was symbolized by eagles, oak trees, and bolts of lightning

Zeus

After having overtaken his father, Cronus, Zeus became the ruler of the whole world—the gods and humanity. His reign was characterized by order and justice, guaranteeing oaths, and maintaining order in the poleis, the Greek city-states. As the king of the kings, he acted as the protector of kingship. Moreover, Zeus was the god of heaven and thunder; therefore, one of his most significant symbols was the thunderbolt alongside the eagle, which symbolized strength and justice.

Zeus's most powerful weapon was his lightning bolt

Zeus was particularly worshiped in the cities of Olympia and Dodona, home of an old oracle. Although he was the highest god, Zeus had almost human qualities, especially his soft spot for the female sex. To the anger of his second wife, the goddess Hera, he had many liaisons with goddesses, nymphs, and mortal women. To succeed in his

Zeus Takes Over As the leader of the rebellion against the Titans, Zeus became the leader of the Olympians (**1**). In spite of this, Zeus took an egalitarian approach and shared dominion over the world equally with his brothers Poseidon and Hades. The three gods drew lots, with Poseidon receiving power over the seas, Hades given the underworld, and Zeus the sky. They shared possession of the earth. As king of the gods, Zeus presided on Mount Olympus, convened councils, issued decrees, and brought order to the stars.

➤➤ **Jupiter:** p. 206

Birth of Zeus When the time came for Zeus to be born, his mother Rhea, fearing that Cronus would devour him like the rest of her children (**2**), fled to Crete. There in a cave, attended by nymphs and guarded by the brave Kouretes, or spirits, Rhea brought Zeus into the world. While the nymphs nursed Zeus, the Kouretes made loud noises striking their shields with their spears to prevent Cronus from hearing the baby's cries. Once the child's safety was assured, Zeus was given to Gaia for safe-keeping. For centuries the young men of Crete performed loud martial dances to commemorate the great god's birth.

The Two Jars of Destiny One of the most vivid illustrations of Zeus's power and his knowledge of the Fates was the two jars (**3**) that stood by his throne. Inside these jars were all the fortunes of humankind: one jar held good luck, the other contained hardship. In his wisdom, Zeus always mixed the contents of both jars whenever he determined someone's destiny. The myth of Zeus's two jars is made all the more poignant because it appears in one of the last books of Homer's *Iliad*, as a story told by the great warrior Achilles to Priam, the king of Troy. Priam, once one of the most blessed of monarchs, lost all of his sons to the Trojan War. Priam had come to Achilles's tent to plead for his son Hector's body, so that he could give him an honorable burial. The mixed nature of fate was further exemplified as the great Achilles, having lost his best friend, was also soon to lose his own life.

The Olympic Games

Beginning in 776 B.C., the first foot-races were held in Zeus's honor in the Greek town of Olympia in the Peloponnese. The "Olympiads," or Olympic Games, were inspired by an oracle as an alternative to warfare. As a cult site associated with both Zeus and his wife, Hera, Olympia also hosted women's games called the Heraia. During the Heraia, women would compete in the same stadium as men. The Olympics were later revived in the late 19th century, but were only for amateur athletes. It was not until the 1970s that professional athletes competed.

(4)

sexual conquests he often used his ability to transform himself and others. He appeared as a bull, fire, rain, an eagle, and a swan, among other forms. With Hera and the other women Zeus (**4**) had many children, such as Apollo and Artemis with Leto, a Titan's daughter. His favorite daughter, Athena, was born from his head after he swallowed her pregnant mother Metis. Without the help of his son Heracles, who he had with Alkmene, the daughter of a Mycenaean king, Zeus would have been overtaken by the Giants, ancient monsters born of castrated Uranus's blood, in the Gigantomachy ("Giant War").

Certain details of Zeus's birth and rise to power mirror those of the Vedic gods, as well as those of the Babylonians and Hittites, while struggles for power are found among the gods as far north as Scandinavia. However, the island of Crete has long been claimed to be Zeus's birthplace.

Figures and Stories Relevant to Zeus

Zeus's Wives Although he had many lovers, Zeus only married twice. His first wife, the Titaness Metis, was forced into marriage. She assumed various disguises to escape him, but Zeus finally trapped her. His next wife was Hera (**5**). As the goddess of marital fidelity, she struggled with Zeus's affairs. Her jealousy was famed.

5

Rape of Europa One day Zeus saw a mortal girl, Europa, picking flowers. Inflamed with lust, Zeus transformed himself into a bull and approached her with a mouthful of crocuses. Then, he kidnapped her and brought her (**6**) to Crete, where he lay with her. They had three children: Sarpedon, the king of Lycia; Rhadamanthys, who became a judge in the underworld after his death; and Minos, the later king of Crete.

Zeus as a Swan Another woman Zeus lusted after was Queen Leda of Sparta, the wife of King Tyndareus. To avoid Hera's jealous gaze (and that of Tyndareus) Zeus transformed into a swan (**8**) and lay with Leda. Together they had two children, Helen and Polydeuces, who were born from an egg. Their mortal siblings, fathered by Tyndareus, were Clytemnestra and Castor. The princesses became queens of Sparta and Mycenae, playing central roles in the Trojan War. Castor and Polydeuces became the celestial constellation of the twins.

Io and Zeus Once, Zeus fell in love with Io, a priestess of his wife Hera, and slept with her. Before Hera could accuse Zeus of infidelity, he turned Io into a cow (**7**) and gave her back to Hera as a gift. Hera placed Io under the guard of "hundred-eyed" Argus, but Hermes (sent by Zeus) killed Argus and freed Io. Hera tormented her with a gadfly and forced Io to flee in madness. The Ionian Sea and the Bosporus ("cow-crossing") were named in honor of Io's many wanderings.

Pandora's Box

Enraged that Prometheus was trying to gain more power for people by giving them fire, Zeus was determined to have his revenge. He commissioned Hephaestus to produce the most beautiful creature man had ever seen, and summoned a council of the gods so that each could give the new creature a special gift. Because she was given special powers by each god, she was named Pandora, "all-endowed." She was sent into the world with a dowry given by Zeus in a closed box (or ceramic vase). Hermes then offered Pandora to Prometheus's brother Epimetheus ("hindsight") as a bride, and he foolishly took her. One day, out of curiosity, Pandora opened her dowry box and unwittingly released plagues upon humanity. Closing it, only hope, which was also in the box, remained.

■ Hera was Zeus's wife and sister, the patron goddess of women, and the goddess of marriage and childbirth

■ She was known as Juno in Roman mythology

■ She represented fidelity and was known for her jealous rages

■ She was often depicted with a pomegranate, representing fertility, life, and regeneration

■ She was symbolized by the peacock for her pride, and a scepter as a symbol of authority

Hera

The daughter of Rhea and Cronus, Hera (**1**, with soldiers during the Gigantomachy) was the most beautiful Olympian goddess. Zeus was in love with Hera, but could not seduce her until he disguised himself as a cuckoo and cuddled against her breast.

As a symbol of pride, the peacock was an attribute of Hera

As the patron goddess of women and Zeus's wife, she presided over marriage. Many myths show her as a jealous wife. In this role, she embodies the concept of monogamy, thus acting as a model of virtue and conjugal fidelity. She also oversaw childbirth. With Zeus she had Ares, the god of war; Eris ("discord"); Eilithyia, the goddess of the birth-bed; and Hebe, the goddess of youth. However, Hera's powers were so great that she also created Hephaestus, the god of fire, by herself.

Many regions in Greece claimed to be Hera's birthplace, such as the island of Samos, Arcadia, Knossos, and Argos. In any case, her cult was revered everywhere.

» Queens of the Gods: pp. 208, 242

A Goddess Scorned Many of Hera's stories revolve around her discovery of Zeus's extra-marital affairs. Once she plotted with the gods to bind Zeus to his bed with 100 cords and take away his thunderbolt. Eventually he was freed by one of the Hecatoncheires; the women he slept with, however, were not so lucky. Hera was wrathful, as seen when she took the voice of Echo (**3**), a nymph, who often distracted Hera during Zeus's affairs.

Garden of the Hesperides When Zeus married Hera, Gaia gave her a bough of golden apples as a wedding present, which gave immortality to the gods. The Hesperides—"nymphs of the evening"—were entrusted with guarding them. Together with the hundred-headed dragon Ladon, they kept watch in a garden far to the west beyond the ocean. Colorful sunsets were said to come from the Hesperides and their garden (**2**). During one of his labors, Heracles journeyed west, killed Ladon, and persuaded Atlas—who was said in some traditions to be the father of the Hesperides—to steal some of the apples for King Eurystheus, but the goddess Athena eventually restored them.

Holy Marriage

Many Greek communities annually practiced the rite of the holy marriage or "hierogamy," which was common in the whole ancient world. There were several forms of such rites. The marriage of Zeus and Hera was consummated by human proxies, or the statues of the two gods were figuratively married. Such festivals show the importance of Hera as queen of the gods. It was typical for ancient artists to depict Hera wearing a bridal veil and Zeus gripping her hand (right).

Holy Marriage: p. 39 | **Gaining Immortality:** p. 289

Poseidon

Poseidon, brother of Zeus, was the god of the sea and rivers. Because of his association with horses and chariots, the Greeks held chariot races in his honor. Through his dominion over the sea, its shores, and riverbanks, he caused storms and earthquakes.

Not content with his own territory, Poseidon often competed with other gods for dominion over parts of Greece. Once, he tried to claim Athens as his own, but his attempt ended in failure.

Poseidon is seldom seen in art without his trident, a symbol of his oceanic realm. He is usually riding a chariot drawn by half-horse and half-serpent creatures with fish tails (**1**). His cult extended throughout the Mediterranean, even into Anatolia and Ethiopia.

The trident was a fisherman's tool

- ■ After the war against the Titans, Poseidon received the sea
- ■ He was god of the oceans, rivers, and horses
- ■ His Roman equivalent is Neptune
- ■ Often represented with his trident, Poseidon would strike the ground when angry causing earthquakes and shipwrecks
- ■ He rode in a chariot drawn by hippocamps (horses with a serpent-like fish tail)

Figures and Stories Relevant to Poseidon

» **Nymphs and Muses:** p. 172

Poseidon's Lovers and Children

Poseidon's wife was the Nereid Amphitrite (**2**). Together they had Triton, who is often depicted with his parents. However, Poseidon shared his brother Zeus's passion for women, sometimes with disastrous results. With a nymph he fathered Polyphemus, the man-eating Cyclops that Odysseus encountered. Through raping Medusa, who was then transformed into a monster, he had the winged horse Pegasus, and the Giant Chrysaor. His brief fling with Demeter produced the flying man-horse Arion and the nymph-horse Despoena. His children from the earth goddess Gaia were the Giant Antaios and the sea monster Charybdis. By the daughter of King Minos of Crete he became father of Orion, a Giant hunter.

Poseidon in the *Iliad* and *Odyssey*

When Poseidon and Apollo offended Zeus, they were commanded to build the long walls of Troy. Yet the Trojan king Laomedon betrayed them by withholding the promised reward. Vengefully, Poseidon sent a sea monster against Troy, which was killed by Heracles. During their war against Troy, the Greeks were mostly supported by Poseidon. After the fall of Troy, Odysseus's voyages landed him on the island of the one-eyed Cyclops Polyphemus, Poseidon's son. When Polyphemus captured Odysseus's men and started devouring them, he was tricked and blinded by Odysseus, whose return to his family in Ithaca was then constantly thwarted by storms, earthquakes, and sea monsters, such as Scylla (**3**), that were sent by Poseidon, until Zeus finally made him stop.

Poseidon and Zeus

Poseidon was described as a god who constantly chafed under Zeus's orders. Once he even conspired with Hera and Athena to overthrow Zeus. While Zeus was found in his bed, powerless, Poseidon debated with the others over who should succeed him on the throne. But before they could decide, Zeus was freed from his bonds. As punishment, Zeus sentenced Poseidon to build the great walls of Troy (**4**). By contrast, Poseidon fought bravely side by side with Zeus in the Titanomachy.

Demeter

As the goddess of corn, crops, and fruit groves, as well as the bringer of the seasons, Demeter (**1**) had a prominent cult in agricultural areas like Attica and Sicily. The daughter of Rhea and Chronus in the Greek tradition, Demeter may have originated from an Indo-European mother-earth deity.

A fruitful harvest was essential to the Greeks

■ Demeter was predominantly a goddess of the fertility of the fields

■ Her Roman equivalent is Ceres

■ She taught humankind agriculture and was particularly venerated in the countryside

■ Her lovers included Zeus and Poseidon

■ Her symbols were either a tuft of grain or a torch to aid her search for her daughter

Demeter's association with the sowing and reaping of crops made her a revered figure among women who worked the fields. Moreover, she protected marriage and well-mannered family life in general. Men dared not chop down her sacred trees for fear of retribution.

The most sacred time of year for Demeter was when the harvest was gathered, winnowed, and celebrated by festivals and secret rituals. Keeping Demeter happy was essential. Although generous by nature, her fury when betrayed was fierce, seen in her reaction to the kidnaping of Persephone.

›› **Teachers of Agriculture:** pp. 24, 335

Demeter's Love Affairs

Demeter was never married, but she attracted some of the Olympians. Even her own brother Zeus became her lover, and a jealous one at that. At the wedding of Cadmus, the founder of Thebes, Demeter had an affair with the young Iasion, son of Zeus and Electra. Upon discovering the couple, Zeus is said to have killed Iasion with a thunderbolt.

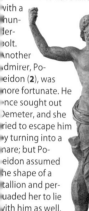

Another admirer, Poseidon (**2**), was more fortunate. He once sought out Demeter, and she tried to escape him by turning into a mare; but Poseidon assumed the shape of a stallion and persuaded her to lie with him as well.

Figures and Stories Relevant to Demeter

Ceres, Demeter's Roman Equivalent, see pp. 316–317

Hades and Persephone, see pp. 154–155

Poseidon, Demeter's Lover, see pp. 128–129

Zeus, Demeter's Lover and Brother, see pp. 120–121

Demeter's Children Demeter had several children. Persephone (**3**, with Demeter), queen of the underworld, and Iacchus, a god of revelry associated with Dionysus, were her offspring from Zeus. Plutus, the god of wealth, was her son from Iasion. Arion, the flying horse that accompanied Heracles, was a result of her affair with Poseidon.

The Eleusinian Mysteries The plains of Eleusis were the center of worship for Demeter (**4**), her daughter Persephone, and her son Iacchus. A renowned temple was built in Eleusis, where Demeter's cult was introduced from Crete. It was also the place where Persephone was reunited with Demeter, and where humanity learned the art of cultivating crops. The focus of the Eleusinian Mysteries was the cycle of death, rebirth, and the promise of everlasting life, as symbolized by the descent and return of Persephone from the underworld. A broth of barley and mint (sacred to Demeter and Persephone, respectively) was drunk as part of these rites, which were simultaneously solemn and boisterous.

Apollo

The god of prophecy, music, and healing, youthful Apollo was also a great archer. Like his twin sister Artemis, he delighted in nature and was often depicted with a chariot, bow, and arrow.

■ Apollo was an ideal figure of youth, and the god of music, poetry, and the arts

■ A complex figure, he was also god of light and the sun, archery, medicine, and healing, but he also had the power to cause plagues and illness

■ As Apollo was a great god of prophecy, the most famous Greek oracle, at Delphi, was dedicated to him

■ He is seen playing a lyre or kithara, but he is also depicted holding quiver, bow, and arrow ready for use

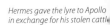

Hermes gave the lyre to Apollo in exchange for his stolen cattle

Apollo's origins show signs of a mixed Hittite and Indo-European heritage; the Greeks say he came from Zeus's union with Leto, who had to hide from Hera's jealous wrath on the island of Delos where the god (and his sister Artemis) could be born in safety. Thus Delos became a prominent place for the worship of Apollo. By slaying Python at Delphi, he established his oracular cult there. With the power to both create and end plagues, Apollo was also the father of Asclepius, god of medicine.

Apart from his arrows, particularly fearsome to the Greeks in the Trojan War, the lyre was also commonly attributed to Apollo. He shared honors with Dionysus at musical and dramatic festivals. On Mount Olympus, Apollo was the choir master of the Muses, with whom he fathered many children.

Battle With Python When Apollo first came to Delphi, he found an ancient oracle of Gaia guarded by the great serpent Python. As Python had threatened and stalked his mother Leto in her pregnancy and had plagued the countryside near Mount Parnassus, Apollo slew the beast (**1**). However, because Python was sacred, Apollo had to undergo a rite of purification. He instituted the Pythian Games at Delphi in the dragon's memory.

1

Competition With Pan Even as a baby, Apollo had mastered the lyre, a stringed instrument played with a plectrum. Yet the shepherds' god Pan, a son of Hermes, believed he was a better player. When the nymph Syrinx turned into a clump of reeds rather than yield to his advances, Pan turned the reeds into a set of pipes and bragged that the tunes he played on them were superior to Apollo's. A contest between the two gods was arranged with the mountain god Tmolus as judge (**2**). Pan's rustic melodies lost out to Apollo's more enjoyable tunes. When a witness, King Midas, protested the decision, he was given donkey's ears.

Apollo and Daphne When Apollo ridiculed the archery skills of Eros, the god of love made him fall for the nymph Daphne, daughter of the river god Peneus and Creusa. Apollo was so enamored that he had another suitor, Leukippos, put to death so he could have Daphne to himself. Determined to remain a virgin, she ran. Standing by the river banks, she called to her father to protect her. He transformed her into a laurel tree—her feet became roots and her arms grew branches (**3**, with Apollo). Apollo wore and gave out laurel wreaths in her memory.

Figures and Stories Relevant to Apollo

Artemis, Apollo's Twin Sister, see pp. 136–137

Eros, Made Apollo Love Daphne, see pp. 146–147

Python, see Monsters and Giants, pp. 174–175

The Trojan War, see pp. 184–185

Zeus, Apollo's Father, see pp. 120–123

The Oracle of Delphi

The oracle at Delphi (**2**), located on the slope of Mount Parnassus, was the most trusted and sought-after in the ancient world. Established in prehistoric times, it belonged to the earth goddess Gaia until the eighth century B.C. when it began to function as the oracle of Apollo. According to legend Apollo slew the serpent Python, who the Pythia—the priestess of the oracle—was named after. In post-classical and Roman times the oracle saw many ups and downs until it was abolished in A.D. 393 by Emperor Theodosius. The oracle complex was marked by the *omphalos*, or "navel" stone of the world. The temple had famous maxims such as "know thyself."

The Pythia was a young virgin (later a woman aged 50 or more) chosen from the local peasantry to serve Apollo (above) at his temple; she had to have led a blameless life and to be clean of physical or moral defects

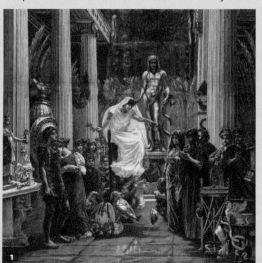

Priestess of Apollo The Pythia, or priestess of Apollo, lived a highly circumscribed life. Regarded as Apollo's bride, the priestess was presented in a traditional wedding dress, and was expected to live as a virgin throughout her years of service. When consulted, the priestess would go to a private room in Apollo's temple and sit on a stool set over a hole (**1**) emitting noxious fumes, which were said to be the remains of Python. Breathing the fumes, she would fall into a trance. While possessed by the god, she would utter a prophecy that was then translated by one of the attending male priests. The procedure was a well-organized, flourishing business.

>> Divination and Prophecy: pp. 120, 207, 217, 447

Artemis

■ Artemis was the virgin goddess of chastity, forests, wild animals, and the hunt, also of childbirth and fertility

■ Her equivalent in the Roman tradition is Diana

■ She often appears in a forest and is represented with quiver, bow, and arrow; she is often accompanied by a deer or stag

Artemis and Apollo were the product of an love affair that Zeus had with his cousin Leto. Hera was displeased and decreed that Leto should find no solid ground to give birth to her offspring. At last, the island Delos was found as a suitable place, and after Artemis was born she even helped her mother to bring forth her twin brother Apollo. Delos later became a center of Artemis's cult. As a girl, Artemis persuaded Zeus to grant her six wishes, among them to remain chaste and unmarried eternally and to be properly equipped for hunting. So she was revered as the goddess of chastity, the hunt, and wild animals. As a former midwife she was invoked in childbirth, but when a woman died after giving birth to a child, it was attributed to Artemis's arrows.

In Greece, Artemis was usually portrayed as a maiden huntress, but her cult had various aspects: In Arcadia she was primarily a goddess of the forest, and her symbol was a bear; in Tauris on Crimea her cult had orgiastic features; and in Ephesus, where a great temple, one of the Seven Wonders of the World, was erected in her honor, Artemis was regarded as a fertility goddess.

Innocence Preserved and Innocence Lost

Artemis always fiercely defended the chastity of herself and of her followers. For example, the giant hunter Orion was once one of her favorite companions. However, when he tried to rape one of her followers (some sources say he tried to rape Artemis), he was promptly killed. When Zeus fell in love with Callisto, a beautiful, chaste nymph in the retinue of Artemis, he transformed himself into Artemis so that he could sleep with her (**1**). As Callisto soon became pregnant, Artemis found out about the affair and turned Callisto into a bear. In her memory, Zeus placed her and their son Arcas in the sky as Ursa Major and Minor.

Niobe's Children In a myth that describes the harshness of the gods, Queen Niobe of Thebes gave birth to seven daughters and seven sons. She boasted that her childbearing was superior to that of Leto, who had only two offspring. Leto's children, Artemis and Apollo, took their revenge by slaying all her children (**2**). Upon seeing his dead children, Niobe's husband, Amphion, committed suicide in his despair. Grief-stricken, Niobe went to Mount Sipylus, carrying her youngest daughter, where they turned into stone. A mountain river sprang from Niobe's tears.

> ### Figures and Stories Relevant to Artemis
>
> **Apollo**, Artemis's Twin Brother, see pp. 132–133
> **House of Atreus**, Family of Iphigeneia, see pp. 190–191
> **Nymphs**, see pp. 172–173
> **Zeus**, Artemis's Father, see pp. 120–123

Hounds of Acteon The hunter Acteon was a descendant of Apollo through his grandmother Cyrene. One day while out hunting in the mountains with his pack of 50 dogs, Acteon stumbled upon Artemis while she was bathing naked in a forest spring. Because Acteon dared to look upon the goddess naked, Artemis in her rage transformed him into a stag. Then Acteon's dogs, no longer recognizing their master, chased the stag and tore him to pieces (**4**).

Iphigeneia at Aulis With the Greek army assembled at Aulis preparing to attack the city of Troy, Agamemnon shot a stag and boasted he was a better archer than Artemis. In revenge, she held back the winds, making it impossible for the army to sail. Agamemnon was forced to sacrifice his daughter Iphigeneia; however, Artemis took pity on her (**3**). Artemis substituted a hind for her on the altar, and sent the princess to Tauris as her priestess.

■ Minerva in the Roman tradition, Athena had many epithets, such as Parthenos ("virgin") and Nike ("victory")

■ She was the goddess of arts, war, and wisdom

■ She was symbolized by an owl, a shield, or an olive tree, and pictured in full armor

Athena

The goddess of war, wisdom, and the arts, Athena was the favorite daughter of Zeus. She was born from Zeus's head, full grown and in armor.

Athena was often accompanied by an owl, as depicted on this Athenian coin

She was referred to as the virgin goddess—Athena Parthenos—by the Greeks. True to this, she never had any love affairs, unlike most of the other Olympic gods and goddesses. She was named the patron goddess of many Greek cities including, most famously, Athens and Sparta. The artistic depictions of her in this role often show her bearing full military arms.

However, she was not only a warrior. She was also the patron of craftsmen and artists. She taught the Greeks how to cook and sew. As a friend of the demigod Prometheus, she gladly shared her wisdom and intelligence with humankind.

The Cult of Athena

As goddess of war, Athena Promachos was associated with defense rather than attack. The Greeks built her shrines on top of their citadels so that she might defend their cities against invaders. The Greeks also built her shrines on the prows of their triremes so that she might protect their ships in battle. As Athena was also the goddess of wisdom and the arts, philosophers, historians, teachers, sculptors, weavers, and potters also built her shrines within their homes.

》 Minerva: p. 210

Athena and Arachne When the mortal woman Arachne, a famous weaver, challenged Athena to a contest (**1**), the goddess could not refuse. She wove a tapestry showing her competition against Poseidon at Athens, while Arachne wove a tapestry showing Zeus's 21 infidelities. Outraged by the subject of Arachne's tapestry, Athena destroyed Arachne's work. Later, when Arachne realized her arrogance, she hung herself, but Athena took pity on her. She brought her back to life as a spider.

Competition With Poseidon Over Attica
When people settled in Attica, both Poseidon and Athena wanted to be the patron god of the new city. Poseidon plunged his trident into the ground and a stream arose, which gave the citizens access to the sea. Athena planted a domesticated olive tree (**3**), which would give them an endless supply of wood, oil, and food. Seeing the value of Athena's gift, the people chose her as their new patron, renaming the city Athens.

Birth of the Monster Medusa One day Poseidon chased a beautiful young girl named Medusa into one of Athena's temples. Catching the girl under the goddess's statue on the altar, he raped her. Furious about what had happened in her temple, Athena transformed Medusa into a hideous, green Gorgon with snakes for hair (**2**). Afterward, all humans who met the gaze of Medusa were turned to stone until she was slain by Perseus.

> ### Figures and Stories Relevant to Athena
>
> Judgment of Paris, see Aphrodite, pp. 142–143
>
> Perseus, Helped by Athena, see pp. 180–181
>
> The Trojan War, see pp. 184–185
>
> Zeus, Athena's Father, see pp. 120–123

Ares

The son of Zeus and Hera, Ares was the god of warfare. Associated with armies and battles, he was also linked with civil wars, insurrections, and violence. Out of his amorous affair with Aphrodite, the goddess of love and beauty, he had several children: Deimos ("fear"), Phobos ("panic"), Eros ("desire"), and Harmonia ("harmony").

Ares, the least favorite of the Olympian gods, had a cult associated with Thrace, where he may have originated before being adopted into the Greek pantheon. Ares also had a substantial following among the Colchians on the Black Sea. He was honored by warriors, despite his general unpopularity.

As a soldier, however, Ares left something to be desired. His sister Athena routinely proved herself superior to him in battle. In the Trojan War he fought by Hector's side against the Greek hero Diomedes who was supported by Athena. She diverted Diomedes' spear so that Ares was injured. When he tried to support his son Cycnus against Heracles he was wounded again. He also fell victim to the twin Giants Otus and Ephialtes when they attacked Mount Olympus. Captured by the twins, Ares was chained inside a cauldron for 13 lunar months, i.e., a year, until the god Hermes finally released him.

■ Ares was the god of war and the spirit of battle

■ His Roman equivalent is Mars

■ He was not a popular god, and represented the brutal and bloody aspects of warfare

■ He was accompanied into battle by his sister Eris ("strife") and his sons Deimos ("fear") and Phobos ("panic")

■ Although there were few cults to Ares he would sometimes be invoked before battle

■ He rode in a chariot pulled by four fire-breathing horses

The Amazons

A tribe of women descended from Ares, the Amazons (right) were, like their father, devoted to warfare and renowned for their courage. Amazon ("breastless") derives from the legend that they cut off their right breasts to improve their archery and javelin-throwing skills.

Affair With Aphrodite When the sun god Helios spotted Ares and Aphrodite (**1**) in an embrace, he told Aphrodite's husband Hephaestus, who fashioned an invisible net around his bed to trap the lovers in the act. Not satisfied with just ensnaring them, Hephaestus invited the gods to see the couple. Caught in the act, they drew the Homeric laughter of the other Olympians.

Trial on the Areopagus One day Ares' daughter, Alcippe, went to a stream at the foot of the Acropolis in Athens. While there, Poseidon's son, Halirrhotius, tried to sexually assault her. Seeing the attack, Ares (**3**) killed him. Outraged, Poseidon held a tribunal of the gods on the hillside which overlooked the stream and charged Ares with murder. Ares successfully pled his case before the Olympians. In memory of this first trial by jury, the Athenians named the place Areopagus (**2**), "hill of Ares," and for centuries reserved the site for trials of men held for murder and impiety.

Aphrodite

As the goddess of love and beauty, Aphrodite is often seen naked or provocatively draped with her sacred bird, the dove, in her hand. Consistent with her dominion over physical love, she was associated with all lovemaking on land, air, and sea.

For all her charms, however, Aphrodite had a dark side. She was frequently unfaithful to her unattractive husband Hephaestus. The most prolific of her affairs were those with Ares, Dionysus, and Hermes. She was notorious for enticing god and man alike into adulterous affairs. Aphrodite boasted that she could make any Olympian god or goddess fall in love with a mortal, and she was blamed for instigating, with the help of her son Eros, a large number of ill-fated romances on Mount Olympus and earth which had dire, and sometimes fatal, consequences.

Aphrodite's chief cult site was in Paphos on the island of Cyprus, which indicates that she was perhaps a fertility goddess of Eastern origin, e.g., related to the Phoenician Astarte.

■ Aphrodite was the goddess of sexual love and beauty, fertility, desire, and the sea

■ She was a tireless lover and matchmaker, equivalent to the Roman goddess Venus

■ Often depicted nude, her attributes were a mirror, apple, and myrtle wreath

Apple of Discord When Eris ("strife") was not invited to the wedding of Peleus and Thetis, she rolled a golden apple among the guests with a simple inscription, "to the fairest." Aphrodite, Hera, and Athena argued over who deserved it, so Zeus selected the Trojan shepherd Paris, son of King Priam, as their judge (**1**, judgment of Paris). The goddesses offered bribes, but Aphrodite's offer of Helen of Sparta won out. Paris's subsequent abduction of Helen provoked the Trojan War.

①

» **Aeneas—Founding of Rome:** p. 198

Myth of Adonis Adonis was a handsome young fertility god. His mother, Princess Myrrha of Assyria, had said that she was more beautiful than Aphrodite. As punishment, the goddess instigated an incestuous union between Myrrha and her father. Full of remorse, Myrrha was transformed into a myrrh tree. When Adonis was born from the tree, Aphrodite sent him to Persephone for safekeeping. Both goddesses loved Adonis (**3**), but the jealous Ares sent a boar to kill him (**2**).

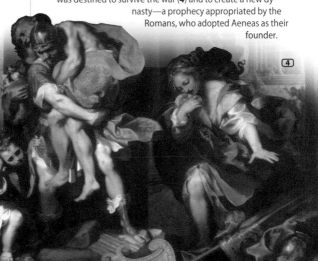

Birth of Aeneas Angered by Aphrodite's amorous schemes, Zeus settled the score by stirring passion in her for Anchises, a handsome Trojan shepherd. Aphrodite assumed a mortal girl's form and, masquerading as a Phrygian princess, claimed that Hermes had sent her to Anchises to be his wife. Believing her, Anchises slept with Aphrodite, who gave birth to their son Aeneas. Aeneas grew to become a leader in the Trojan War and was second only to Hector in bravery. According to Homer, Aeneas was destined to survive the war (**4**) and to create a new dynasty—a prophecy appropriated by the Romans, who adopted Aeneas as their founder.

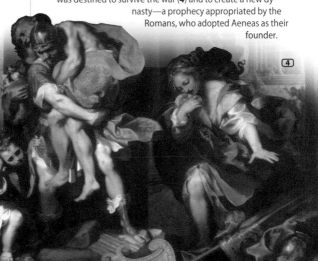

The Birth of Aphrodite

When Cronus castrated Uranus with a scythe, he cast his father's genitals into the sea. As foam formed around them, a young maiden emerged from it, the goddess Aphrodite, so named because she was born from the foam (*aphros*) of the sea.

Because she first set foot on dry land at the island of Cyprus, Aphrodite was said to have been born there. Because she also drifted within sight of Cythera before arriving at Cyprus, she came to be known by two nicknames: "the Cytherean" and "Cyprus-born." The birth of Aphrodite has been a popular subject among artists since antiquity.

Eros

According to the *Theogony* by the Greek poet Hesiod, Eros ("desire"), the god of love and sexual desire, was born from primordial chaos together with Gaia ("earth") and Tartarus ("underworld"). He was seen as the incarnation of sexual love, which was considered the impetus of all life. Having initiated the unification of Gaia and Uranus, Eros became the guardian of the marriages of gods and people. However, he was also a destabilizing force capable of depriving god and man alike of their reason. Because he spread chaos with his bow and arrow, a symbol of the sudden, often unreasoned, happening of love, he was also said to be Aphrodite's son. In this manifestation he appears as a young, athletic man.

Among the mystery cults, Eros was identified with Phanes ("enlightener"), who was born from the first world-egg and created the universe. For the philosopher Plato, Eros drew the eye to physical beauty, not as an end in itself, but as a way to direct the mind toward contemplation of the idea of beauty.

- Eros ("desire"), god of sexual love, brought together Uranus and Gaia

- He was the guardian of marriage, as well as the protector of homosexual love between men

- As a son of Aphrodite, he was depicted as a young man, later as a winged infant

- He carried a bow and arrow, which he used to incite often disastrous love affairs

- His Roman equivalent was Amor or Cupid

Figures and Stories Relevant to Eros

From Elder to an Infantile Trickster In the hands of the poets, Eros seems to have undergone a transformation from esteemed elder to a youthful—even infantile—trickster. In the fourth century B.C., Apollonius of Rhodes portrayed Eros as a juvenile delinquent who cheated at dice when he was not busy meddling in human affairs by forcing ill-matched couples to fall in love. The contrast between these two forms of Eros, however, is not as great as it appears. From the beginning, ① desire could always be destructive and immature.

➤➤ **Tricksters:** pp. 148, 166, 170, 234, 360, 440

Medea and Jason Some love affairs prompted by Eros reflect the delirious power of desire that makes people forget reason and social rules, such as Medea and Jason. When Jason arrived in Colchis to take the golden fleece, he had to perform a series of impossible tasks. Hera plotted with Aphrodite to help Jason by forcing the Colchian princess Medea to fall in love with him and help him with her magic (**3**, Medea making Jason a potion). Aphrodite asked Eros to shoot Medea with one of his arrows, promising that he would get a toy that once belonged to Zeus in return: a golden ball that left a fiery trail every time it was thrown. Eager for the toy, Eros shot Medea, instantly setting her passion aflame. So powerful was Eros's work that Medea not only helped Jason get the fleece, she also killed her own brother before sailing off with Jason. However, Jason later divorced Medea for a Greek princess, so she slew both their children and the princess in revenge—a symbol of the destructive power of Eros.

Eros and Psyche Princess Psyche ("soul") was so beautiful that her subjects abandoned Aphrodite's temples to worship her instead. Aphrodite became so jealous, she demanded that Eros force Psyche to fall in love with the most hideous thing alive: but the plot went wrong and instead, Eros himself fell in love with the princess. Eros courted her in secret and, after many adventures, Psyche was made a goddess and married the god of love (**2**).

- Hermes was identified with the Roman god Mercury
- He served the Olympic gods as herald and led the souls of the dead to Hades
- He was a trickster who protected both merchants and thieves
- His many inventions included the Greek alphabet, the lyre, fire, and ritual sacrifice
- He was portrayed as a bearded man wearing a long tunic, winged sandals, and cap
- He carried a herald's staff; also associated with fertility, he was depicted with a phallus

Hermes

Originally an Arcadian fertility god linked with animal husbandry, Hermes eventually became the most devious and quick-witted of all the gods. He was the son of Zeus and his mistress, Maia, and was born in a remote cave. Later he served his father and the other gods as a herald and led the souls of the dead into the underworld. Perhaps Hermes' most famous exploit was the murder of Argus, the hundred-eyed beast, to liberate Zeus's lover, Io.

He was the patron of merchants, but, as a trickster, he was also the god of thieves. He protected the travelers who built *hermae*, rectangular pillars, as tributes to him along roads to protect their journeys. Because he invented dice, gamblers also paid him tribute as the god of wealth and good fortune. Hermes was also credited with a myriad of inventions adopted by humankind, such as musical instruments, fire, the alphabet, and ritual sacrifice. In light of his diplomatic skills, he became the patron god of language and rhetoric. Later Hermes watched over men engaged in athletics, and his image graced gymnasium entrances.

Figures and Stories Relevant to Hermes

Apollo, Hermes Stole His Cattle, see pp. 132–133

Hades and Persephone, see pp. 154–155

Odysseus, Helped by Hermes, see the *Iliad* and the *Odyssey*, pp. 186–187

Perseus, Helped by Hermes, see pp. 180–181

Zeus, Hermes' Father, see pp. 120–123

The First Musician On the day he was born, Hermes crafted the first lyre (**1**). Using the shell of a tortoise he found grazing outside his cave, he made the lyre's strings from sheep guts. He was also the first to tie reeds together to make pan pipes, and he played both instruments so beautifully that Apollo swapped his cattle and his golden shepherd's rod for them.

①

» **Tricksters:** pp. 146, 166, 170, 234, 360, 440

Stealing Apollo's Herd

Even as a baby, Hermes was a trickster. One day he was put in the cradle for a nap, but he toddled out of his cave-nursery and found a herd of cattle (**2**) watched by the god Apollo. Reversing their hooves and fashioning soft sandals for himself, he drove them back home, while the tracks the cattle left behind only led back to the place they had left. Apollo had a hard time figuring out where the herd had been taken, and an even harder time placing the blame on Hermes, a baby. From that time on, Hermes was also worshiped as the patron god of thieves.

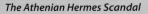

Herald of the Gods

When Hermes (**3**) first met Zeus, the king of the gods was so impressed by his son's shameless lies that he made him the herald and ambassador of Mount Olympus. Hermes went on to play important roles in many of the most famous myths of the gods, aiding mortals and immortals alike. He communicated regularly with the underworld, overseeing Persephone's return to her mother, Demeter, and leading the souls of the dead to the afterlife. It was Hermes who warned Odysseus about the witch, Circe, and gave him an antidote to her potion, and Hermes who gave Perseus an unbreakable sword and guided him to the Graeae ("gray women") so he could find the equipment he needed to behead Medusa. Hermes was also the god of sleep, through whom Zeus would send prophetic dreams.

The Athenian Hermes Scandal

As a sign of piety to Hermes, the Athenians traditionally used to place hermae (right, from Cyrene) in the doorways of their homes and in the streets. During the Peloponnesian War, on the eve of Athens' expedition against Syracuse (Sicily), a gang of delinquents defaced the hermae throughout the city. The act of sacrilege was regarded as an evil omen and was blamed on the expedition's leader, Alcibiades. Although he claimed that he was innocent, Alcibiades was exiled from Athens. The expedition to Syracuse met with defeat.

Stolen Cattle: p. 281

Hephaestus

■ Hephaestus was known as Vulcan in the Roman tradition, where he was said to have his forge under Mount Etna in Sicily

■ He was the god of blacksmiths, craftsmen, artisans, metallurgy, and fire

■ His mother was Hera and his wife was the goddess of love, Aphrodite, who betrayed him

■ Lame since his birth, he was known for his ugliness

■ His symbols are a hammer and anvil—a smith's tools

The god of fire and craftsmen, as well as the blacksmith of Mount Olympus, Hephaestus was birthed by Hera without the aid of Zeus in revenge for his giving birth to Athena by himself. Rejected by Hera for his ugliness and his lame feet, Hephaestus was thrown into the sea. He was later thrown out of Mount Olympus again, this time by Zeus, for defending his mother. Hephaestus lived and worked for years on the isle of Lemnos—a mythical reference to metallurgy's origins in the Greek islands.

In spite of his looks, Hephaestus managed to marry the most beautiful goddesses. According to the Greek poet Hesiod, Aglaia ("glory"), the youngest of the Graces, was his wife. But traditionally he was married to Aphrodite (**1**, in the forge of Hephaestus). She betrayed him with Ares and the horned god was cruelly taunted by all the other gods. However, a consummate craftsman, Hephaestus served them by creating fantastic items, such as Hermes' helmet, Aphrodite's girdle, armors for heroes, and even Pandora, the first woman.

1

Marriage to Aphrodite

Because of his hideous appearance, Hera threw Hephaestus off Mount Olympus. To punish his mother, he made her a golden throne from which she could not escape, and then ran away. As no one but Hephaestus could release her, the gods begged him to come back to Mount Olympus. Yet, it was not until the god of wine, Dionysus, got him drunk that he returned. Yet Hephaestus refused to release Hera until she offered him Aphrodite as his bride in exchange for freedom, and they were wed (**2**).

Figures and Stories Relevant to Hephaestus

Aphrodite, Hephaestus's Wife, see pp. 142–143

Ares, Had a Love Affair With Aphrodite, see pp. 140–141

Hera, Hephaestus's Mother, see pp. 126–127

The Trojan War, Achilles' Shield, see pp. 184–185

Shield of Achilles As a favor to the goddess Thetis, who had sheltered him when he was a boy, Hephaestus made a shield (**4**, Thetis giving Achilles the shield) for her son, Achilles, to use during the Trojan War. The shield was embellished with vivid scenes.

Harmonia's Necklace

Through her affair with the god Ares, Aphrodite had many children, which the jealous Hephaestus vowed to curse. When Ares' and Aphrodite's daughter, Harmonia ("harmony"), was to wed Cadmus, the founder of Thebes, Hephaestus was determined to curse their marriage. At their wedding, he gave Harmonia a cursed necklace he had made. Because of the necklace, Harmonia and Cadmus suffered during their reign in Thebes, and ended up being transformed into serpents (**3**).

Hestia

■ The daughter of Cronus and Rhea, Hestia was protector of the household and ensured the hearth fire always burned

■ In the Roman tradition, she was known as Vesta and was served by virginal priestesses called Vestal Virgins

■ As virgin goddess, she was often shown modestly cloaked

①

The eldest child of Cronus and Rhea, Hestia was the first to be swallowed by her father in a vain attempt to avoid being overthrown. Because she was the last one he vomited out, she is known as both the eldest and youngest of her siblings.

Hestia was the kindest and most easygoing of the gods, refusing to take part in the many quarrels that raged at the palace on Mount Olympus. Zeus honored Hestia for her good character, and named her the protector of the household and the hearth fire that was not allowed to go out.

In Rome, her name was Vesta, and her cult may have been more prominent there than in Greece. She became patron goddess of the Roman state and the eternal flames at her temple (**1**) were the symbol of the welfare of Rome. Maiden daughters of the elite, known as the Vestal Virgins, were servants of the maiden goddess and tended the flames. Raping a Vestal Virgin was one of the most sacrilegious crimes in Rome.

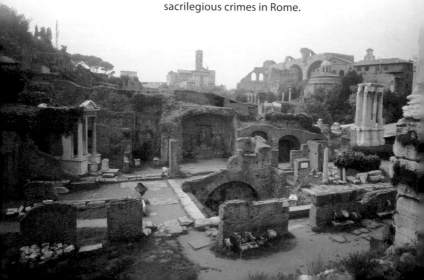

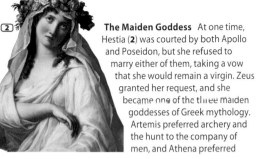

The Maiden Goddess At one time, Hestia (**2**) was courted by both Apollo and Poseidon, but she refused to marry either of them, taking a vow that she would remain a virgin. Zeus granted her request, and she became one of the three maiden goddesses of Greek mythology. Artemis preferred archery and the hunt to the company of men, and Athena preferred warfare and the craftsman's shop; Hestia, meanwhile, preferred the hearth fires of both home and public places. In the Roman tradition, her priestesses also had to be virgins.

Vesta and Priapus In a Roman myth, Priapus (**3**), the impudent god of gardens and male fertility, lusted after Vesta. During a feast of the gods, he tried to sneak up on her once everyone had fallen asleep. As Vesta slept, Priapus set to have his way with her. However, just as he was about to, a nearby donkey let out a loud bray. As Vesta awoke, Priapus narrowly escaped being caught, and in doing so avoided Vesta's wrath.

③

Home, Hearth, and Altar As goddess of the hearth and the hearth fire, Hestia was the protector of domestic harmony, of hospitality, and of the preparation of food and bread. Cooking at the hearth fire (**4**) was sacred to her, as was the kettle that stood on it. As her hearth fire was at the center of every temple, Hestia received the first offerings of a sacrifice, even before the gods for whom the ceremonies took place.

Figures and Stories Relevant to Hestia

Cronus and Rhea, Hestia's Parents, see the Titans, pp. 116–117

Zeus, Granted Hestia's Virginal Request, see pp. 120–123

Hades and Persephone

■ Hades, Pluto in the Roman tradition, was the "Zeus of the underworld" and, like Demeter, made the corn grow

■ Persephone, Proserpina in the Roman tradition, was kidnapped by Hades

■ As guardian of the underworld, his symbol was a key

Hades, a brother of Zeus, was given rule over the underworld in the aftermath of the Titanomachy. Depicted as merciless, he was as dark as his realm, which was more a prison for the souls of the dead than a hell in the Christian sense. The souls lived there as shadows of their former selves. As the Greek were afraid to speak his name, Hades was given epithets like Eubuleus ("giving good advice").

When Hades fell in love with Demeter and Zeus's daughter, Persephone, he kidnapped her (**1**), taking her into the underworld. Later, a compromise was reached that she would divide the year between residing in the underworld and above ground.

The kidnapping of Persephone is one of the most famous Greek myths. The story was used to explain the changing of the seasons, as Demeter caused all crops to die because her daughter was not with her.

1

▶▶ **Hel:** p. 236

Demeter's Disguise When Demeter (**2**) learned that Persephone was in the underworld, she was distraught. Shunning Mount Olympus, she wandered around the world. When she reached Eleusis, the kingdom of Celeus, she turned into an old woman. She sat by the town's well, where she met Celeus's daughters. Pretending to be a refugee from Crete, Demeter let the girls bring her to the palace to work as a nursemaid. Celeus and his wife entrusted Demeter with their son Demophoön. To repay their kindness, Demeter tried to make the boy immortal by curing him over a hearth fire, but the queen saw her and the spell was broken. Demeter revealed herself, ordered that a temple be built at Eleusis, and taught them her secret rituals.

The Pomegranate Seed When Hermes discovered Persephone in the underworld and demanded that she be returned to Demeter, it was decided she could return to her mother forever under one condition: if she had not eaten any of Hades' food while she was down below. Hades, seizing his last chance, tricked Persephone into eating a pomegranate seed (**3**) before her return. Because of this, she could never fully escape from Hades' realm, and was forced to remain his wife.

Figures and Stories Relevant to Hades and Persephone

Demeter, Persephone's Mother, see pp. 130–131	Erinyes, see pp. 190–191
The House of Atreus, Orestes Was Plagued by the	**Zeus**, Persephone's Father and Hades' Brother, see pp. 120–123

The Erinyes The Erinyes, or the Furies, were born from the blood of castrated Uranus that fell on their mother, Gaia. As spirits of vengeance, they persecuted anyone guilty of perjury, murder, or crimes committed against one's own family. Symbolizing pangs of guilt, they inflicted evildoers with madness. In the underworld, they enforced the torture of the dead. After plaguing Orestes (**4**, with his sister, Iphigeneia) for murdering his mother, Clytemnestra, Athena calmed them. They became the Eumenides ("kind ones").

The Underworld

The underworld was conceived by the Greeks as the bottom half of the universe. It was also referred to as Hades, after the name of its ruler. The kingdom of Hades was divided in several parts, the lowest being Tartarus, where the damned suffered awful torments. While a few lucky souls spent eternity in the Elysian Fields, the rest were led by Hermes to the banks of the river Styx where, for a fee, they were taken on a boat steered by Charon to the kingdom's gates. Cerberus, the many-headed dog, guarded the gates. Family members placed a silver coin in the mouth of the deceased to ensure their safe passage. Those who went unburied, or whose families could not afford the fare, were condemned for eternity to wander the earth as ghosts.

Orpheus

■ Orpheus was a demigod with a magical ability to play the lyre

■ He taught the Greeks agriculture, medicine, and writing

■ With Apollo as his teacher, he became the greatest minstrel

■ He could enthrall all creatures with his music and singing; he even overpowered the Sirens

■ His lyre was made into a constellation in the night sky

As the son of King Oeagrus (some sources say the god Apollo) and Calliope, the muse of epic poetry, Orpheus was a demigod, as well as an inimitable musician and singer. His highly complex and beautiful music was prized for its intricacy.

When Orpheus played his favorite instrument, the lyre, the melodies were so beautiful that they calmed the beasts of earth, sea, and air, and enthralled the hills, rocks, and streams. These skills came in handy when Orpheus accompanied Jason and the Argonauts on their expedition to find and capture the golden fleece.

Orpheus's life is remembered in Greek tradition because of three major episodes: the tragic loss of his wife Eurydice, the expedition of the Argonauts, and his brutal end at the hands of the Maenads. During his life he was also said to have improved the daily life of the Thracians by introducing agricultural and medical techniques; he also fostered the religious cults of the gods Apollo and Dionysus.

Savior of the Argonauts As an Argonaut, Orpheus was often called upon to play and sing—sometimes to inspire the rowers with fresh energy, sometimes to stop the fights that arose among the crew. One day, the Argonauts' boat (**1**) encountered the Sirens, creatures whose song made sailors stop at their island and never want to go home. Orpheus strummed and sang so loudly that he drowned out the song of the Sirens and ensured the Argonauts could continue safely.

①

Loss of Eurydice Orpheus was married to Eurydice (**2**), and together they settled in Thrace. One day, perhaps even their wedding day, Eurydice was killed by a snake. Distraught, Orpheus went to the underworld looking for her. When he reached the underworld throne of

Hades and Persephone (**3**), he pled for the return of his wife in such a moving song that his wish was granted, but only on one condition: he could not turn to look at her until they were both completely above ground. Thus the couple walked back up to earth, Orpheus leading the way. As he emerged, he turned to look at Eurydice, who was not yet above ground. The agreement broken, she faded back into the shadows of death forever.

Death of Orpheus Following the loss of Eurydice, Orpheus foreswore the love of all women and the worship of all gods except Apollo and wandered the wilds of Thrace, avoiding the company of men. So when he encountered some Maenads, followers of Dionysus, they attacked him with sticks and stones, but his magical song kept them from hitting him. Enraged, the Maenads tore Orpheus limb from limb, casting his head into the sea, where it floated to the island of Lesbos. Here it was buried in sacred ground, but its

Figures and Stories Relevant to Orpheus

Hades and Persephone, see pp. 154–155

Jason and the Argonauts, Orpheus Assisted the Argonauts, see pp. 182–183

Muses, Calliope Was Orpheus's Mother, see pp. 172–173

continued singing was stopped by Apollo. The Muses collected the rest (**4**) of Orpheus's body, burying it at the foot of Mount Olympus, where the nightingales sang in his honor. Zeus made Orpheus's lyre into a constellation in the sky.

Journeys in the Underworld: pp. 39, 41, 353, 407

Dionysus

The Greek god Dionysus was the patron of wine, vegetation, and orgiastic ecstasy. He was the son of Zeus and the mortal Semele, who was the daughter of Camus, the founder of Thebes. To protect him from the jealous Hera, Dionysus was raised in far-off Mount Nysa. When he grew older, he traveled throughout the Eastern lands, where he taught the cultivation of the vine. Dionysus had great powers; he even raised his mother Semele from the dead and brought her to Mount Olympus.

As Dionysus was the god of liberation from societal worries, his followers (**1**, dancing Maenads) had a reputation for debauchery. Legends state that as a result Greek kings like Lycurgus and Pentheus rejected his cult, usually with dire consequences. The god's origin is unknown, but the Greeks regarded him as a foreign god from the East. Dionysus was also celebrated in the Eleusinian Mysteries, along with Demeter and Persephone.

■ Dionysus was the god of wine, vegetation, and revelry

■ His Roman equivalent is Bacchus

■ Festivals were held in honor of him as the patron of theater

■ His attributes were the flute, thyrsus, and a bunch of grapes

1

▷▷ **Deities of Wine—Hathor:** p. 92

Birth of Dionysus

There are two different tales about Dionysus's birth. In one myth, the pregnant Semele was killed by the blaze from Zeus's thunderbolts (**2**) because, doubting that he was a god, she insisted he reveal his true nature. Hermes rescued the unborn god from his mother's ashes and sewed Dionysus into Zeus's thigh, from where he was born months later. Another story says that the child Dionysus was dismembered on Hera's orders. Athena or Rhea recovered his heart, which was reimplanted by Zeus into Semele's womb so that Dionysus could be reborn.

Figures and Stories Relevant to Dionysus

The Dionysia, see pp. 162–163	Hermes, Helped Dionysus, see pp. 148–149
Hera, Pursued Dionysus, see pp. 126–127	Minos and the Minotaur, see pp. 178–179

Marriage With Ariadne After betraying her father, King Minos, by helping the hero Theseus escape the labyrinth where he had killed the Minotaur, Ariadne fled with Theseus on his return voyage to Athens. However, he abandoned her some say at the demand of Dionysus) on the island of Naxos. Finding her there (**3**), Dionysus took her as his bride. She bore several children, and upon her death Dionysus set her wedding diadem in the sky as the constellation Corona.

Dionysus and His Travels to the East

After inventing the cultivation of the vine, Dionysus was said to have visited a number of Eastern lands: Lydia, Phrygia, Egypt, and even India, where he remained for several years. One myth explaining his travels says the goddess Hera drove him mad, and he was forced to wander aimlessly in the East until the Phrygian goddess Cybele (**4**, with Dionysus) purified him and taught him her religious rites. This is fitting because Cybele was an earth goddess who, like Dionysus, was associated with orgiastic rituals. Her pinecone sat at the tip of his *thyrsus*, or staff.

The Dionysia

Dionysus, in Rome known as Bacchus, was celebrated in ancient Greece in festivals named Dionysia. Perhaps originally a Thracian fertility ritual, the mysterious Dionysia were known for their feasting, drinking, and orgies. In Athens they became an urban festival, several days long, with a procession and performances. According to myth, Dionysus was often accompanied by a wild retinue, consisting of Satyrs (half-man, half-goat) and Centaurs (half-man, half-horse) both notorious for drunkenness and lust; and Silenus, an older Satyr, sometimes considered to be Dionysus's tutor. The wine god's darker side was represented by the Maenads or Bacchantes, women driven mad by wine, who in their frenzy could rip a man or beast apart with their bare hands.

- As the son of Zeus and Alcmene, Heracles was a demigod, but was allowed to live on Mount Olympus after his death

- With his superhuman strength and a lion skin that made him invulnerable, he passed many trials, including the famous 12 labors

- He was represented as a strong man and amorous lover who enjoyed eating and drinking

- His weapon was the bow and sometimes he used a club

Heracles

The demigod Heracles, famous for his superhuman strength and innumerable acts of heroism, was the son of Zeus and Alcmene, princess of Mycenae. Best known for his successful completion of the 12 labors, Heracles also freed Prometheus from his torture. Although Heracles' name means "Hera's glory," the queen of the gods was furious with her husband's infidelity, and always plotted against him.

Heracles' strength was obvious from the beginning. Before he was a teenager, he could kill a lion with his bare hands. This strength made him an important ally in the Olympian gods' fight against the giants. However, Hera afflicted him with a tragic madness. In a senseless rage he murdered his wife, the Princess Megara of Thebes, and their children.

Always helpful, Heracles once fought Hades to bring Queen Alcestis back from the dead for King Admetus; he joined the hunt of the Calydonian boar and accompanied the Argonauts on their search for the golden fleece. The Greeks worshiped Heracles as a protector of humanity; however, he was parodied in their comedies as an excessive eater and drinker.

Plotting of Hera Moments before Heracles' birth, Zeus proclaimed that the next royal child to be born in the kingdom would rule over Mycenae. Enraged to learn of yet another of her husband's affairs, Hera delayed Alcmene's delivery of Heracles and made Eurystheus's mother give birth to him early. Thus, Heracles lost his inheritance and Eurystheus became the king of Mycenae. After Heracles' birth, Hera sent two mighty snakes to kill him inside his cradle, but he strangled them (**1**).

12 Labors After killing his wife and children, Heracles was sent by the oracle of Delphi to serve the Mycenaean king Eurystheus as punishment. Eurystheus gave Heracles 12 tasks: killing the Nemean lion (**2**), the Hydra, and the Stymphalis birds; capturing the Erymanthian boar, the Ceryneian hind, the Cretan bull, Diomedes' horses, Geryon's cattle, and Cerberus; cleaning Augeas's stables; and fetching an Amazon's girdle and the apples of the Hesperides.

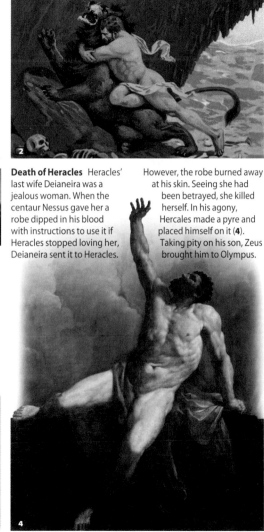

The Final Labor By making the labors so difficult, Eurystheus was trying to kill Heracles. Yet, Heracles had the last laugh. After completing 11 of Eurystheus's labors, only one remained: to capture Hades' guard dog Cerberus. When Heracles dragged the dog to Eurystheus's court, the cowardly king leapt into an urn (**3**).

Death of Heracles Heracles' last wife Deianeira was a jealous woman. When the centaur Nessus gave her a robe dipped in his blood with instructions to use it if Heracles stopped loving her, Deianeira sent it to Heracles.

However, the robe burned away at his skin. Seeing she had been betrayed, she killed herself. In his agony, Hercales made a pyre and placed himself on it (**4**). Taking pity on his son, Zeus brought him to Olympus.

Figures and Stories Relevant to Heracles

⏩ **Heroes Fighting Against Monsters:** pp. 27, 181, 251, 315, 361

Prometheus

■ Prometheus was a Titan who created people from clay

■ He gave crafts and sciences to humankind

■ He stole fire from the gods and gave it to humankind

■ Because he tricked the gods to help the people he had created, he was punished by Zeus

■ He was chained to Mount Caucasus, and an eagle ate every day from his liver; thus, he paid for his ingenious and rebellious spirit

Prometheus, meaning "foresight," played an important role in early human history. The Greeks viewed him as their creator and giver of culture. He and his brother Epimetheus ("hindsight") were also entrusted with creating all the world's animals. The Greeks commemorated Prometheus's most important gift, that of fire, with an annual torch race, starting from Plato's Academy. Along with fire, Prometheus gave people the mechanical arts, sciences, and wisdom. His generosity toward humanity led him to be punished eternally on Mount Caucasus by Zeus. However, it was not just Prometheus who suffered. Zeus also cursed humanity by creating a woman named Pandora, who unleashed evil on the world.

As the son of the Titan Iapetus and the Oceanid Klymene, Prometheus was a trickster. During the war of the Titans, he counseled the Titans to use trickery instead of open warfare against the Olympian gods. It was their refusal to take his advice that led him to side with Zeus. Prometheus's son Deucalion lived to survive the great flood in an ark and, with his wife Pyrrha, reestablished humankind by throwing rocks behind their shoulders.

Creation of People In Plato's *Protagoras*, the world was populated by the gods, who created mortal creatures from the elements. Prometheus and his twin Epimetheus were asked to give the animals features and means for survival. Epimetheus supplied them with claws, hooves, and the like, before they were sent into the world. Finally, when it was time to create humans, the brothers realized they had given away everything that would help them survive. Thus

Prometheus formed people from clay (1) watered with tears to symbolize the hardships they would endure.

Figures and Stories Relevant to Prometheus

Heracles, Saves Prometheus, see pp. 164–165

Pandora's Box, see pp. 124–125

Zeus, Adversary of Prometheus, see pp. 120–123

⟩⟩ Creation of People With Clay: pp. 22, 100

Testing Zeus's Omniscience To settle a dispute between people and the gods, Prometheus created two different temple offerings, and gave Zeus the first choice. One was wrapped in an ugly ox's (**2**) stomach, but contained choice meats, and the other was wrapped in attractive white fat, but contained only bones. Although he knew it was a trick, Zeus chose the offering with the more pleasant exterior in order to create an everlasting hostility between the divine and mortal worlds. From then on, when humankind sacrificed to the gods, only the fat and bones would be burned at the altar.

Gift of Fire

As Zeus was angered by Prometheus's trickery, he tried to deprive people of fire so that their meat would always be raw and inedible. Yet, by means of a fennel stalk, which he ignited from the chariot of the sun god Helios, Prometheus brought the fire back to the people. This gift of fire (**3**) ensured humanity's survival. Enraged, Zeus plotted with Hephaestus and the other gods to make human life one of hard labor and misery. They created a beguiling woman named Pandora ("all-endowed") and sent her with a box to Epimetheus. Unsuspecting, she opened it and unleashed miseries among humankind.

Prometheus's Punishment By Zeus In revenge for stealing fire, Zeus devised a cruel punishment for Prometheus. He ordered the blacksmith god Hephaestus to nail Prometheus to a rock on Mount Caucasus, located at the end of the earth. Then Zeus sent an eagle to peck and eat at his flesh (**4**). Every day the bird would eat Prometheus's liver, and every night the liver would grow back, ensuring that he would live in a constant state of misery. Prometheus's ordeal was not over until the hero Heracles shot the eagle with an arrow and freed Prometheus from his fetters. However, he had to wear a ring with a stone from Caucasus, so that Zeus could still claim that Prometheus was fastened to it. Another source says that even after the eagle's death, Prometheus remained stuck on Mount Caucasus until the Centaur Cheiron, mortally wounded by Heracles, agreed to take Prometheus's place. In doing so he gave his immortality to Prometheus, who was finally free.

Tricksters: pp. 146, 148, 170, 234, 360, 440 | **Bringers of Culture:** pp. 24, 32, 41, 442

Cultural Heroes

The first cultural heroes of the Greeks were mostly gods or demigods. However, as mythology slowly gave way to history, the Greeks switched over to praise the merits of humans. Something arose that could be called "the spirit of *agon*" ("competition"), which was universal in Greece. Members of all poleis vied for prizes and praise from their fellow citizens, whether in the arenas of sports, drama, rhetoric, philosophy (**3**, Plato and Aristotle in discussion), or the sciences. The most famous contest was perhaps the Olympics, whose winners were honored as favorites of the gods. In Athens, honorees in various spheres of public life were commemorated through statues, and their names were inscribed on archive walls to see and to admire.

The Olympics
Although there were always quarrels between the Greek poleis, sporting contests, such as the Olympics, existed as sanctuaries for civic competition. Athletes (**1**) from the different cities competed there against each other, thus providing an opportunity for peaceful competition. The Olympics were held in honor of Zeus.

Thespis Thespis of Icaria (**2**, theater troupe) was the poet credited with writing and performing the first traditional drama. He was likely the first to enact a story at the Athenian festival of the Great Dionysia, playing the character of Dionysus opposite the chorus. He also helped create competitions in dramatic tragedy, and won the first competition in 534 B.C. in Athens.

3

Sisyphus

The trickery of Sisyphus, King of Corinth, was almost proverbial. He earned Zeus's wrath by telling the river god Asopus where the king of the gods had taken his daughter, Aegina, a river nymph. Zeus ordered the god Thanatos ("death") to escort Sisyphus in person to the underworld, but because of Sisyphus's trickery Thanatos was imprisoned instead. While he was trapped, no one on earth could perish. Annoyed that his opponents would not die, Ares, the god of war, intervened and released Thanatos. Before he was again brought to the underworld, Sisyphus told his wife, Merope, not to bury him and to refuse the rites of the dead. Angry, Hades sent Sisyphus back to earth with orders to punish his wife; however, Sisyphus stayed and happily lived out the rest of his natural life. But, upon his death, his eternal punishment in the underworld was that he had to push a rock up a hill, only to have it get away from him once he reached the top, and roll back down each time. In this, Sisyphus became a symbol for human labor done in vain.

Tricksters: pp. 146, 148, 166, 234, 360, 440

- The Muses were the nine goddesses of the liberal arts
- They were mostly depicted with wings
- The nymphs were connected to nature, fertility, and growth; they were not immortal, but lived very long lives
- In art they appear as lightly dressed young women

Nymphs and Muses

The Muses (**1**, with Apollo, their leader) and nymphs were graceful female goddesses whose allure enticed both Greek gods and kings, who often became their lovers, along with countless artists.

Daughters of Zeus and the Titan Mnemosyne, the Muses were said to live on mountains, especially on Mount Helicon in Boeotia, where the center of their cult was situated. There were nine Muses: Clio (history), Euterpe (flute playing), Thalia (comedy), Melpomene (tragedy), Terpsichore (dance), Erato (singing), Polyhymnia (mime), Urania (astronomy), and Calliope (epics). They were especially beloved by the artists who looked to them for inspiration.

The nymphs, natural spirits appearing as beautiful women, reflected the belief that the divine was present throughout nature. There were flower nymphs, water nymphs, and nymphs who existed as cooling breezes.

1

Daughters of Memory When the Titan goddess of memory, Mnemosyne, slept with Zeus for nine nights, she bore nine daughters called the Muses (**3**). Each of them had a special function in the cultural life of Mount Olympus. Originally there were only three Muses: Melete ("meditation" or "practice"), Mneme ("memory"), and Aoede ("song").

Figures and Stories Relevant to Nymphs and Muses

Apollo, Leader of the Muses, see pp. 132–133

Gaia and Uranus, Castration of Uranus, see p. 115

The Titans, Mnemosyne Was the Mother of the Muses; Birth of the Oceanides, see p. 117

Zeus, Father of the Muses, see pp. 120–123

Tree Spirits The Dryads ("tree-daughters") (**2**), nymphs of the wood, were the spirits who presided over cultivated groves and wild forests alike. Each species of tree had its own group of tree spirits, and in addition each tree had a spirit of its own. Among the more important tree spirits were the Meliai ("ash"), who were born from the blood of Uranus when he was castrated, and the nymphs of the laurel tree, the Daphnaie, who were sacred to Apollo. Because lowland trees were usually cut down for farming and grazing, the spirits of mountain pine trees, the Oreads, received special reverence along with their fellow mountain spirits, the Satyrs.

Nymphs of the Water There were numerous types of water nymphs. Alongside the 3,000 nymphs of the ocean, the Oceanides (**4**), were the nymphs of the Mediterranean, the Nereids. Another group of nymphs, the Naiads, ruled over fresh water and were found in springs, rivers, and lakes.

Monsters and Giants

The realm of Greek myth was filled with giants and monsters, beings in animal and/or human form who both served and threatened god and man alike. They may have been symbols of the bold and untamed forces of nature, as in the case of the ship-devouring beasts, Scylla and Charybdis. But they could also have been explanations for large fossilized remains turned up by a farmer's plow, which may have given rise to the giants. In either case, they spoke directly to humankind's experience of the world in all its grandeur and horror.

Some creatures, like the elder Cyclopes and Hecatoncheires, became important allies of the Olympian gods in their struggle for dominance. The Giants (or Gigantes) and the Titans, both children of Gaia and Uranus, made war on Zeus. One unique aspect of their fearsome powers was that often these mythic beasts could only be subdued by demigods like Heracles and Perseus, and not by the gods.

■ The monsters and giants in Greek myth personified the uncontrollable forces of nature

■ Most of the giants—like the Cyclopes, the Hecatoncheires, the Giants (or Gigantes), and the Titans—were the monstrous children of Gaia and Uranus

■ Famous monsters of Greek mythology were the Gorgons, the Hydra, the Chimera, the Harpies, and the Cerberus

Hecatoncheires The Hecatoncheires (**1**), the sons of Uranus and Gaia, had fifty heads on their broad shoulders and one hundred arms. Uranus hated them from birth and forced them into a secret place under Gaia, who resented this. It was Uranus's cruelty to the Hecatoncheires that prompted his castration at the hands of his son, Cronus. But like his father, Cronus made the mistake of imprisoning them. Zeus liberated them to fight against the Titans; however, they were later banned from heaven and earth, the fate of many monsters. They guarded the gates to the underworld.

1

The Cyclopes The Cyclopes ("orb-eyed") (**2**) were a breed of giants with an eye in the middle of their foreheads. The first generation were sons of Uranus and Gaia, who were imprisoned beneath their mother along with the Hecatoncheires. Like them, the Cyclopes were imprisoned by Cronus. They played a pivotal role in the War of the Titans, fashioning Zeus's lightning bolts, Poseidon's trident, and Hades' invisible helmet. A younger generation of Cyclopes lived in Sicily. One of them, Polyphemus, terrorized Odysseus on his journey from Troy.

> ### Figures and Stories Relevant to Monsters and Giants
>
> **Gaia and Uranus**, Mother and Father of Many Monsters and Giants, see pp. 114–115
>
> The *Iliad* and the *Odyssey*, Odysseus Blinded Polyphemus, see pp. 186–187
>
> **Magical Creatures**, More Monsters, see pp. 176–177
>
> **The Titans**, see pp. 116–117
>
> **The War of the Giants**, see pp. 118–119

Harpies Winged daughters of a sea god and a nymph of the storm clouds, the Harpies ("snatchers") (**3**) were known for their swiftness. When a person disappeared, the Harpies were said to have carried him away. They were originally portrayed as fair-haired and pretty, but later poets described them as hideous half-birds with faces emaciated from hunger, who derived pleasure from destroying meals by seizing food and fouling the table with their droppings. The Harpies are famous for harassing the blind King Phineus, who had the gift of prophecy but lacked Zeus's discretion. The Harpies stole his food before he could eat it. They were driven away by the Boreades along with the Argonauts.

Magical Creatures

Among the many dramatic elements of Greek myth there was a large supporting cast of magical creatures, who usually appeared as freakish combinations of humans and animals. Their origins are complex; they were often seen as alien peoples, barbarian and hostile to life, or as inhabitants of other continents, who the heroes had to fight and dominate. The killing of these creatures by the heroes can also be interpreted as a symbol of the Greeks bringing culture to barbarian areas.

Some appear to have roots in the constellations, and in the variety of interpretations the stars inspire; astronomical myths, in turn, represent an attempt to relate them to their heavenly neighbors. Natural phenomena like volcanoes, hot springs, and dinosaur fossils also figure prominently in the lore associated with them. Although sometimes a benign feature of the sea and countryside, many of these creatures were violent and wreaked havoc on humankind.

■ Some creatures of Greek myth were fearsome humanoid figures, such as the Gorgons

■ Others were made from mixtures of human and animal forms

■ The Centaurs were half man and half horse, while Pegasus, born of the neck of Medusa, was a winged horse

■ The Chimera and the Hydra were siblings of the hellhound Cerberus and the Sphinx

■ Dragons, ghosts, vampires, and unicorns are also found in Greek mythology

Chimera Chimera (**1**) was a triple-headed, triple-bodied beast with the head and forepaws of a lion, the head and torso of a goat, and the head and body of a dragon as a tail. A fire-breathing monster, Chimera was raised by the king of Caria and ordered to lay waste to the countryside of Lycia. After many had tried and failed, it was Bellerophon, flying on Pegasus the winged horse, who slew her with a lead spear.

(1)

2

Centaurs Half man and half horse, the Centaurs ("bull killers") (**2**) may have originated from the equestrian hunting culture of Thessaly, where bulls were hunted on horseback. In myth, they were the children of the nymph Nephele and King Ixion. Characterized by a vivacious sexual appetite, they once provoked a war with their kinsmen the Lapiths, after carrying off women from a wedding party to which they had been invited. With a weakness for wine, Centaurs were not known for their ingenuity. The most famous Centaur, Charon, became the boatman who ferried the souls of the dead to the underworld. Heracles was entertained by one during his labors, but—typically—had to fight and kill a number of them.

Gorgons With a woman's body and serpents for hair, the three Gorgons (**3**) were so terrifying that looking at them turned a person to stone. However, Asclepius, god of medicine, discovered that their blood could raise mortals from the dead. While the Gorgons Sthenno and Euryale could not be killed, Medusa was mortal. On the order of Athena, she was killed by Perseus. The goddess kept her head hidden in her armor.

3

Figures and Stories Relevant to Magical Creatures

The Dionysia, Centaurs Made up the Retinue, see pp. 162–163

Heracles, see pp. 164–165

Monsters and Giants, More Magical Creatures, see pp. 174–175

Perseus, Killed Medusa, see pp. 180–181

Hydra and Heracles Not far from Argos in the swamps of Lerna lived a Hydra ("water serpent") with the body of a lion and nine serpentine heads—one of them immortal. The Lernaean Hydra was sacred to Hera, but it was such a terror that King Eurystheus ordered Heracles to kill it. Armed with his sword, Heracles attacked the Hydra (**4**) and got ensnared in its heads; he found that for each mortal head he cut off, two grew in its place. But his charioteer Iolaus brought a firebrand and started to scorch the necks each time Heracles cut off a head; this prevented them from growing back. Heracles buried the Hydra's last, immortal head under a great stone and dipped his arrows in its poisonous blood.

Dragon Deities: p. 342

4

Minos and the Minotaur

The son of Zeus and Europa, Minos was adopted by the Cretan King Asterius when he married Europa. After having ascended the throne Minos became a mighty king, establishing the first laws in Crete, which he received from Zeus. Because of this, upon his death he was made a judge in the underworld, judging the souls of the dead. However, he is most famous for his stepson, the Minotaur. Minos summoned a bull from the sea, a gift from Poseidon; but instead of sacrificing it to the sea god, he kept it in his stables. In revenge, Poseidon made Minos's wife, Pasiphaë, fall in love with the bull; soon after, she bore the Minotaur ("Minos's bull"), a monster with a man's body and a bull's head. Minos hired the craftsman Daedalus to build a labyrinth where he could hide the Minotaur from the world. The Minotaur, however, demanded human sacrifices. Athens, a rival city-state, had killed Minos's son Androgenos, and Minos laid siege to the city. When a terrible plague hit Athens, the oracle of Delphi said that they had to provide seven young men and seven maidens to feed the Minotaur every nine years. This was observed until the arrival of the Athenian prince Theseus. He killed the beast and found the way out of the labyrinth with the aid of Minos's daughter Ariadne, who gave him a ball of string.

»» Gods as Law Givers: pp. 30, 40

Perseus

Like many heroes, Perseus faced great adversity from birth and was forced to undergo many trials before he rose to power. He was the son of Zeus and Danae, princess of Argos.

Before Danae gave birth to Perseus, it was prophesied that he would kill his grandfather, Acrisius. So the king forced the two of them into a wooden box and set it adrift at sea. The box washed up near the island of Seriphus, ruled by Polydectes. As he grew up, Perseus learned that Polydectes wanted to marry Danae. Wanting to protect his mother, Perseus rebelled. In order to get rid of Perseus, Polydectes sent him out on an impossible task. After many adventures, Perseus returned to Argos, where he fulfilled the oracle's prophecy by accidentally killing Acrisius.

- Perseus was a demigod, the son of Zeus and the mortal princess Danae
- He succeeded in a quest to behead the Gorgon Medusa with the help of the deities Athena and Hermes
- He married the Ethiopian princess Andromeda, after having saved her from a sea monster
- He was given objects to aid him in his tasks, including a helmet of invisibility, a satchel, a polished shield, a sword, and a pair of winged boots

Danae and the Shower of Gold When King Acrisius was told by an oracle that his daughter, Danae, would bear a son who would kill him, he desperately tried to avoid this fate. To keep her from getting pregnant, he imprisoned her in a bronzed cell with only a small opening for air and food. As Zeus desired her, he poured himself through the opening as a golden shower, falling into Danae's lap (**1**). As a result of this union, Danae gave birth to Perseus.

Slaying of Medusa

Seeing that Perseus was standing in the way of him marrying Danae, Polydectes of Seriphus pretended he was marrying another princess and asked Perseus for a wedding gift.

He asked him for the head of Medusa, the Gorgon whose looks turned men to stone. This was a nearly impossible task; however, Athena and Hermes aided Perseus in his quest. They sent him first to the Graeae,

goddesses who shared one eye and one tooth between them. After stealing their eye, he asked them to tell him Medusa's whereabouts. Nymphs, living nearby, gave him a pair of winged boots, a helmet of invisibility, and a sack. When he found Medusa, he looked at her through the reflection of the shield Athena had given him and, using the sickle of Hermes, slew her (**2**). Placing her head in his sack, he headed back to Polydectes. The king did not believe Perseus until he saw the head for himself, which instantly turned him into stone.

Figures and Stories Relevant to Perseus

Athena, Helped Perseus, see pp. 138–139	**Nereids**, see Nymphs and Muses, pp. 172–173
Hermes, Helped Perseus, see pp. 148–149	**Poseidon**, Demanded Andromeda's Sacrifice, see pp. 128–129
Medusa, see Magical Creatures, pp. 176–177	**Zeus**, Perseus's Father, see pp. 120–123

Saving Andromeda

When the Ethiopian queen Cassiopeia boasted that she and her daughter, Andromeda, were more beautiful than the Nereids, sea nymphs who served the goddess Thetis, the kingdom was in peril. As punishment, Poseidon flooded King Cepheus's lands, and demanded Andromeda's sacrifice to appease him. When Perseus, who was traveling through Ethiopia, discovered Andromeda chained to a rock and threatened by a sea monster, he fell in love with her. Going to her parents, he promised to slay the monster if he could marry her and take her home as his queen. Cepheus and Cassiopeia agreed and Perseus, using his winged boots and adamantine sickle, beheaded the beast. Although he had saved Andromeda (**3**), Perseus still had to fight her suitor, Phineus. Showing him Medusa's head, Phineus was turned to stone.

Heroes Fighting Against Monsters: pp. 27, 165, 251, 315, 361

Jason and the Argonauts

Prince Jason of Thessaly was deprived of his birthright by his uncle, Pelias. After being raised by the centaur Chiron, Jason returned to Thessaly, determined to reclaim his father's throne. Pelias agreed to return the throne if Jason brought him the golden fleece of a sacred winged ram hanging in Ares' grove in Colchis. Jason and a crew of heroes set off on the Argo (**1**), the first Greek longship, built with the help of Athena.

After many adventures on the way, the Argonauts reached Colchis. King Æetes was willing to give up the golden fleece only if Jason completed a series of impossible tasks. With the help of Æetes' daughter Medea, who was skilled in magic, Jason finished the tasks. However, when Æetes refused to give him the golden fleece, Jason stole it and fled, taking Medea with him. Ultimately, he did not ascend the throne of Thessaly as he was unfavored by the gods. This was because of the murder of Medea's brother Apsyrtus, by which he became "impure" in their eyes.

The myth of Jason has been told in various forms. The only complete version is preserved in the *Argonautica* of Apollonius of Rhodes.

■ Along with the Trojan War, the story of Jason and the Argonauts is one of the greatest Greek myths

■ Jason, prince of Thessaly, had to retrieve the golden fleece of a sacred ram to win back the throne of his father

■ He assembled a group of heroes and sailed with the Argo to Colchis

■ Heracles, Orpheus, Polydeuces, Castor, and Atalanta were among the crew

■ The myth of Jason is intimately connected with the myth of Medea

Figures and Stories Relevant to Jason and the Argonauts

❯❯ **The Golden Fleece in Ancient Middle Eastern Mythology:** p. 51

History of the Golden Fleece

Historians have long wondered about the origin of the golden fleece myth. One theory suggests it might have had something to do with the large amount of gold found in the rivers of the Caucasus Mountains (site of Colchis), where people panned for it with the help of sheepskins, according to the historian Appian. Others say that the myth of the Argonauts refers to the colonization of the Black Sea region by the Greeks in the 13th century B.C.

Women of Lemnos En route to Colchis, the Argonauts stopped at the island of Lemnos. Aphrodite had cursed the island not long before by planting rumors in the women's heads that their husbands, who were returning from war, had brought home their slave girls as mistresses. In a jealous rage, the women slaughtered all the men. With no men left to procreate with, they were facing extinction. Thus, the Argonauts were given such a warm and lusty reception by the women (**2**) that they stayed. After a long time, Heracles, who had guarded the ship, reproached Jason and his crew. They returned and the Argo sailed on, filled with wine and provisions from their grateful hostesses.

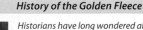

The Robbery of the Golden Fleece When the Argonauts arrived at Colchis, King Æetes said he would give Jason the golden fleece if he could harness two fire-breathing bulls, sow dragon's teeth, and slay the warriors born from those teeth. Medea, Æetes' daughter and a priestess of Hecate, fell in love with Jason and helped him accomplish his tasks. When Æetes refused to hand over the fleece, Medea helped Jason steal it (**3**) by using her knowledge of potions to make the dragon guarding the fleece fall asleep. Then Medea murdered and dismembered her brother, Apsyrtus, to keep the Colchians from pursuing them.

The Trojan War

■ Found in Homer's epics, the *Iliad* and the *Odyssey*, the Trojan War was extremely important in Greek mythology

■ The Greeks and the Trojans fought over the abduction of Helen from the Spartan court

■ The most famous Greek warriors were Achilles, Ajax, and Odysseus

■ The most famous Trojan heroes were Hector and Aeneas

■ Historians and archaeologists still debate over the physical evidence relating to these stories; the Trojan War could have occurred around 1200 B.C.

The legendary fight between the Trojans and the Achaeans (the Greeks) is one of the most famous wars in history due to the epics of Homer. It is still discussed whether the war took place or if an earthquake destroyed the city of Troy around 1200 B.C.

The war began when the Trojan prince Paris abducted Helen (**1**), the wife of the Spartan king Menelaus. Paris felt that he had the right to take Helen, the most beautiful woman on earth, because he had been promised her by Aphrodite. For Helen, he had voted Aphrodite as the most beautiful in a contest between Hera, Athena, and the goddess of love. Yet Menelaus wanted Helen back, and mobilized an unprecedented force of Achaean armies with his brother, the Mycenaean king Agamemnon. As Troy was a well-fortified city and the gods fought for both sides, the siege dragged on for ten years.

Among the many heroes of the war, two stood out: the Trojan Hector, Paris's brother, and the Achaean warrior Achilles. The latter was nearly invulnerable, except for his heel. Yet, both ultimately lost their lives. The end of the war saw an Achaean victory, which was masterminded by Odysseus.

Figures and Stories Relevant to the Trojan War

Aeneas, Trojan Hero, see pp. 198–199

Aphrodite, Offered Helen to Paris, see pp. 142–143

Athena, Hera, and Poseidon, Fought on the Side of the Greeks, see pp. 138–139, 126–127, 128–129

The *Iliad* and the *Odyssey*, Main Sources for the Myths of the Trojan War, pp. 186–187

Zeus, Helen's Father, see pp. 120–123

The Rage of Achilles The bravest, strongest, and most handsome of Agamemnon's warriors (**3**), Achilles suffered from extreme rage and pride. When he had to surrender his slave and mistress Briseis to Agamemnon, he refused to fight. As a result the Achaeans suffered heavy losses. When the Trojans torched Achaean ships, Achilles' friend Patroclus fought in his place—and in his armor—and was slain by Hector. Achilles, mad with grief, killed Hector and desecrated his body, dragging it behind his chariot to the Achaean camp.

The Trojan Horse When the war remained unresolved after ten years, the wily king of Ithaca, Odysseus, devised a scheme for taking Troy by stealth. The Achaeans built a massive wooden horse that was hollowed to hold warriors inside. After the horse had been loaded with Odysseus and many others, it was rolled before the gates of Troy. The Achaeans struck camp and pretended to sail away. Thinking the Greeks had lifted the siege and left the horse as an offering, the Trojans threw open the gates, brought in the horse (**2**), and celebrated into the night. Later, as the city of Troy slept, Odysseus and his men climbed from the horse and opened the gates for the Achaeans, who had returned on their ships. Troy was overrun, pillaged, and utterly destroyed.

Schliemann and the Birth of Archaeology

Even though 19th-century historians saw Homer's epics and Troy as pure fiction, Frank Calvert, an English archaeologist, purchased a site in Hissarlik, Turkey, in the 1860s. Heinrich Schliemann (right), a German businessman with a passion for Homer, took over Calvert's operations and uncovered the remains of Troy. Although an amateur whose methods were often questionable, Schliemann made many important finds, which he paired with Homer's heroes, e.g., the mask of Agamemnon. His work laid the foundation for archaeology and invigorated interest in Greek mythology.

The Iliad *and the* Odyssey

Much of what is known about the Trojan War and its after-math comes from two epics written by the Greek Homer (**1**) in the second half of the eighth century B.C.: the *Iliad* and the *Odyssey*. The first epic, which takes its title from Troy's ancient name of Ilium, recounts the origins and conse-quences of Achilles' (**3**) anger with the Achaean leader Agamemnon against the background of the Trojan War. The *Odyssey*, set ten years after the war, de-scribes the Ithacan king Odysseus's long journey home. Even early readers understood Odysseus's hopes and failures as a symbol for human life, with all its adventures, tests, and dangers. Both poems are rich in descriptions of the Greek gods, their constant quarrels and plots on Mount Olympus, as well as their many interventions in human affairs.

Wanderings of Odysseus The journey home from Troy took Odysseus ten years. A cunning advisor during the Trojan War, he later became a victim of the power play of the gods. Because he had blinded Poseidon's son, the Cyclops Polyphemus, the sea god was Odysseus's worst enemy. After much of his fleet was destroyed by the Laestrygons, man-eating Giants, he and his men were enchanted by the goddess Circe, who tried to hold Odysseus on her island forever. Next, Odysseus faced the Sirens (**2**), who he survived by filling his men's ears with wax while he alone, tied to the mast, resisted their alluring songs. His ship even escaped the sea monsters Scylla and Charybdis. However, when his men killed oxen sacred to the god Helios, their ship sank and all the men lost their lives. Odysseus washed up on the island of the nymph Calypso, who held him prisoner for years. When Odysseus finally came home to Ithaca, he killed his wife Penelope's numerous suitors before taking back his throne.

Oedipus

When King Laius of Thebes was told by the oracle at Delphi that his son would kill him, both he and his wife Jocasta agreed to abandon their newborn child in the wilderness. However, the baby was found by a shepherd, who brought him to Corinth where he was adopted by the king. When he was almost grown up, he was told by a drunken companion that he was not the son of the royal couple of Corinth. Deeply troubled and not content with his parents' evasive answer, Oedipus went to the oracle to find out the truth. The oracle told him that he would not only kill his father, but he would also marry his mother. To prevent this, he left Corinth. On the road he was

accosted by a man and slew him, not suspecting for a moment that this was his real father Laius. Arriving at Thebes, he liberated the city from the oppression of a sphinx by answering her riddle: What creature went on four feet in the morning, on two at noon, and on three in the evening? A human. Gratefully, the Thebans made him their new king, and the widowed queen Jocasta gave him her hand. When a plague came to Thebes some years later, an oracle demanded justice for Laius's murder. As Oedipus hunted for his predecessor's killer, he learned the truth and blinded himself in punishment. After wandering in exile, the repentant sinner was accepted by the gods of the underworld.

The House of Atreus

Few families have as brutal a history as the house of Atreus. Thus, they were a popular subject of tragedies, from ancient authors like Aeschylus (*The Oresteia*) and Euripides to authors of the modern era like Goethe and Racine. The line began with Tantalus, whose atrocious act against the gods damned his dynasty. Pelops, Tantalus's son, and Atreus, his grandson, further illustrated the family's lust for blood. Atreus and his brother, Thyestes, murdered their half brother and then fled to Mycenae.

- The House of Atreus was a damned dynasty that became the subject of many epics
- The cursed family began with Tantalus, who proved the omniscience of the gods
- Tantalus's grandson, Atreus, was the king of Mycenae
- The sons of Atreus, Menelaus and Agamemnon, were major players in the Trojan War
- Agamemnon's children, Orestes and Electra, avenged their father's murder

In Mycenae, Atreus became king, but was murdered by Aegisthus, the son of his predecessor. Atreus's son, Menelaus, later succeeded to the throne of Sparta while his other son, Agamemnon, became king in Mycenae. The brothers married Menelaus's predecessor's daughters, Helen and Clytemnestra. Menelaus's wife caused the Trojan War, during which the brothers fought successfully together. After his return to Mycenae, Agamemnon was murdered by Clytemnestra. Agamemnon's children avenged him, which had tragic results for all.

Tantalus and Pelops Tantalus, king of Sipylus in Lydia, is notorious for committing a truly impious act: he once invited the gods to eat at his palace, and—either because the pantry was empty or to test the gods' powers—cut up his son Pelops, cooked him in a stew, and served him for dinner. All the gods except Demeter, who ate Pelops's shoulder, realized at once what had happened, and Tantalus was banished and condemned to perpetual hunger and thirst in the underworld (**1**). Although standing in water, he could not reach down to drink it, and the branches of a fruit tree hung close to him, but shied away when he tried to pick a fruit. This is the origin of the word tantalizing. At the same time, Pelops was reassembled with an ivory shoulder made by Hephaestus as the only reminder of his ordeal.

Atreus and Thyestes

When Atreus, the son of Pelops, learned that his wife Aerope had slept with his brother, Thyestes, he punished him by murdering his children and feeding them to him as a meal. Thyestes suspected nothing until Atreus brought out the heads and hands of his victims. Seeing this, Thyestes vomited up his children and put a dark curse on all of Atreus's children. Thyestes went into exile but was later brought back by Atreus's sons, Menelaus and Agamemnon, and imprisoned. Atreus tried to persuade Aegisthus (**2**, later murdered by Agamemnon's son Orestes), Thyestes' son, to murder his father. Instead, Aegisthus avenged his father by killing Atreus and helping Thyestes take his brother's throne.

Agamemnon and Clytemnestra

Clytemnestra was forced to marry Agamemnon, who had murdered her first husband. She hated him because he was willing to sacrifice their daughter, Iphigeneia, for a favorable wind to attack Troy. Although Iphigeneia was saved by Artemis, Clytemnestra, together with her lover, Aegisthus, took revenge when Agamemnon returned home (**3**).

Orestes and Electra

After she killed Agamemnon, Clytemnestra forced their daughter Electra into poverty. Their son Orestes, living in exile, wanted to avenge his father's murder, but to do so he would have to murder his own mother. After gaining the

oracle at Delphi's approval, he returned to Mycenae. Then, pretending to be a messenger with word of his own death, he entered the palace and killed her (**4**), but was hounded by the Furies as punishment.

> ### Figures and Stories Relevant to the House of Atreus
>
> **Artemis**, Saved Iphigeneia, see pp. 136–137
>
> **The Trojan War**, Involved Menelaus and Agamemnon, see pp. 184–185

Roman Mythology

One of Rome's most famous founding myths was that of Romulus and Remus, who were weaned by a wolf

Roman Mythology

Roman religion had its origins with the arrival of diverse nomadic peoples around the Tiber River in central Italy. This immigration began as far back as the Stone Age. The Latins, Rome's direct ancestors, migrated from central Europe to the region south of the Tiber River during the second millennium B.C.; their language and traditions would eventually come to prominence but for some time they were under the influence of the Etruscans, a people of possibly Anatolian origin who can be traced as living north of the Tiber as early as 1400 B.C.

The Etruscans came to rule much of north-central Italy, with foreign alliances that included the Phoenician colony of Carthage; it is through contact with either the Phoenicians or the Greeks that they developed the first alphabet used in that region. Etruscan culture reached its height during the eighth century B.C., and a succession of their kings ruled over the Latin city of Rome, which was founded in 753. Although the Latins overthrew the Etruscans (**1**, Etruscan soldier) and founded the Roman Republic in 510 B.C., Etruscan priests were retained and their religious traditions and practices, such as divination (**2**, model of a sheep's liver for divination), were carefully preserved, laying the foundations for later Roman practices.

The next influences on Roman religion and mythology were the Greek-speaking colonies along Italy's eastern coast and on the island of Sicily. Having migrated there during the Dark Ages (1200–800 B.C.), the Greeks brought their polytheistic beliefs and introduced Romans to their colorful accounts of the gods and heroes. Romans assimilated many Greek gods into their pantheon, such as

Jupiter (Zeus) and Juno (Hera). However, the Greek passion for mythology, as found in the epic poems of Homer and Hesiod, did not take root in Roman soil at first.

One reason for the lack of interest in mythology was that Romans did not conceive their gods as human-like figures with minds and behaviors. Thus, their religion was also not as concerned with giving the gods names. In many cases the Romans only prayed and made offerings to the *genus loci* ("spirit of the place") without any further designation. What was more important was to invoke the god's *numen* ("presence") to ensure success in all endeavors.

The Romans believed in ever-present natural divinities whose will was consulted on important matters primarily through *haruspices* ("organ gazing"), the examination of the organs of sacrificial animals. Priests or augurs (**3**) also interpreted natural events (e.g., the flights of birds and lightning) as messages from the gods—practices they adopted from the Etruscans. The *pontifex maximus* ("great bridge-builder") supervised all of Rome's cults, which were administered in turn by a college of *flamines*, state-appointed priests. A separate official, the *aedile*, was responsible for athletic and theatrical festivals held in the gods' honor. Under the empire, however, the emperor assumed the title of Pontifex and eventually became a god in his own right, with his own priests appointed to perform rites for the imperial cult. Officially, this was portrayed as

a natural extension of his power over the state's religious matters. Prayers to the emperor and his family's patron gods ensured the stability of the state's sacred rites. The emperor's status as a civic and spiritual leader had enormous consequences for the rise of Christianity and

the development of the Church's hierarchy. Whatever oral traditions may have existed in Rome's early days, many myths were not written down in standard form until the time of Emperor Augustus (27 B.C.–A.D. 14) (**4**, posing as Jupiter with a scepter, laurel wreath, and *lituus*, an augur's staff). Augustus gave Roman religion its Greek veneer, creating the false impression (still popular today) that Roman religion was the same as the Greeks'. Augustus commissioned Virgil's *Aeneid*, an epic about Rome's legendary forefather Aeneas of Troy. Livy wrote a comprehensive history of Rome from the city's founding brothers Romulus and Remus to the Caesars; and Ovid wrote *Metamorphoses*, a poetic catalogue of miracle tales drawn mostly from Greek mythology. Works like the *Aeneid*, which celebrated the magnitude and eternal reign of the Roman Empire, demonstrate the Romans' pragmatic outlook on their myths. They were used to uphold the Roman state and legitimize its territorial and cultural expansion.

Even as Rome's poets and historians established a mythic past, the state embraced the present and future. New gods, new theologies, and cult practices were constantly emerging as Rome's sphere of influence expanded. There were multiple mechanisms of change. Foreign cults were often introduced to Rome through the political tradition of *evocatio* ("summoning"). During the evocatio, the deities of conquered peoples were sent for, and if these gods responded to the summons, the triumphal procession that introduced their sacred idols into the city (whether through military conquest or theft) was a sign that Rome honored these gods more and offered them better protection. Thus, the evocatio did not disrupt Roman state rites. Another method of change was syncretism, in which any god from the Roman pantheon could be assimilated with a foreign god whose powers and position were similar. The process was dynamic, and sometimes involved the adoption of a new cult in Rome, or the recognition of a new aspect to their old gods. Many of these cults were first worshiped by the Roman army before being practiced by a broader part of the population, like the cult of Mithras.

Among Rome's patrician ruling class, piety was a dominant concern, hence it was important to respect all the gods in their myriad forms, whoever and wherever they may be. Not least, piety, or *pietas,* helped to ensure the stability of social structures, demanding respect for parents, the Senate, or the emperors. Myths propagated a patriarchic order, giving power to the patriarch of the household (*pater familias*) and to the upper classes.

Romans believed that the highest expression of religion was in public displays of generosity and regular attendance at festivals and public sacrifices. In the early days of the republic, Rome only enjoyed a handful of athletic competitions in honor of the gods. But, with the addition of Greek-style dramatic plays, and the constant competition among the patricians for public favor, the number of games vastly increased (**5**, Colosseum). By the fourth century A.D., nearly half the year was devoted to sacred festivals, with at least a hundred days set aside for stage shows. This explains why early Christians, rejecting Roman piety as hypocrisy, were condemned as "atheists" because they avoided the theater and refused to participate in public sacrifices.

5

Aeneas

From the earliest days of the Roman Republic, Rome claimed Aeneas, the son of Venus and a key figure in the Trojan War, as their founding father.

Telling a different story than the *Iliad* of Homer, Virgil's Roman epic poem, the *Aeneid*, held that the Trojan hero Aeneas escaped the ruins of Troy with some companions. Led by a prophecy that he would settle on the Tiber River and establish a new Troy, he set sail. As an adversary of the Trojans, the goddess Juno tried on several occasions to foil the prophecy. After a stay in Carthage and a fateful encounter with its queen, Dido, Aeneas consulted a Sibyl and visited his dead father, Anchises, in the underworld. Encouraged by him, Aeneas sailed up the Tiber to Latium in central Italy. At first receiving a friendly welcome, a war later ensued between the Trojans and the Latins. Finally, Aeneas achieved his goal by establishing Lavinium. His son Iulus later founded Alba Longa, the precursor of Rome.

- Aeneas, son of Venus, was a heroic figure from Troy
- According to legend, he founded Lavinium in central Italy
- He was worshiped as the god Jupiter Indiges after his death
- Julius Caesar claimed to be of the line of Aeneas
- His story is transmitted in the *Aeneid* of Virgil

Aeneas and Dido One of the most famous episodes in Virgil's *Aeneid* was Aeneas's affair with Queen Dido of Carthage. The Phoenician princess Dido, like Aeneas, had been forced into exile after losing her husband. When Aeneas landed in Carthage, Venus and Juno directed the romance, each to her own ends. The results were tragic: Cupid wiped clean Dido's memory of her lost husband, and she fell madly in love. When Aeneas left to fulfill his destiny, Dido committed suicide (**1**) on a funeral pyre. Dido's fate can be connected to Carthage's relations with, and later destruction by, Rome.

City/State Founders: pp. 200, 353, 383

War Against Turnus

Upon Aeneas's arrival in Latium, he was greeted by King Latinus, who had been told in a prophecy that he should marry his daughter Lavinia to a foreign guest. Aeneas was warmly welcomed and offered Lavinia's hand in marriage. However, this infuriated Queen Amata and the Rutulian king Turnus, Lavinia's suitor. Juno, ever eager to foil Aeneas's plans, stirred up a deadly war between the Latins and Aeneas's men, forcing Aeneas to seek an alliance with the neighboring Etruscans. Although Jupiter, the king of the gods, initially pledged to remain neutral, he eventually intervened on Aeneas's behalf after much blood was spilled. Finally, Turnus and Aeneas faced each other in a duel. Turnus was wounded and put mercilessly to death (**2**).

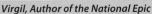

Virgil, Author of the National Epic

Emperor Augustus commissioned the poet Virgil to take the myth of Aeneas and create a national epic that glorified his empire. Virgil, born near Mantua ca 70 B.C., had studied literature and philosophy for years in Rome, and was already famous for his pastoral poem, Georgics. Originally asked to write a paean to Augustus's military conquests, Virgil instead crafted a poem that wove traditional myth together with contemporary history, which he cast as bold "prophecies" of future glory.

Figures and Stories Relevant to Aeneas

Aphrodite, Greek Equivalent to Venus, Mother of Aeneas, see pp. 142–143

The Iliad and the Odyssey, see pp. 188–189

Romulus and Remus, Another Foundation Myth of Rome, see pp. 200–201

The Trojan War, Aeneas Was a Trojan Hero, see pp. 186–187

Anchises and the Household Gods

Ancient temples are famous for their statues, but each household had its own personal idols—small images of the gods who watch over the family. These *penates*, or household gods, were a central feature of Roman worship and may have been of greater importance than public statuary. When Aeneas fled from Troy, he not only carried his crippled father Anchises (**3**), he also took the household gods that had protected them through the generations. The image of Aeneas and his burden symbolized the virtues of loyalty to family and to the gods.

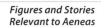

Romulus and Remus

When Numitor, the king of Alba Longa, a city in Lazio, was overthrown by his brother Amulius, his daughter Rhea Silvia was forced to become a Vestal Virgin and could not conceive heirs to the throne of Alba Longa. However, when she was raped by the war god Mars, she had the twins Romulus and Remus. Amulius imprisoned Rhea Silvia and left her sons on the banks of the Tiber River. A she-wolf saw the twins and suckled them (**1**) until they were discovered by the shepherd Faustulus.

Unaware they were royalty, the twins were raised by Faustulus near Palatine Hill. When they learned of their royal lineage, they helped Numitor regain his throne. In return, he allowed them to establish a city of their own, which was named Rome. After murdering Remus, Romulus ruled the city and increased its population by offering asylum to exiles and abducting women from their neighbors.

The legend of Romulus and Remus was formulated around the fourth century B.C. By having the city's founders derived from the god Mars, Rome was given sacred status.

■ Romulus and Remus were twin brothers who founded Rome

■ The legend of Romulus and Remus is the most popular of Rome's multiple founding myths

■ This ancient Roman legend was transmitted in written form by writers such as Plutarch and Livy

■ Suckled by a she-wolf who rescued them, they were raised by a shepherd

■ Romulus was the first of seven mythical kings of Rome

■ Deified, Romulus was identified with the war god Quirinus

Figures and Stories Relevant to Romulus and Remus

Aeneas, Sometimes Portrayed as Romulus and Remus's Grandfather, see pp. 198–199

Ares, Greek Equivalent to Mars, Father of Romulus and Remus, see pp. 140–141

Rape of the Sabines, Under the Reign of Romulus, see pp. 202–203

(**1**)

➤➤ **City/State Founders:** pp. 198, 353, 383

Rape of Rhea Silvia One day Princess Rhea Silvia left the temple of Vesta to fetch water, and took a nap down by the river. While she was sleeping, Mars caught sight of her and was determined to lie with her (**2**). As he was doing so, Rhea Silvia dreamed she was at Troy. When she dropped her hairpin, she saw twin trees grow where it fell. One of the trees grew tall and broad enough to shade the entire world. When Rhea Silvia awoke, she found herself pregnant with Romulus and Remus.

Founding of Rome After restoring Numitor to the throne, Romulus and Remus founded a new city in the hills where they grew up. Romulus was named the city's ruler (**3**) and built a small stone wall to mark its borders, warning that anyone coming over the wall would be killed. Mockingly, Remus jumped over the wall and was slain by Romulus. After this Romulus said: "The fate of my brother should be the fate of anyone who dares to jump over the wall of my city!"

The Cult of Quirinus

One of the original triad of Roman gods, along with Jupiter and Mars, Quirinus was a god of war. A temple named the Quirinal that stood on one of the seven hills of Rome was dedicated to him. He also had his own priest, the Flamen Quirinalis. Later, the Romans came to believe that their founder Romulus had himself become Quirinus. It is said that Romulus was in the Field of Mars (right) one day with his Senate, when he disappeared in a storm heralded by dark clouds and lightning. Many suspected murder, but a divine vision announced he had been transformed into the god.

Divine Rulers: pp. 48, 84, 220, 336, 368

Rape of the Sabines

After the founding of Rome, Romulus met with nearby communities to find wives for his men. When his embassies were rejected, he organized a festival in honor of Consus, the god of harvest. The Sabines, a neighboring tribe, attended in large numbers, but while they were watching the day's spectacle, Romulus gave a signal, and his men seized the women of their choice and carried them off as brides. The Sabine leaders declared war over the rape of their daughters. However, the Sabine women intervened when they saw their Roman husbands and children fighting against their fathers and brothers, and the tribesmen were declared Roman citizens.

Curiatii and Horatii

In order to resolve the war between the neighboring kingdoms of Alba Longa and Rome, both sides agreed to have three Alban brothers, the Curiatii, battle against three Roman brothers, the Horatii (**1**), on behalf of their armies.

When two of the Horatii were killed quickly, it appeared the Curiatii would win. However, the surviving Horatius ran, and in so doing separated the wounded Curiatii who pursued him. He then turned, fought, and killed each of the Alban brothers one by one, giving Rome the victory. The king of Rome, Tullus Hostilius, oversaw the destruction of Alba Longa and forced the Albans to emigrate to Rome.

Set around the sixth century B.C., when Rome was beginning its expansion, the legend of the Curiatii and the Horatii not only demonstrated courage in battle and willingness to die for the greatness of Rome, but also symbolized the military emancipation of the young Roman state from the domination of Alba Longa and gave rise to legal practices.

■ The myth of the Curiatii and Horatii illustrates the conflicts between Alba Longa and Rome, and the victory of the latter

■ Two groups of male triplets, the Horatii from Rome and the Curiatii from Alba Longa, were set against one another to settle the Alban-Roman war

■ Horatius, who slew the Curiatii alone, later slew his sister who mourned for a Curiatii who had been her husband

☐ 1

Rome and Alba Longa

Although often at odds (**2**, Romans and Albans fighting), the citizens of Rome and Alba Longa both descended from Trojan refugees who settled in Italy at Lavinium, named after their leader Aeneas's Latin wife. As Lavinium was prosperous, Aeneas's son Ascanius founded the nearby kingdom of Alba Longa. After many generations of Alban kings, Romulus and Remus founded Rome where they had grown up.

Trial of Horatius

When the victorious Horatius came home and saw his sister weeping for her fiancé, one of the fallen Curiatii, he killed her and said: "So perish any Roman woman who mourns the enemy." For taking the law into his own hands, Horatius was condemned to death (**3**). However, he was saved when he appealed to the people. As penance, he had to pass through a door of spears. Thus, no one was above the written law, not even a hero.

Figures and Stories Relevant to Curiatii and Horatii

Aeneas, Father of Ascanius, the Founder of Alba Longa; the Curiatii Were Albans, see pp. 198–199

Romulus and Remus, Founders of Rome; the Horatii Were Roman, see pp. 200–201

The Trojan War, Aeneas Fled from Troy to Italy; His Son Founded Alba Longa, see pp. 184–185

Jupiter

As king of the gods, Jupiter presided over public morality and the Roman government's most important actions: its treaties, declarations of war, and public oaths. Although Jupiter shared some key aspects with the Greek god Zeus—their position as father of the gods, which guaranteed the patriarchical family order—the rites and temples dedicated to Jupiter in and around Rome speak to his distinctly Roman character.

As the god of the air, the realm that fed the soil, Jupiter was responsible for the fertility of fields. In times of drought, processions and ceremonies like the Nudipedalia (conducted with bare feet) were offered to appease Jupiter in his aspect as Pluvius, "rain-bringer." Generals built temples to Jupiter Stator ("stander") when Roman forces won against overwhelming odds. Jupiter even claimed Romulus and Remus, Rome's founders, as his grandsons. The early kings and later emperors styled themselves as earthly kin of the god, and Jupiter was known as the defender of the Roman Republic and worshiped as Jupiter Liber ("freedom") for centuries.

■ Jupiter was the chief god of the Roman pantheon, as well as a part of the Capitoline triad with Juno and Minerva

■ As Jupiter Optimus Maximus Soter ("Jupiter best, greatest, savior"), he was the protective god of the free empire

■ As with his Greek equivalent, Zeus, he is symbolized by a lightning bolt, and an eagle served as his messenger

Jupiter Capitolinus The temple of Jupiter (**1**) in his aspect of Optimus Maximus ("best" and "greatest") was built on the Capitoline hill by the Etruscan kings, but was dedicated in the era of the republic. When complete it housed the triad of gods—Jupiter, Juno, and Minerva—and became the focus of all Roman civic ritual. Its dedication date, September 13, was the day Roman officials were sworn into office. The temple housed engraved copies of treaties, as well as the spoils of victorious battles.

》 Zeus: p. 120 | **Triads of Gods:** pp. 264, 308

(2)

Rise of the Cult of Jupiter

In Virgil's *Aeneid*, King Latinus favored the god Saturn while Aeneas, guided from Troy to Italy by Jupiter's prophecy, heralded the introduction of Jupiter's cult. This reflects the idea that although he later became the chief god of the state, Jupiter (**2**) was a relatively new addition to Roman mythology. Saturn, who first came to Italy seeking refuge after his expulsion from Mount Olympus, was already worshiped as the god of sowing (*sata*) along with a number of Latin agricultural gods. The war between Turnus and Aeneas was in part a battle for the primacy of Saturn or Jupiter, and Aeneas's victory marked the elevation of Jupiter's cult above all.

Forms of Jupiter

As the Romans made contact with foreign cultures, native gods were often integrated into the Roman pantheon. Because Jupiter was the patron god of Roman legions, local gods displaying warrior-like strength were easily identified with him. One example is Jupiter Dolichenus (**3**), originally known as Baal, a thunder and fertility god of Syrian origin. Jupiter Dolichenus is so named because he originated in the town of Doliche in Asia Minor. As a military god, Dolichenus had his own temples in Rome; however, only Eastern priests were allowed to conduct his rites.

(3)

Figures and Stories Relevant to Jupiter

Augurs and Auspicia

The art of divination was highly developed in Rome. Augurs (right) were high priests responsible for interpreting various signs from the gods. Roman authorities always consulted augurs to see whether a proposed course of action met with the gods' approval. A variety of natural phenomena, such as thunder and lightning, earthquakes, and the behavior of animals on the ground or birds (above) in the air (auspicia means literally "bird-watching"), were interpreted as divine signs. Another practice of the Augurs was to read the future in the organs of sacrificed animals.

Baal: p. 52 | **Divination and Prophecy:** pp. 120, 134, 217, 447

■ The patron of women, Juno was a fertility goddess, and the wife and sister of Jupiter

■ She was part of the Capitoline triad with Jupiter and Minerva

■ Juno was also worshiped as the patron goddess of Rome

■ Like her Greek counterpart, Hera, she was associated with marriage and childbirth

■ As personal guardian spirit, *juno* was the female counterpart of the male *genius*

■ She usually appears as an extremely beautiful matron figure and sometimes with military characteristics

■ Her sacred animal was the goose

Figures and Stories Relevant to Juno

Aeneas, Juno Tried to Hinder Aeneas, see pp. 198–199

Jupiter, Juno's Husband, see pp. 206–207

Minerva, Worshiped With Juno and Jupiter in the Capitoline Triad, see pp. 210–211

Romulus and Remus, see pp. 200–201

Juno

Juno (**1**, creating the Milky Way) was originally an Italian fertility goddess and patron of women, who was later identified with the Greek goddess Hera. Many of her aspects demonstrate her governance over all stages of women's lives. On a woman's wedding day, Juno Interduca led the bride from her home to the marriage ceremony, then Juno Domiduca conducted her to her husband's home. As the most auspicious time of year for marriage was during June, the month was dedicated to Juno. However, the main festival in honor of Juno, the Matronalia, was held annually on the first of March.

As the savior of the Roman state, Juno was often seen with a Roman soldier's cloak and armed with a spear. Incredibly popular, her cult was found throughout Italy. In the Capitoline Temple she was worshiped as Juno Regina, "queen" of the gods.

⏭ **Hera:** p. 126 | **Queens of the Gods:** pp. 126, 242

Juno Moneta During the early days of the republic it was said a flock of geese (**2**) sacred to Juno Regina, enshrined on the Capitoline Hill, once warned Rome of an impending Gallic invasion. In thanks, Rome recognized and worshiped the goddess in her new aspect as Moneta, "the warner." Shortly after, a temple was dedicated to Juno Moneta on the Arx (a secondary Capitoline Hill) and it served as a repository for the *libri lentei*, important civic records recorded on linen. As the temple also protected the city's mint, the term "moneta" came to be synonymous in Latin with money.

The Matronalia

The Matronalia was an opportunity for Rome's wives to give thanks to Juno Lucina. They commemorated the marriages between the Romans and the Sabines, as well as the general sanctity of marriage (left). Husbands also used to give presents to their wives.

Juno Lucina Mothers worshiped Juno Lucina (**4**, Temple of Juno Lucina in Agrigento), the "light bringer," who brought their children to the light of day. This aspect of Juno played a key role when Romulus and his men kidnapped the Sabine women. At first, their marriages were childless. When they prayed to Juno in her sacred grove, she revealed a fertility rite—whipping their wives' backs with thongs of goat skin. This was so successful that it was reenacted every year at the Lupercalia festival in February.

Juno Sospita While intimately connected to women and lunar cycles, Juno also protected Rome from foreign invaders in her aspect as Juno Sospita ("savior") (**3**). The center of this cult was Lanuvium, south of Rome in the province of Latium. Strange portents at this temple were seen as signs of impending losses in battle. The cult became so important during the republic that a temple was dedicated to Juno Sospita Mater Regina ("savior," "mother," and "queen") in the Forum Holitorium.

■ Minerva was the Roman goddess of warriors, commerce, and medicine

■ She invented music and numbers, and was the goddess of poetry, wisdom, and crafts

■ She was the goddess of domestic crafts, and also the patron of tradesmen's guilds and male handicrafts

■ She was Jupiter's daughter and was born from his head

■ Minerva formed part of the Capitoline triad with her father Jupiter and Juno

■ She shared many attributes with her Greek equivalent, Athena

■ She sometimes appeared in the garments of a warrior, with a shield and breastplate

Figures and Stories Relevant to Minerva

Minerva

Born from her father Jupiter's head, Minerva was the virgin goddess of handicrafts, the arts, wisdom, medicine, commerce, and war. She shared similar attributes and functions with her Greek equivalent, Athena. However, Minerva owes her name and some attributes to the Etruscan goddess Menrva. Nerio, the native Roman goddess of war, can also be seen as a precursor of Minerva.

As the personified goddess of Roma was often represented as Minerva, it is not surprising that the worship of Minerva was found most prominently in the city of Rome, where she was honored within the Capitoline temple with Jupiter and Juno. Another important site was the Temple of Minerva Medica (**1**). It was said that an idol in her image was first brought by Aeneas from Troy, where she had reigned as the "fortune of the city." In Rome the idol was housed in the Temple of Vesta. According to this legend, so long as the idol was preserved, the descendants of Troy would prosper. The Quinquatria, which fell on the fifth day after the ides, was Minerva's greatest festival. Beginning on her birthday, March 19, the games lasted for five days, three of which included gladiator contests.

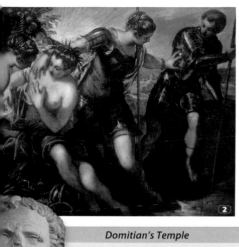

Anna Perenna Disguised as Minerva

When Mars, the god of war, fell in love with Minerva, a virgin goddess, she refused his advances (**2**). Sick with love, he enlisted the help of Anna Perenna ("occurring each year"), the Roman goddess of the new year and the mother of time. Instead, Anna Perenna dressed up as Minerva and came to Mars veiled. He was fooled into marrying the aged goddess. During Anna Perenna's annual festival held on the ides of March (March 15), young Roman girls used to sing racy songs in honor of this famous trick.

Domitian's Temple

Emperor Domitian (left), who ruled between A.D. 51–96, honored Minerva as his personal patron goddess. He built a great temple (right) to Minerva at the Nerva Forum in Rome. *It featured relief sculptures depicting her mythology and cult. In later years, the temple housed statues of the deified emperors, reinforcing the ideological connection between the imperial house and the Roman pantheon. The temple was destroyed by Pope Paul V in 1606.*

Goddess of Handcrafters and Artists

As the goddess of crafts, Minerva was the patron of tradesmen's guilds. In pre-Roman times, Minerva was probably a household goddess that watched over women as they did their spinning and weaving. Her Roman cult expanded from her domestic role to include traditionally male handcrafts, as well as the performing arts (**3**, Minerva with the Muses). She was the inventor of the *aulos*, a double-piped instrument, which she gave to the mortal Marsyas. Along with Liber Pater ("free one," known as Bacchus) and Apollo, she oversaw music, poetry, and theater.

Ovid's Metamorphoses

1 Ovid (**1**) was a poet of the early empire, famous for his racy love songs and the *Ars amatoria* ("Art of Love"), for which he was exiled by Emperor Augustus. His *Metamorphoses* are a humorous anthology of miracles from the time of creation onward, in which mortal and immortal figures of Greek mythology were transformed into, among others, animals, trees, and bodies of water. He mingles his stories (**4**, Icarus and Daedalus) with ironic and philosophical observations, including a paean to the deified Julius Caesar.

Pygmalion Once, a lonely sculptor, Pygmalion, carved an ivory statue of a beautiful woman, and fell in love with her (**2**). On the feast day of Aphrodite, he prayed to the goddess, asking for a wife as lovely as his statue. However, she understood what he actually wanted. Coming home, he touched and cuddled the statue, which began to move. The woman came to life, and the couple were married and had a daughter, Paphos.

Philemon and Baucis
Disguised as travelers, Jupiter and his son Mercury sought shelter. Only one kindly old couple, Philemon and Baucis, welcomed and fed them (**3**). The couple were rewarded by the gods, who turned their home into a temple. However, all the elderly couple wanted was to never be separated. So after their deaths they were transformed into two trees standing side by side, branching out into each other

4

Janus

Janus, the god of doorways (**1**, Arch of Janus), thresholds, fountains, and civil law, is one of the few genuinely Roman gods. His role in the Roman pantheon could be described as a mediator between the gods and humanity; the young and old; and the primitive and modern. Janus was also the founder of agriculture and the father of Rome's Tiber River.

Janus's two-headed appearance reflects his position as the gods' doorkeeper, but also his ability to look forward and backward in time. It was this power that made him the god of beginnings and endings. Janus was even said to have ruled Latium during the golden age of peace and harmony.

The worship of Janus existed throughout the Roman period. He received the first fruits of the harvest to ensure its success. The Roman New Year was heralded by gift-giving and prayers to Janus.

■ Janus was the god of gates, doorways, beginnings, and endings

■ He had two faces, both young and old; one looked to the future, and one to the past

■ The month of January was named after Janus

■ Occasionally, he was depicted with four faces

①

Gates of Janus

When Romulus's successor, Numa Pompilius, inherited the city of Rome, it was constantly at war. Numa Pompilius dedicated a temple to Janus Geminus ("twin") near the Roman Forum, which featured a bridge and bronze doors facing east and west, to be opened during times of war and closed at times of peace. Unfortunately, Rome's history was such that the doors were only closed once during the history of the republic. The next time they were shut, which was under the reign of Augustus (**3**, Augustus shutting the doors), heralded the beginning of the empire.

Janus and the Sabines When Titus Tatius, the king of the Sabines, went to war against Romulus over the abduction of his kingdom's women (**2**, rape of the Sabines), he led his army to try to take Rome by stealth. Tarpeia, the daughter of a Roman commander, was bribed and let Tatius's men enter. The goddess Juno also lent the Sabines a hand by prying the gates open so that the troops could enter the city. However, Janus aimed a geyser of hot, sulfurous water at the advancing troops and forced them back.

Figures and Stories Relevant to Janus

The Deified Emperors, Emperor Augustus, see pp. 220–221

Juno, Assists the Sabines, see pp. 208–209

Rape of the Sabines, see pp. 202–203

Romulus, see Romulus and Remus, pp. 200–201

Roman Gods and the Months

The ancient Roman year (right, calendar) had ten months, a number of which were named in honor of the gods. The first month Ianuarius (January) was named for Janus while Martius (March) and Venereus (April) were dedicated to Mars and Venus, the divine parents of Romulus and Aeneas. Februarius (February) was the month of Februa, a ritual purification. The Roman goddess of fertility, Maius, and Juno gave names to the months of May and June. At first, the remaining calendar months were simply numbered. With the deification of Julius Caesar and Augustus, their names were honored as the months of July and August.

▶▶ Ganesha, Indian God of Beginnings: p. 304

Ceres

The daughter of Saturn and the ancient Roman goddess Ops, Ceres was the Roman goddess of grain and agricultural fertility. Originally of Sicilian origin, she is often linked with the earth goddess Tellus. With Jupiter, she had a daughter named Proserpina, who was abducted by Pluto, god of the underworld. Ceres' temple on the Aventine Hill, modeled after Jupiter's Capitoline Temple, explicitly linked her with the gods of Greek origin. The temple was constructed in consultation with the Sibyl of Cumae and featured the triad of Ceres, Proserpina, and Pater Liber, which corresponds to the triad of Greek gods who presided over the Eleusinian mysteries, Demeter, Persephone, and Dionysus (sometimes Pluto).

Ceres was also associated with death, not only because her daughter reigned in the underworld as Pluto's queen, but also because the cycle of life and death in nature parallels that of human life. Rituals throughout the year attested to this role, such as paying tribute to Ceres to purify a household when a family member died.

■ Ceres was an ancient Italian goddess of grain and agriculture

■ She was associated with the Greek goddess of grain, Demeter

■ Her and Jupiter's daughter, Proserpina, was abducted by Pluto

■ Her temple on the Aventine Hill was a center for plebeian activities

■ She formed a trinity with Pater Liber and Proserpina

■ Initially worshiped alongside the earth goddess Tellus, her cult was later replaced by that of Demeter

■ She is depicted holding a torch and wearing a garland made from ears of corn; another symbol was a snake, representing her connection to earth

The Cerealia

The Cerealia, which began on April 12, was celebrated in honor of Ceres. At first, the festival was only held in times of drought. By the time of the early empire, the Cerealia was an annual event and had grown to eight days, during which women ran through the streets with torches, symbolizing Ceres' search for Proserpina in the underworld. On the fourth day of the festival, the Fordicidia ("cow-killing") celebrated Ceres in her aspect as the earth goddess Tellus. Pregnant cows were sacrificed and their unborn calves were burned, creating ash used to purify sheep herds. The last day of Cerealia featured chariot races at the Circus Maximus that began when foxes were let loose with torches tied to their tails, symbolizing the path of the sun.

The Sibylline Books Sibyls were state oracles who gave their advice in riddles. Once, an unnamed Sibyl (**1**) offered to sell nine books of her oracular prophesies to the Etruscan king Tarquinius Priscus. However, he refused her offer because he thought her price was too high. After she burned six of them, he relented and paid full price for the remaining three. These books were housed in the Capitoline Temple and consulted during wars or outbreaks of disease.

Her oracles led to the introduction of many Greek gods, such as Demeter, into the Roman pantheon.

> ### Figures and Stories Relevant to Ceres
>
> **Demeter**, Ceres' Greek Equivalent, see pp. 130–131
>
> **Hades and Persephone**, Greek Equivalent to Pluto and Proserpina, the Abduction of Ceres' Daughter, see pp. 154–155
>
> **Jupiter**, Had a Daughter With Ceres, see pp. 206–207

Goddess of Plebeians As the patron goddess of farmers and grain, Ceres (**3**) was strongly associated with the plebeian class (**2**, film scene), which grew and sold her crops. Her temple on the Aventine became a major political center as an archive for both senatorial and plebeian legislation. Plebeian aediles, officials responsible for the Cerealia and other festivals, had their headquarters there and supervised the temple's various functions. Among these functions was the distribution of free grain to the poor, which was regarded as a gift from the goddess herself.

» Divination and Prophecy: pp. 120, 134, 207, 447

Personified Virtues

The virtues were in fact abstract principles, which were personified by the Romans as gods to make them visible. Nearly all of them were political or civic virtues and were regarded as distinctively Roman. They were originally virtues of the republic, but were later also assumed by the emperors. They included Justitia ("justice") (**2**), Libertas ("freedom"), Salus ("public welfare"), Fides ("loyalty to the state"), and Victoria ("victory in war") (**4**, together with the emperor Trajan). The virtues, as well as the goddess Roma, the personified city of Rome (**1**), were depicted on coins of the republic along with the emperors. Temples with statues of the virtues were dedicated in honor of military victories. Early in the republic, a temple was dedicated to Concordia ("harmony") (**5**) to celebrate the political reconciliation of the nobility with the people. The temple became a meeting place for the Roman Senate.

Virtues in Christian Times

Christianity had its own virtues that were derived from the Bible, mainly the Sermon on the Mount and Paul's Epistle to the Corinthians. Here, Paul mentions faith, love, and hope as the main Christian virtues. Although the Christians rejected the pagan religion of the Romans, they adapted the personification of virtues as an artistic concept. Often in Christian art, particularly during the Italian Renaissance, the virtues appear as putti (**3**), naked figures of male babies, who are seen accompanying saints or figures of the Bible.

The Deified Emperors

■ Romulus was worshiped after his death as the god Quirinus

■ The concept of sacred kingship had Eastern origins

■ The deification of the Roman emperors was introduced to assure loyalty to the state

■ The deification of Roman emperors began with Caesar, called a living god, and Augustus, called god's son

■ As deified figures, sacrifice to the emperors was important

■ When Rome was Christianized, the ruling figures were regarded as the deputies of Christ on earth

Deification, or *apotheosis,* was a Roman tradition that began with Romulus, the city's first king. However, this practice was inherited from Eastern influenced Hellenism, using the archetype of Alexander the Great. Initially, emperors were deified only after their deaths. It was not until Caesar and Augustus that the imperial cult was established while the ruler was alive. However, deification referred less to the person than to the state order, which the emperor represented. Worship of the emperor as god was demanded as proof of one's allegiance to Rome.

With the conversion of the imperial house to Christianity under Constantine (r. A.D. 306–337), emperors abandoned all claims of divinity or godly descent. Instead, the emperor, as the vicar of Christ (*Vicarius Christi*), became engaged in the affairs and theological disputes of the new Church, convening and presiding over *ecumenical* ("world") councils as bishops. This was later expanded by Justinian (r. A.D. 527–565) with his idea of Caesaropapism, which made the emperor the highest authority on political, spiritual, and ecclesiastical questions.

Early Christians and the Imperial Cult

The imperial cult was firmly established by the reign of Augustus. However, early Christians, rejecting polytheism and idolatry, refused to participate in public sacrifices regardless of whether they were to a pagan deity or to a "divine" emperor. Failure to perform sacrifices to the emperor was regarded as treason, thus many Christians were persecuted as a result.

➤➤ **Divine Rulers:** pp. 48, 84, 201, 336, 368

Augustus Emperor Augustus (**1**, r. 43 B.C.–A.D. 14) was Julius Caesar's adopted son and designated successor. Because Caesar had already accepted honors as a living god before his assassination, Augustus was soon known as *divi filius* ("god's son") and *primus inter pares* ("the first among equals"). Upon Augustus's death, he was given the status of *divus* ("divine") by the Senate and worshiped as a god. He was seen as a messianic figure for his labors of restoring peace (*Pax Romana*), ending the civil wars, and expanding the empire's borders.

Titus Titus Flavius Vespasianus (r. A.D. 79–81) was famous for his effective rule. He believed that the role of the emperor was to benefit the lives of his subjects, thus he was known as Euergetes, or "bringer of benefits." Known today for the destruction of the Temple in Jerusalem, he also completed the Colosseum begun by his father Vespasian (**2**, Titus and Vespasian), and aided victims of the eruption of Mount Vesuvius in A.D. 79. After his death, he was deified by his followers.

Damnatio Memoriae In Roman law the crime of treason was punishable by Damnatio Memoriae, which involved the confiscation of property and wiping out of all traces of the person's existence: his or her name was etched out of public inscriptions, statues were disfigured, and coinage defaced. Patricians were especially vulnerable to this charge. After an emperor's death, the Senate would convene, deciding whether to deify or damn the emperor. For example, Nero (**3**, A.D. 54–68), rumored to be an arsonist, was declared the enemy of the Romans while he was still living, and was damned after his death. Caligula (r. A.D. 37–41), a frenzied tyrant, was assassinated (**4**) and also underwent damnation. The number of emperors who suffered damnation was high—as many as 30 —but they were often rehabilitated for political reasons. Damnation was, in a sense, also a precarious act. It was important that it lay on a person, not the station of emperor, which was holy.

Eastern Gods and Cults in Rome

During the era of the Roman Empire, some new cults spread in Rome, many of which derived from the East, such as the cult of the Egyptian goddess Isis, the Phrygian goddess Cybele (**3**), or the cult of the Persian god Mithras. Mainly during the late empire, there was a noticeable increasing influence of Eastern cultures in Rome. This development coincided with a rising need felt among the populace for personal religion and salvation. A common principle of the Eastern cults, which were often mystery cults, was the retracing of the death and awakening of the god. An influx of Eastern cults came to Rome during the Severus dynasty (A.D. 193–235), which began with the reign of Septimius Severus, born in Libya, who married the daughter of a Syrian sun priest.

Heliogabalus and Elah-Gabal
Heliogabalus (**1**) is the epithet for the flamboyant Roman emperor Marcus Aurelius Antoninus (r. A.D. 218–222), who was born and raised in the city of Emesa in Syria, a center for worship of the Syrian sun god Elah-Gabal. The emperor became a priest of his patron god's cult as a young man. Upon his coronation, he introduced the Elah-Gabal cult, which was connected with that of the Roman god Sol Invictus ("invincible sun"). But he was unsuccessful at creating a consistent state cult, as he claimed that Sol Invictus was synonymous with all high gods, including Jupiter.

» Mithra: p. 58

Mithras Between the first and fourth centuries A.D., the Persian cult of Mithras was adopted by Roman armies, who came into contact with it during military campaigns. A mystery religion (**2**, Saturn in the Mithras cult) with a strict hierarchy and rites of initiation, little is known of its mythology. The cult's central image was the Tauroctony ("bull-slaying"), depicting Mithras in Persian dress killing a bull thought to symbolize the spirit of spring. The temple, or Mithraeum, was a cave that served as an image of the universe, equipped with side-benches for communal meals.

Norse Mythology

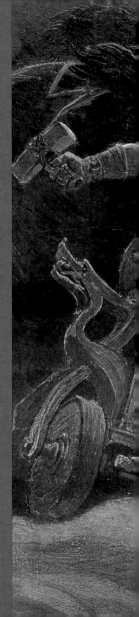

Thor is one of the most popular figures of Norse mythology

Norse Mythology

In ancient Northern Europe a complex set of beliefs flourished celebrating individual courage and victory on the battlefield. With its dramatic tales of heroism, in which the experiences of humans and gods were interlaced, Norse mythology has remained popular to this day. It became the inspiration for many great artists and thinkers, including the German Romantic composer Richard Wagner (**1**, Wotan in Richard Wagner's *Ring des Nibelungen*, 1910), who recognized a timeless quality in the characters portrayed in the myths.

Norse mythology refers to the myths of the Germanic tribes that settled in the area of modern Scandinavia and Central Europe. By A.D. 1000 its influence extended over parts of western Russia and across to Vinland on the eastern coast of North America. From 400 B.C. to the tenth century A.D., the Germanic tribes encompassed different civilizations like the Lombards in northern Italy and the Icelandic people. All these cultures were built with similar religious beliefs, mythology, and cosmology. The myths as well as the names of the gods differed very little between the tribes. For example, Odin, the main god of the Nordic pantheon, was known as Wotan amid the southern Germanic tribes.

As the myths were transmitted by oral tradition, there are few contemporary written sources about gods and beliefs. Many of those that remain are archaeological artifacts. Apart from some runic inscriptions, the main written sources available come from the Roman writer Tacitus, who described the customs and religion of the Germanic tribes around A.D. 100 by contrasting them with the opinions and beliefs of the Romans, and the

①

Eddas, writings from the 13th century A.D. in old Icelandic script. As the *Eddas* were written during the infusion of Christianity, their value as a reference for Norse mythology is disputed. Although their authenticity is contestable, they remain the most important sources on the gods and myths.

Living in the unstable and unsettling times of ancient and medieval Europe, when people were in competition for food and land, it is not surprising that themes of betrayal and disloyalty are found within Norse myths. Breaches of trust could lead to internecine fighting (**2**), which undermined and weakened the tribe—often to the benefit of a rival clan. At this time, Germanic society was based on loyalties to a common ancestor or leader and, as a result, many mythological tales are concerned with familial betrayal. The gods, too, were organized in much the same way as humans, in a civilization composed of husbands and wives, sons and daughters, and brothers and sisters. The potential problems that stemmed from these familial relationships, and the infighting that occurred between the gods, were obviously of intense interest.

The Norse gods were perceived to have both physical and human attributes. At times their representations can be unforgettably vivid, such as Odin with one eye and his hat pulled down over his face. The gods even behaved like humans, motivated by fundamentally human emotions such as anger, jealousy, love, and fear. Such human feelings were naturally accompanied by human failings. Odin, for example, also known as "the father of all," was god of language and poetry and he was known to exploit these skills for cunning and

deceitful ends, even breaking oaths.

Norse mythology tells of many violent encounters with their old adversaries, the giants. Yet the tales also describe the battles the gods fought among themselves. The gods were divided into two families—the Aesir and Vanir. The battle between the two clans was called the "first war of the world." Paradoxically, while the more peaceful Vanir were gaining the advantage in the war, the aggressive Aesir suffered one defeat after another. As a result of their increasingly weak position, the Aesir eventually agreed to end hostilities and to grant the Vanir equal status. Further developments ensured that the truce was unstable, and both sides remained in a perpetual state of unease. The notion of everlasting and unresolved battles, caused by such stalemates, saturates Norse mythology. They indicate a preoccupation with the duality of life on earth and of individual death with the possibility of resurrection. Most important, a new world cannot arise until the battle of Ragnarok—the end of the world—a concept that is uniquely Norse within European mythology.

Such glimpses into the thoughts and views of the Germanic people are of paramount importance when trying to gain an understanding about how the gods were worshiped. The myths themselves offer little insight, and certainly no liturgy or doctrine pertaining to them. Due to the peripatetic lifestyle of the Norse people—who lacked the cohesion of large settlements and any kind of centralized government—religion was fairly disorganized. Temples were rare, with most rituals and ceremonies being held outdoors in sacred locations.

The most common ritual performed in honor of the gods was known as the *blot*, during which animals, usually pigs or horses, were sacrificed (**3**). The blood—which was considered to have special powers—is believed to have been sprinkled over both the statues of the gods and the worshipers themselves. Blots were used to appeal to, and appease, the gods. For instance, Thor, the god of lightning and thunder, would have had immense significance for the seafaring (**4**) Nordic people, and it is likely a blot would have taken place for him before a sea journey.

From the myths, something is also learned about the worldview of the Germanic tribes. They believed the world began with chaos and a chasm between the elemental opposites of ice and fire. The first being, named Ymir, grew out of the collision of these two opposites. He was a primeval giant, who became the father of a race of frost giants. Out of these giants, the gods were born, including Odin. Ymir grew so large and so evil that Odin and his two brothers killed him. The blood that flowed from his body was of such magnitude that almost all the frost-giants drowned. Odin and his brothers used Ymir's dead body to create the universe, which consisted of nine worlds. From his eyebrows, the gods created a place for people to live, which was called Midgard. A great ash tree called Yggdrasil, the world tree, supported the universe with roots that connected the nine worlds together.

The richness and potency of the Norse myths no doubt resulted from the freedom of this great oral tradition. The tales remained fluid—growing and developing with the people who created them—and acted as a reflection of the fears and hopes of their times, offering a great wealth of insight into the human condition and into the minds of the Germanic people.

4

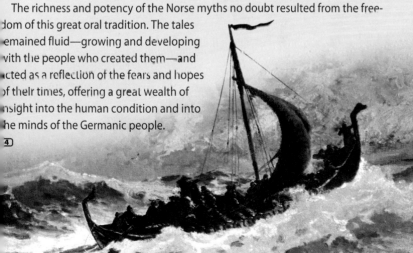

Odin

- Odin was the leader of the Norse gods and the creator of both the world and people

- He was also known to the Germanic tribes as Woden, from which the name for Wednesday originated

- Tacitus associated him with the Roman god Mercury

- He was a god of war and was often depicted with his spear, Gungnir, which never missed its target, and his ring, Draupnir

- He was also a god of wisdom, magic, poetry, prophecy, victory, hunting, and death

- Odin's symbol is the *valknut*, a knot of three triangles

- He had two ravens, Huginn and Muninn; two wolves, Freki and Feri; and an eight-legged horse named Sleipnir

Figures and Stories Relevant to Odin

One of Odin's ravens

As the chief god of the Aesir, one of two dynasties of Norse gods, Odin was the creator of the world and of the first man. Although a god of war, he was also known for his interest in magic, poetry, and the arts. Many of his tales reflect his ongoing search for knowledge and wisdom.

Odin's ravens Huginn and Muninn helped him by flying around the universe, gathering news. Also accompanying him was his mount Sleipnir (**1**), an eight-legged horse that could travel through the air. Odin had many children, including the gods Thor and Baldur, with several goddesses and giantesses. Odin's hall in Asgard was Valhalla, where all courageous warriors went after death. To the Norse, Odin was the personification of strength and power. Because of this, he was credited as having started numerous royal lineages.

①

》 Animals in Myth: pp. 104, 322, 424

Odin Learns to Read Runes By Hanging From Yggdrasil

Odin was always seeking more knowledge. In order to learn the divine secrets of the runes (**2**) he hung by his feet from the branches of the world tree Yggdrasil. If he succeeded in learning the language of the runes, he would then understand the workings of the universe. He remained hanging there for nine days and nights without food or water as his spear, Gungnir, continually pierced his side. To reward his suffering, the universe showed him the secrets of the runes, as well as nine magical songs, or spells. For this accomplishment, he was sometimes referred to by the Norse as Hangatyr, "god of the hanged." The knowledge of the runes was diffused to humanity

when the god Heimdall taught them to his mortal son, Jarl.

Runes

Runes are an alphabet, as well as a tool for divination. For divination, each letter is marked on a stone or chip of wood. They were drawn or spread to reveal the meaning behind each symbol. Though Norse mythology often refers to the secrets of the runes, there is no record detailing how they were actually used. There have been many stones uncovered with inscriptions written in runic, showing that the script was used in an everyday manner, as well as a mystical one.

Odin Sacrifices His Eye for Wisdom

Odin tried to find the "well of the highest wisdom," which sat under the roots of Yggdrasil. While drinking from the well would give one extraordinary insight, it was guarded by the fierce giant Mimir. Disguised as a traveler, Odin tried to access the well, but was stopped by Mimir. He told Odin that he would first have to make a sacrifice. Cutting out his eye (**3**), Odin was granted a single drink and saw the past, present, and future. His eye stayed at the bottom of the well as a reminder that great wisdom comes at a price.

Thoth—Invented Hieroglyphics: p. 99

■ Thor was the Norse god of thunder and lightning

■ Many called on Thor for protection; he was also associated with faithful marriages

■ He was often represented with his hammer, Mjolnir, riding through the clouds in a cart drawn by two goats

Thor's Hammer, Mjolnir Thor is seldom seen in myth without his mighty hammer, called Mjolnir (**1**). When thrown, Mjolnir would always strike its target and return back to the hand of Thor. Its name is often translated as "lightning," reflecting Thor's rule over stormy elements. The hammer was created by the dwarves of Nidavellir, as part of a bet from the trickster god Loki. Loki tried to interfere with the making of Mjolnir, by becoming a fly to bite one of the dwarves who was working the forge. This is why the hammer's handle was short and crooked.

Thor

Thor (**1**), the powerful god of thunder, is one of the best-known figures in all of Norse mythology. He was the son of Odin, and shared his volatile temper and love of battle. Married to the corn goddess Sif, Thor had two sons named Magni ("strength") and Modi ("courage"). When Thor rode in his bronze chariot, which was pulled by two goats, the noise of it created the roar of thunder.

Mjolnir was a symbol of defiance against the Christianization of Scandinavia from the eighth century

Like other Norse gods, Thor had his own hall in Asgard known as Bilskirnir. He played a pivotal role at Ragnarok, the mythical end of the world. Here, he again confronted the Midgard serpent and finally slew it. Yet, he ultimately lost his life in this battle.

Seen as a god who watched over the common man because he welcomed the souls of slaves into his hall after death, Thor was very popular. Thursday, named for Thor, was one of the holiest days of the week to the Norse.

Thor's Fight Against the Giants

One day Thrymr, the king of the giants, stole Thor's hammer Mjolnir. Thrymr would not return the hammer until the goddess Freya agreed to be his bride. When she refused, the gods decided to trick Thrymr. He was told that Freya had agreed, and the wedding was arranged. Dressed as a bride, Thor went in Freya's stead. Thrymr was suspicious, but brought Mjolnir out and gave it to "Freya." Thor threw away his disguise and leapt into battle, defeating the giants (**2**).

Thor and the Midgard Serpent

Disguised as a young man, Thor visited the giant Hymir. When Hymir decided to go fishing, Thor was permitted to join him, provided that Thor supply his own bait. With Thor's hook baited with an ox's head, they rowed out to sea. Thor rowed them farther out than Hymir liked, for fear of the Midgard serpent who lived under the sea. Indeed, the serpent took the bait and was hooked (**3**). Thor battled with the poison-spewing beast, pulling so hard on the line that his feet broke through the bottom of the boat and dug into the seafloor. Afraid, Hymir cut the line and freed the serpent. Thor was so angry that he knocked Hymir right out of the boat, before wading to shore himself.

3

Figures and Stories Relevant to Thor

Loki, Involved in the Creation of Thor's Hammer, see pp. 234–235

Odin, Thor's Father, see pp. 230–231

Ragnarok, see pp. 238–239

⏩ The Dagda—Celtic Thunder God: p. 258 | **Battles Against Serpents:** pp. 51, 291

Loki

■ Loki was both a giant and a god of the Aesir, which he joined by swearing a blood oath with Odin

■ He was a trickster god who used his ability to change shape to lie and steal from the other gods

■ Although Loki often deceived the gods, sometimes he used his villainous skills to help them

■ He was associated with fire and magic

Loki Gives Birth to Sleipnir One day a frost giant came to Asgard, the world of the gods, and offered to build the gods a wall in exchange for the sun, the moon, and the goddess Freya. When Loki agreed to the deal, the gods did not worry as they expected the giant to fail at this great task.

Loki was predominantly known as a sly trickster god, a deity who repeatedly caused problems with his deceptions. His talent for changing shape helped him fool both gods and humans on many occasions. Loki crossed paths with many powerful gods, such as his blood brother Odin and Thor. Loki's actions were the root of many conflicts; however, when threatened, he helped the gods on more than one occasion.

Although considered one of the Aesir, Loki was actually a giant. He swore a blood oath with Odin, which bound them together as blood brothers. Though married to the goddess Sigyn, Loki had his most famous children with the giantess Angrboda: the Midgard serpent, the Fenrir wolf, and the goddess of the underworld Hel. During one of his ruses, he took the form of a mare, and then gave birth to Odin's eight-legged horse. The gods continued to tolerate his deceptive ways until he crossed the line and had Baldur killed. Ultimately, Loki fought against the gods at the battle of Ragnarok.

However, they soon saw that he had a magic stallion to help him keep his end of the deal. To sabotage the giant, Loki transformed himself into a white mare and distracted the stallion so that the wall could not be completed. Thus, the giant could not fulfill his side of the agreement. Soon after, Loki gave birth to Sleipnir, an eight-legged horse that later became Odin's steed (**2**, top).

» **Tricksters:** pp. 146, 148, 166, 170, 360, 440

The Killing of Baldur and the Punishment of Loki

After Frigg had a dream foretelling the death of her son Baldur, she made everything on earth swear not to harm him. However, she forgot to ask the mistletoe, making it his one weakness. When Loki learned this, he tricked the blind god Hodr into killing Baldur with an arrow made from mistletoe. Because Baldur was the favorite son of Odin, Loki was severely punished. He was chained underneath the world tree to three rock slabs, where snake's venom continually dripped on his face. Sigyn, his wife, held a wooden bowl over his face to collect the venom (**2**). However, whenever she left to empty it, the venom dripped on his face and he thrashed violently in pain, which for the Norse was the cause of earthquakes.

②

The Fenrir Wolf

Fenrir was one of three children that Loki had with Angrboda, the giantess. A terrible wolf, Fenrir was kept chained up by the gods because of a prophecy that he and Loki's two other children—the Midgard serpent and the goddess Hel—would one day destroy the gods. Only the god Tyr was brave enough to feed Fenrir when he was a pup. The one thing stopping the powerful Fenrir was a magic thread called Gleipnir that the dwarves made specifically for this purpose. With it he was bound to a rock a mile under the earth. His two sons, Hati and Skoll, were said to chase the horses that pulled the sun and moon across the sky each day. Fenrir later broke free and ate Odin during the battle of Ragnarok (right). Odin was avenged by his son, Vidar, who finally killed the wolf.

- Freya was the goddess of battle, war, love, fertility, and magic
- She was the patron of crops and the spring
- She rode in a chariot that was pulled by two cats
- Hel ruled the underworld and she had power over the souls of those who did not die in glory
- Her dog, Garmr, guarded the underworld
- Her body was half living flesh, while the other half was dead and festering

Goddesses—Freya and Hel

Goddesses of death and love respectively, Hel and Freya both had the responsibility of receiving the souls of the dead.

Freya and her twin brother Freyr were from the older Vanir dynasty, the group of Norse gods who preceded the Aesir. Dually associated with war and love, Freya shared half of all slain warriors' souls with Odin. They went to her hall in Asgard, called Sessrumnir. The goddess of love was irresistible to men and gods alike, and her worship was quite widespread among the Norse.

As one of Loki's three children, Hel was cast out of Asgard out of fear they her and her siblings would eventually overtake the gods. She ruled the dark underworld, which was home to the souls of those not killed in battle. Her hall there was called Niflheim. Like the rest of Loki's offspring (the Midgard serpent and the Fenrir wolf), she was considered somewhat monstrous herself. Hel is described in Norse mythology as being alive on one side of her body, but dead on the other. It was said that when the Danish king Dyggvi died of natural causes, Hel took his soul for her own royal husband.

The Valkyries

The Valkyries were warrior maidens who would go to battlefields and pick through the bodies of those who had fallen. After finding the most worthy of the dead, they took the warriors' souls to Asgard, where half would go to Valhalla and half to Freya's hall, Sessrumnir. Between battles, the Valkyries served Odin in his hall, serving food and drinks. They are often portrayed in art as riding on winged or flying horses, but that is due to a mistranslation of "Valkyrie horse," which was actually a metaphor for a wolf. Some of the Valkyries are given names in Norse mythology, although they seldom play individual roles.

>> The Morrigan—Picking Through the Dead: p. 265

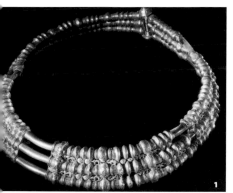

Freya's Necklace Freya wore a magic necklace (**1**) that made her irresistible to any male who saw her. The necklace—called Brisingamen—was made by four dwarves, who each represented one of the four elements. When Freya tried to pay them for forging the necklace, they rejected her gold, wanting only a night with her. Because she loved the necklace and would have done anything to have it, she slept with each dwarf. In one myth, Loki tried to steal the Brisingamen, but the giant Heimdall spotted him as he was escaping from Freya's hall. Loki was stopped and Freya regained her necklace.

Hel's Bargain Over Baldur's Soul After the death of Baldur (**2**) from a sprig of mistletoe, his soul was taken to the underworld of Hel. Given his favored status as the son of Frigg and Odin, the gods persuaded Hel to let Baldur come back to Asgard. She agreed to this on one condition: that everything on earth—living or dead—cried for his soul. Because Baldur was so loved, all things wept when told about his untimely death; all things except a giantess named Thokk. Thokk—who was actually Loki in disguise—refused to mourn him. Because of this, Baldur remained with Hel until Ragnarok. When the gods discovered Loki's trick to keep Baldur in the underworld, they chained him beneath the earth as punishment.

Hel in the Underworld The realm of the Norse underworld was named after the goddess who ruled there, Hel (**3**). It was also referred to as Helheim. Very different from the Christian version of Hell, there were no flames or torment. Hel was a cold world of shadow, where the souls of the sick and the elderly went after death. Only those who died in battle were given access to Asgard, so the rest came to Hel. This world was the very lowest, located far beneath the roots of the world tree Yggdrasil.

Hades: p. 154

Ragnarok—The Final Battle

As a three-year-long winter raged, the earth was plunged into darkness. Humanity was overrun by war. The earth began to shake, ripping up the trees and crumbling the mountains. The Midgard serpent came ashore, bringing tidal waves with him. Breaking their chains, Loki and Fenrir joined the giants in an assault on Asgard. The gods prepared themselves for battle, as the call of war was spread throughout the nine worlds. Even the warriors' souls in Valhalla fought for the Aesir. Ultimately, the battle between the gods and giants left many dead and the world destroyed. A new earth rose out of the flames. Two survivors, Lif and Lifthrasir, who had hid in Yggdrasil's branches, continued the human race.

Odin (above, the Andreas Stone) fought valiantly against the ferocious Fenrir wolf, but was finally devoured by him; after Odin's death, Baldur replaced him as the head of the new Norse pantheon
At the end of Richard Wagner's opera Götterdämmerung ("twilight of the gods"), the old world and the gods perish, clearing the way for a better world (right, scene)

» **Fighting Between the Gods:** pp. 26, 117, 118, 245, 458
End of the World: p. 313

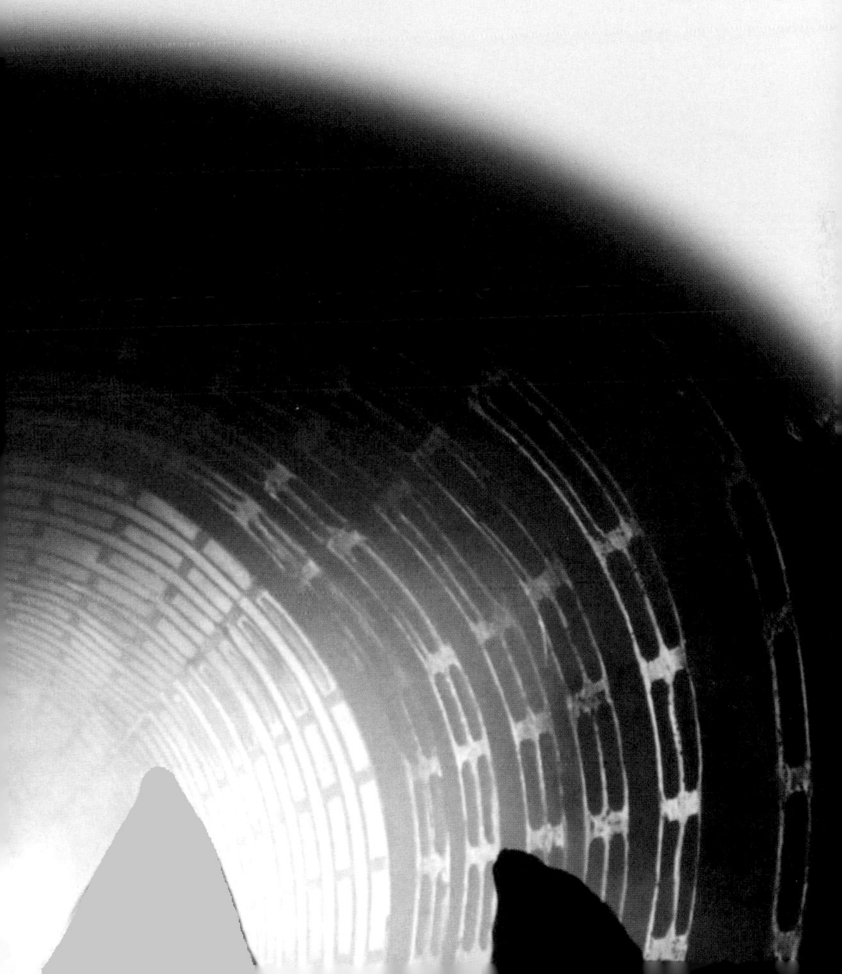

The World Tree Yggdrasil

The Norse universe contained nine worlds, all connected by the world tree, called Yggdrasil (**3**), which grew up through them all. Described as an ash tree, its name often translates as "terrible steed," in reference to Odin.

While some interpretations put all the worlds beneath the roots of the great tree, it is commonly accepted that the gods lived in Asgard, located in the upper branches. Beneath Yggdrasil's roots lay the underworld of Hel. In between were the world of the Vanir, Vanaheimr; the world of frost giants, Jotunheim; the world of fire giants, Muspelheim; the world of dark elves, Svartalfheim; the world of elves, Alfheim; the world of dwarfs, Nidavellir; and the world of humanity, Midgard. Midgard was surrounded by an ocean and a protective wall made by the gods to keep humanity safe from the giants.

At each of Yggdrasil's roots were three sacred wells—one of fate, one of wisdom, and one that sourced the rivers. The well of fate was the home of the Norns (**2**), who tended the roots. With the end of the world, only two people survived, Lif and Lifthrasir, who hid in Yggdrasil's branches.

Beings in Yggdrasil Aside from the nine worlds, a population of creatures lived in Yggdrasil (**1**). At the base of the tree, a serpent or dragon named Nidhogg lived there, gnawing on the roots. At the very top of the tree, there was an unnamed eagle who had great wisdom. On his head sat the hawk Vedrfolnir. A red squirrel named Ratatosk ran between Nidhogg and the eagle, bringing gossip and insults as he traveled along the trunk of Yggdrasil. There were also four deer that ran across the tree's branches. They possibly represent the four elements, the compass directions, or the seasons.

World Tree of the Maya: p. 395

Frigg

Frigg was the goddess of marriage, love, fertility, and the household. Her many similarities to the goddess Freya suggest that they might have been different forms of the same deity.

As the wife of Odin, Frigg was the queen of the Aesir. Aside from Odin, only she was allowed to sit on the great throne, Hlidskjalf, where she counseled her husband on important matters. Her primary roles were as Odin's wife and the mother of Baldur and Hodr. She had the power of prophecy and could see into the future. Although she had this great ability to read other people's fates, she never shared what she knew.

Unlike many other Norse gods and goddesses who had animal companions, Frigg was typically accompanied by her dozen handmaids. Together in her hall of Fensalir, they spun the clouds and the golden threads of fate. Each of them had specific roles to play, such as Gna, who took Frigg's orders to all parts of the nine worlds. Fulla, Frigg's favorite handmaid, carried her lady's jewel box full of magical tools used for special ceremonies.

- Frigg was the wife of Odin, the leader of the gods
- Her name translates as "beloved one"
- She was the goddess of love, marriage, and motherhood, and had the gift of prophecy
- She was also the goddess of the sky and is often portrayed with a spinning wheel because she spun the clouds

Frigg's Envy While Frigg (1) was the patron goddess of marriage, some myths detail her questionable morality. In one tale she became envious of a gold statue fashioned by Odin's devotees. She slept with a servant to persuade him to completely destroy the statue bearing her husband's likeness.

(1)

>> Queens of the Gods: pp. 126, 208

Frigg Tricks Odin One day Frigg and Odin started arguing over the fate of two warring tribes: the Winnilers and the Vandals (**2**, helmet). Odin preferred the Vandals, but Frigg wanted the Winnilers to be victorious. The fight continued until Odin said that whichever tribe he saw first in the morning would win the war. Since his bed faced the Vandals, he knew that his tribe would win.

However, Frigg cleverly turned his bed around to face the other way, and made the Winniler women comb their long hair down over their faces. When Odin woke up the next morning, he did not know who these long-bearded men were. He realized that he had been tricked by Frigg, but kept his word. The Winnilers won the war, and from then on were known as the Longbeards.

②

Figures and Stories Relevant to Frigg

The Aesir, see p. 245

Hel's Bargain Over Baldur's Soul, see Freya and Hel, p. 237

Odin, Frigg's Husband, see pp. 230–231

Frigg's Attempt to Save Baldur Seeing her son Baldur's death in a dream, Frigg tried to prevent it from happening. She asked everything on earth, living and dead, to swear an oath not to harm him (**3**, with animals). Unfortunately, Frigg forgot to ask the mistletoe (**4**), which ultimately led to Baldur's doom. This single weakness left Baldur having to suffer in the underworld of Hel until after the final battle of Ragnarok.

④

3

Asgard

Of the nine worlds in Norse mythology, Asgard (**1**) was home to the gods. It is described in great detail within Norse textual sources, with the gods each having their own regions, fields, and great halls. The deities convened to discuss important matters in the field of Idavoll, at the center of Asgard.

Asgard was located on the great ash tree, Ygg-drasil. Descriptions usually place it in the high branches, but some tales say that Asgard lay beneath Yggdrasil's roots. The realm of Asgard was connected to the world of men by the Bifrost Bridge.

Asgard also housed the honored dead, namely those who died in battle. The most glorious hall in Asgard, called Valhalla, belonged to Odin. All Norse warriors hoped to go there after death so as to take part in the continuous feasting and drinking. Later, Asgard was invaded by the giants during the apocalyptic battle of Ragnarok.

■ Asgard was the world of the Norse gods and lay in the world tree, Yggdrasil

■ Each of the gods had their own hall in Asgard

■ The greatest hall was Odin's hall, Valhalla, the home of those who died in glory

■ Asgard is the Norse version of heaven and exists in contrast to the underworld, Hel

■ Both the Aesir and Vanir lived in Asgard

■ The bridge to Asgard was a rainbow, which was watched over by Heimdall, the guardian of the gods

Figures and Stories Relevant to Asgard

Hel's Underworld, see Hel and Freya, p. 237

Odin, Ruler of the Gods in Asgard, see pp. 230–231

Ragnarok, Battle of the Gods and Giants in Asgard, see pp. 238–239

Valhalla, Greatest Hall in Asgard, see pp. 246–247

Bifrost Bridge A bridge made of a rainbow (**2**) spanned between the world of humanity and Asgard. Known as the Bifrost Bridge, it was guarded by a god named Heimdall, who had his own hall just over the bridge, called Himinbjorg. Aided by his acute hearing—which was said to be able to hear the wool growing on sheep—and no need to sleep, Heimdall protected Asgard. He was the first to spot the legions of giants going over the Bifrost Bridge at Ragnarok. He blew the great Gjallarhorn to alert the Aesir of the upcoming attack.

2

The Aesir and the Vanir

The Norse pantheon originally consisted of two separate families: the Aesir and the Vanir. Once at war, they were finally able to find peace after both sides exchanged hostages. The only remaining Vanir deities to live in Asgard were Freya (left) and her brother Freyr. Their father Njord was also a Vanir, but did not play much of a role in any Norse myths. It is likely that the Vanir were an older and simpler fertility pantheon that was overtaken as Norse society changed and became more civilized. The Aesir headed by Odin (right) came to dominate mythology. The battle between the dynasties symbolizes the change of humankind's outlook and shift in beliefs.

⏵ **Fighting Between the Gods:** pp. 26, 117, 118, 238, 458

Valhalla—Warrior Paradise

The greatest hall in Asgard, the uppermost world in Norse mythology, was Valhalla, the hall of the god Odin. There were 540 doors to the hall, each large enough so that 800 warriors could pass through at once. Only the warriors who showed great courage and skill in battle were chosen to enter Valhalla. The souls of these fallen warriors, known as the Einherjar, were taken to the hall by the Valkyries. Once in Valhalla, the warriors spent their time feasting on wild boar, drinking mead, and readying themselves for the great battle of Ragnarok. At the end of the world, these souls in Valhalla joined the gods to fight against the giants. The rooster Gullinkambi lived here, crowing to wake the warriors each morning. He also crowed to alert the warriors at the beginning of Ragnarok.

The Eddas

The term *Eddas* refers to two books, both written independently of each other. They are the main sources for Norse and Germanic mythology. However, both are much younger than the myths and tales they describe. Because the *Eddas* were written during medieval times, they are influenced by Christian ideas.

The *Prose Edda*, written by Snorri Sturluson in the 13th century, contains three books: the *Gylfaginning*, the *Skaldskaparmal*, and the *Hattatal*. Norse myths are found in each section, although the Gylfaginning has the most mythological material. The *Skaldskaparmal* is written as a conversation between the gods Aegir and Bragi, who discuss both mythology and poetic styles. The final section of the *Prose Edda*, the *Hattatal*, focuses primarily on Norse poetic verse structure.

The *Poetic Edda* (**3**) is a collection of 34 heroic and mythological poems, which were orally transmitted and then compiled together.

Interpreting the *Eddas*
Today, there are many different translations (**1**) and interpretations of both *Eddas*. The *Prose Edda*, for example, was written by Sturluson, a converted Christian. He often changed the gods' roles to make them mortal rather than divine. It is believed that this was his editing.

Sigurd the Dragon Slayer A (**2**) hero of the *Poetic Edda*, Sigurd was born after the death of his father. Sigurd's mother gave him the broken shards of his father's sword, which later was remelded to help Sigurd kill the dragon Fafnir. The sword was so strong that it cut through the anvil used to make it. Odin told Sigurd to dig trenches to hide in as he stabbed at Fafnir. Odin also told him to bathe in the dragon's blood. Following Odin's advice, Sigurd killed the dragon (**2**) and bathed in his blood, which touched all his body except for his shoulder where a leaf had stuck. Next, he drank the blood and could speak to birds. Roasting the heart and eating it, he gained the gift of prophecy.

≫ Odin: p. 230

Beowulf

■ Beowulf was a hero of the North Germanic tribe, the Geats

■ He defended the Danish court from monsters and was later made king

■ In his youth, Beowulf symbolized heroic virtue and honor, and as king, the ideal wise ruler

■ He was aided by his magic sword Hrunting

As a heroic warrior-king of Geats, Beowulf is the main character of an epic poem of the same name. Scholars have often debated about the origin of Beowulf, some saying that he originated from a Germanic god named Beowa. Although *Beowulf* is written in the Anglo-Saxon language, the story takes place in medieval Scandinavia.

Beowulf was the son of the Swedish warrior Ecgtheow. While in service of the Geatish king Hredel, Ecgtheow married Hredel's daughter and together they had Beowulf. The first part of the epic tells the story of young Beowulf's battle against the monster Grendel, who attacked the Danish court. In the second part, Beowulf becomes the king of Geatland. After ruling for 50 years in peace, a fire-breathing dragon attacked his land. Although aged, Beowulf readied himself for battle. He eventually overwhelmed the dragon, but was fatally injured during the fight.

Beowulf was given the sword Naegling for defeating Grendel and his mother

Beowulf, the Manuscript

Only a single handwritten manuscript of Beowulf *survived to the modern era. For many centuries it was forgotten and it was nearly destroyed by a fire. The epic is found within the Nowell Codex, which dates from around A.D. 1000. This makes* Beowulf, *and the rest of the Nowell Codex, among the oldest works of*

English literature. It is believed that this surviving manuscript is not an original, and that Beowulf *was likely composed hundreds of years earlier. The oral tale, however, could be even older. Scholars have long debated over the presence of biblical symbolism in* Beowulf, *which was transcribed during the Christianization of Britain.*

➤➤ **Heroes Fighting Against Monsters:** pp. 27, 165, 181, 315, 361

Fight Against Grendel Heorot, the hall of the Danish king Hrothgar, was once plagued by a beast called Grendel (**1**). Each night he snuck into the hall and killed the warriors while they slept. The men could not defend themselves and were forced to abandon the great hall. Hearing about the situation, Beowulf traveled to Geatland to defeat the monster. King Hrothgar welcomed the confident hero, leaving him in charge. As night fell, Beowulf pretended to be asleep and waited for Grendel to attack Heorot again. When the beast tore through the doors, Beowulf jumped up to fight. However, his men could not help because their weapons were enchanted. Beowulf managed to fatally wound Grendel by tearing off his arm. Grendel retreated to the swamps to die and the hall celebrated.

Battle With Grendel's Mother Although Grendel was dead, the troubles at Heorot were not over. Grendel's mother (**2**, *Beowulf* film scene) attacked the hall in revenge for her son's death. Beowulf and his men followed her back to her home in the lake. Using his magical sword, Hrunting, he dove into the water after Grendel's mother. Attacking him, she dragged him to the bottom of the lake. Hrunting was useless against her so Beowulf threw it away, grabbed one of her own swords, and sliced her head off. Then Beowulf found the corpse of Grendel in her lair, so he chopped off Grendel's head as well. When he returned to Heorot, King Hrothgar gave him another sword, called Naegling.

Celtic Mythology

The Gundestrup cauldron, a silver ritual vessel depicting multiple Celtic gods, dates from around the first century B.C.

Celtic Mythology

The Celtic people are a group of related Indo-Germanic tribes who colonized France (Gaul), Spain, southern Germany, Hungary, and northern Italy from the sixth century B.C. to approximately 50 B.C. From 400 B.C. until the Roman period of Julius Caesar, many mainland Celts also moved into Britannia (Great Britain). Mainland Celts shaped the Hallstatt culture in Central Europe during the early Iron Age. A cultural peak began during the La Tène period of the

fifth century B.C., which was characterized by Mediterranean influence, and ended with Caesar's conquest of the region around 50 B.C. In contrast, "island Celts," who shared the Irish-Gaelic and British-Welsh cultural sphere, were able to carry their cultural life on into the Middle Ages by harmonizing their culture with the early Christian culture.

Myths of the island Celts of Great Britain and Ireland were introduced into medieval culture and thus survived to the present day, although in a Christianized form. Parts of myths reappear in several major legendary cycles, including the Ulster Cycle about the achievements of the Irish hero Cúchulainn. The Mythological Cycle tells the stories of several prehistoric migrations to Ireland. Another important source is *The Mabinogion*, a collection of Welsh prose. Traces of Celtic mythology can be found in all these stories in which ancient gods are now represented as various heroes. Animals play an important role in these myths and are a reminder of the special status of honor they were accorded in Celtic culture. The Celtic mythological romances about King Arthur (**1**) of Britain were probably the most influential in literature. Legends about this ideal ruler, who became a role model of medieval chivalry, were also influenced by mythological elements. These elements were not only the fairies and dragons that populated his world, but also motifs such as the Christian

element of a Holy Grail. King Arthur's temporary stays on the mysterious island Avalon indicate Celtic ideas of an afterworld.

Certain elements of Celtic mythology from the islands have survived to the present, for example, Halloween celebrations, and some elements are currently being revived. It is curious that neo-pagans or neo-druids have chosen Stonehenge (**3**), a circle of megaliths, as their center and that this

site is frequently associated with the Celts, even though it is older by about 500 years. Today, many people know Celtic mythology from video games, the *Asterix* comics, or Tolkien's *Lord of the Rings* (**2**, movie scene).

Although relatively recent sources are available about the Celtic people of the islands, the mythology and religion of the mainland Celts are only known from accounts by Roman authors and from archaeological finds.

The names of several hundred names Celtic gods are known from inscriptions. It is thought that most of them were local or regional names and probably not known across the entire Celtic culture. A likely reason is that there was never a unified Celtic kingdom. Furthermore, Roman authors often compared them to Roman gods in order to illustrate their function and attributes. Very often they were associated with features of the landscape, such as rivers and mountains. Notably, animals also had a special status as companions or manifestations of the gods. It is most likely that animal, river, spring (**4**), mountain, and tree cults preceded the worship of gods. Mother goddesses and matrons also played an important part in the pantheon. The same role was later

frequently taken over by Christian saints. Originally, they were associated with fertility cults.

Teutates, the god of war, Taranis, the god of the sky and thunder (similar to the Roman god Jupiter), and Belenus, the god of fire (compared to the Greek-Roman god Apollo), were some of the more popular Gallic gods. The goddess Belisama reminded the Roman authors of Minerva. Epona, the goddess of the horses, later came to be worshiped in Rome. Both cultures were mixed to some extent during the Roman occupation of Gaul, which explains how the names and functions of Celtic and Roman gods came to be frequently combined.

Offerings and funeral rites played a major role in Celtic religious culture. As with many other nature-oriented religions, offerings were given to appease the gods whose territory the humans were intruding upon. Animals were commonly sacrificed or weapons offered before battles and wars. There were also various forms of human sacrifices. People believed that this would maintain the cycle of life. New life would come from death. Valuable burial objects (**5**) were found which indicates that the Celts believed in an afterlife. Caesar also claimed in his *De bello gallico* that Celtic people believed in the transmigration of the soul.

Both Celtic groups, the island and mainland Celts, had the *Druids* ("knowing the oak tree") as their spiritual leaders. The main source for the knowledge of the Druids comes from Julius Caesar. The noble priests were highly respected. Not only were they responsible for carrying out sacrifices, they were also skilled fortune-tellers, judges, dream interpreters, and so on. They only passed on their knowledge orally. After A.D. 14, the Druids were suppressed by the Roman emperor Tiberius. Since the 18th and 19th centuries, which saw a revived interest in the Druids, they have been glorified in popular culture in mystic-romantic ways.

The Dagda

As the son of the mother goddess Danu, the Dagda was the leader of the Celtic gods and king of the mythical Tuatha Dé Danann ("people of the goddess Danu"). He led them to victory over the Fomorians, who were living in Ireland when the Tuatha Dé Danann arrived. Aside from his status as king of the gods, the Dagda was the patron of warfare, wisdom, and magic. Because he was able to summon the seasons, he was worshiped in connection with crops. His sexual appetite is the theme of many myths, which reflect his connection to fertility rites. The Dagda and his consort the Morrigan (he is also linked with the goddess Breg) represent the duality of masculine and feminine aspects. He was also father to numerous gods, including Brigid.

The Dagda was described as a huge man who carried a club that was capable of both killing as many as nine men with one swing, as well as bringing them back to life. He also possessed a cauldron that was never empty and a harp named Uaithne, which played magical music that changed the seasons. He was often unflatteringly depicted in a short tunic that usually left his backside exposed.

■ The Dagda ("the good god") was the chief of the Celtic gods and the Tuatha Dé Danann

■ He was the god of life and death, the earth, and treaties

■ He had a cauldron that fed all people, an allusion to his role as a vegetation god

■ Each year, he slept with the Morrigan, the goddess of war

■ He brought on the seasons with his magic harp

■ He carried a staff, one end of which could kill nine men at a time, the other could bring them back to life

■ He had superhuman strength and a strong sexual appetite

Figures and Stories Relevant to the Dagda

Brigid, the Dagda's Daughter, see pp. 262–263

Elves and the Otherworld, the Tuatha Dé Danann Were Said to Have Moved to the Otherworld, see pp. 266–267

The Morrigan, the Dagda's Consort, see Celtic Goddesses, pp. 264–265

Samhain, pp. 272–273

Uaithne Harp and the Fomorians The powers of the Dagda's magical harp (**1**) were associated with the music it played. It played three songs, each named after one of the harp's children: Goltraiges ("sorrow"), Gentraiges ("joy"), and Suantraiges ("sleep"). During a war between the Tuatha Dé Danann and the Fomorians, the Fomorians stole the harp. Going to the Fomorians' hall to retrieve it, the Dagda had the harp play its three tunes. After the three songs had been played, the Fomorians were fast alseep and the Dagda brought back the harp.

①

Taranis and the Dagda

Taranis (**2**, Gundestrup cauldron with broken spoke wheel, his symbol) was the god of thunder in the continental Celtic pantheon, but is often thought to be related to the Dagda. It is likely that the Romans associated the Dagda with the role of thunder god because he was the leader of the Celtic gods and the leader of their Roman pantheon, Jupiter, ruled over thunder. The only specfic reference to Taranis is in the Roman epic *Pharsalia* written by Lucan in the first century A.D.

Sleeping With the Morrigan

Each year on the festival of Samhain, the Dagda was said to sleep with the Morrigan (**3**, as a raven) on the banks of the Unius River. This ritual affair was believed to ensure fertility and success for the Celtic people for the coming year. The site by the river is still called "the bed of the couple" today. Some variations to the myth refer to them sleeping together only once. In one tale, the Dagda sought advice from the Morrigan before battling the Fomorians. But then to coerce her into giving him the details needed to win the war, he copulated with her as she stood with one foot on either bank, washing the blood from the warriors' clothes who would die in the battle to come.

Birth of Aengus When the Dagda had an affair with Boann, goddess of the Boyne River (**4**), she became pregnant. Afraid that she would be found out by her husband, Nechtan, owner of the well of knowledge, the Dagda held the sun in place for nine months while Boann was pregnant. When their son, Aengus, was born, only one day had passed. For all the effort made to hide his parentage, many myths name the Dagda and Aengus as father and son. Due to the circumstances of his birth, Aengus was said to have power over time. He is sometimes seen as a Celtic Cupid, the Roman god of love.

▶▶ **Thor—Norse Thunder God:** p. 232

Belenus and Belisama

Belenus was one of the most ancient and wide-spread Celtic deities. He was not only worshiped in Celtic Britain, but also in Gaul, Austria, Italy, and Spain. Belenus ("bright one") likely gave his name to the fire festival of Beltane, which was originally linked with his cult. Although the Celts also associated him with pastoralism, healing, and fountains, the Romans connected Belenus as the god of light with their light god Apollo.

His consort or wife was Belisama ("summer bright"), the goddess of fire, bodies of water (**1**), and metalworking. She shared common traits with the goddess Brigid, as well as the Roman goddess Minerva. Many inscriptions bearing the name "Belisama Minerva" reflect the blending of deities and traditions that often occurred in Roman-occupied lands.

No myths of Belenus or Belisama have survived to modern times. Their names have been found only in classical texts and stone inscriptions, suggesting the presence of sanctuaries. The names of geographic features also hint at the existence of their cults.

- Belenus ("bright one") was the god of light and was associated with pastoralism
- His consort was Belisama
- His worship spread from northern Italy to southern Gaul and Celtic Britain
- Belisama ("summer bright") was the goddess of fire, light, water, and metallurgy
- Worshiped in Britain and Gaul, she was associated with the Roman goddess Minerva and the Celtic Brigid

River of Belisama Many Celtic goddesses were linked to various bodies of water, usually rivers or wells. The Greek scholar Ptolemy described a "Belisama Aest" in his mapping of northern Britain, leading some to think he was talking about the Mersey River (**2**). However, since his map was not completely accurate, some scholars hold the view that the Ribble River in Lancashire, England, was being referred to.

2

Belenus and Bile Belenus (**3**) is often mistakenly associated with Bile, an archaic Irish master god of life and death, due to the similarity of their names. However, as Belenus was a bright god of light and Bile was a dark god associated with death and the underworld, it is highly unlikely that these two deities were ever one and the same. The Welsh god Beli Mawr may have actually been a later version of Belenus. However, Beli Mawr may have also been a historical person, specifically, one of the kings of early Britain. Several lines of Welsh ancestry lead back to Beli Mawr. **3**

Figures and Stories Relevant to Belenus and Belisama

Brigid, Associated With Belisama, see pp. 262–263

Celtic Goddesses, Belisama Was a Celtic Goddess, see pp. 264–265

The Beltane Festival in Ireland

The festival of Beltane, held on May 1 in Ireland and Scotland, marked the start of summer and open pasturing. Cattle were led between two bonfires to purify and protect them before they were led into summer pastures. Households would put out their hearth fires and relight them from the Beltane fires. The holiday is still celebrated today by neo-Pagans (left).

Minerva: p. 210

Brigid

Daughter of the Dagda, Brigid is one of the best known and most loved goddesses of the Celtic pantheon. Her popularity likely comes from her down-to-earth and helpful demeanor. As a tripartite goddess, she was represented by three sisters, each of which had a specific function. Altogether she was the patron of poetry, metallurgy, fire, fertility, and divination. She married the Formorian king Bres in an attempt to reconcile the conflict between his people and her own, the Tuatha Dé Danann. Their son, who was named Ruadan, was later killed in battle. Brigid's cries at his death began the Irish tradition of keening while mourning.

■ Brigid ("exalted one") was the Dagda's daughter

■ She was a tripartite goddess: the patroness of smithcraft, poetry, prophecy, and fertility

■ She was a very popular figure, and when Christianity came to Ireland, she was adopted into the Catholic Church as St. Brigid

■ She owned the king of boars, the king of sheep, and two oxen

With the infusion of Christianity, Brigid was one of many Celtic deities incorporated into the Christian tradition. The goddess was merged with the fifth-century Catholic saint Brigid of Kildare, who was said to have founded the first female Christian church community in Ireland. Another story says that she was Mary's midwife during the birth of Christ. With the transportation of Irish slaves to the Caribbean by the English, a Voodoo goddess named Maman Brigitte may also have derived from Brigid.

Festival of Imbolc

The Celtic festival of Imbolc, also called Oimelc ("ewe's milk"), took place on the first of February to celebrate the first signs of spring and the newly milking ewes. Special foods, lighting of candles (right), and divination marked the occasion. Originally dedicated to Brigid, the festival later became the feast day of St. Brigid.

Voodoo—Originated From the Fon: p. 446

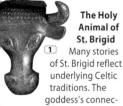

The Holy Animal of St. Brigid

① Many stories of St. Brigid reflect underlying Celtic traditions. The goddess's connection to milk—best demonstrated by the festival of Imbolc—was present in the Catholic tradition, which names the cow (**1**) as her holy animal. When St. Brigid was a child, her mother had only one red-eared cow to give milk; however, there was always more than enough. Some sources say the cow was supernatural, possibly from Tír na nÓg, the land of the elves. Other tales of St. Brigid describe how she traveled the countryside, accompanied by her white cow, spreading the Christian message throughout Ireland. In religious art, she is usually portrayed with a cow lying at her feet.

Sacred Flame at Kildare As the patron goddess of metalworking, Brigid was closely associated with fire and flame. Her most sacred shrine was an eternally burning flame in Kildare, Ireland. The flame was cared for by 19 priestesses who were dedicated to Brigid. After Christianity swept through the land, many of the ancient Celtic deities were given up, but Brigid was transformed and reborn as St. Brigid (**2**). In Kildare, a Catholic monastery was founded at the site of the shrine, and the flame continued to be tended by 19 nuns. Each woman would watch over the flame for a day, but on the 20th day, Brigid herself tended the fire. The flame burned on for hundreds of years until it was finally extinguished in the 16th century during the Reformation because of its underlying Pagan history. In 1993, the sacred flame of Brigid was lit again in the town square of Kildare and continues to burn today. It is maintained by the still existing order of Brigidine sisters.

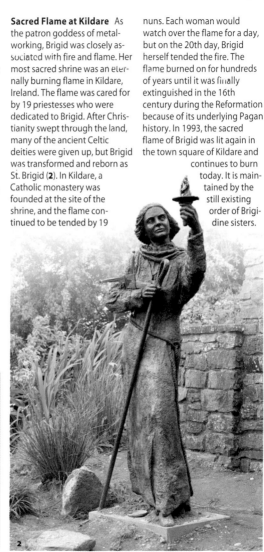

2

》 Animals in Myth: pp. 104, 230, 322, 424

Celtic Goddesses

Goddesses played an important role in the Celtic pantheon. Each of them had various roles, which associated them with multiple aspects of Celtic life. Three was a sacred number to the Celts, and is reflected in their female pantheon. Several goddesses are grouped in threes, such as the Matronae, goddesses of motherhood and fertility (**1**, altar in Germany). Morrigan was also a tripartite goddess with her two other aspects, Badb, a crow, and Macha, a warrior goddess. Sacred rivers and springs were frequently associated with Celtic goddesses, whose myths often involved water. Many of the Celtic goddesses were discarded with the coming of the Roman Empire and the eventual conversion to Christianity of the Celtic and Gaulish lands. While some of them, like Brigid, were incorporated into Christianity, others lived on in Roman cults. Thus, the goddess of horses Epona was also honored by the Roman cavalry in Gaul and continental Europe.

■ The number three was sacred to the Celts, and this was reflected in the tripartite aspects of the goddesses

■ Examples of tripartite goddesses include the Matronae (mother goddesses), the Morrigan, and Cerridwen

■ Some Celtic goddesses were adopted into Christianity

1

» **Triads of Gods:** pp. 206, 308

(2)

Cerridwen and Her Cauldron
The Welsh goddess Cerridwen represented wisdom, knowledge, and transformation. Her cauldron (**2**), the Amen, was used to brew potions. She was assisted by a blind man named Morda, who tended the fire, and a boy named Gwion, who stirred the potions. Once, Cerridwen was tending a knowledge potion, which required a year and a day to cook. When drops of the potion were accidentally ingested by Gwion, he gained great knowledge. Enraged, Cerridwen went after him, but he kept changing into different animals to escape. When he turned into a chicken, she caught and ate him. However, he turned into a seed and nine months later she gave birth to him as the bard Taliesin.

The Battle Goddess Morrigan
As a dark goddess of war and conflict, the Morrigan was often seen on the field of battle (**3**). Her most common form was as an old woman on the banks of a river, washing the clothes of the men who would later die in battle. In the form of a crow, she then picked through the dead bodies in search of souls. Besides knowing the outcome of all wars, she was also known to interfere in a battle on behalf of one side or the other. She was adapted into the Arthurian legend as Morgan le Fay.

Figures and Stories Relevant to Celtic Goddesses

Belisama, Celtic Goddess, see Belenus and Belisama, pp. 260–261

Brigid, see pp. 262–263

The Morrigan, Slept With the Dagda Each Year, see the Dagda, pp. 258–259

The Tripartite Nature of Celtic Goddesses

Although not unique to Celtic mythology, the concept of a tripartite goddess is particularly prevalent among the Celtic pantheon. Sometimes it refers to one goddess with three specific aspects, such as Cerridwen who had qualities of the traditional maiden, mother, and crone phases of life. Brigid ruled over three distinctly different areas: inspiration, metalcraft, and healing. On the other hand, some Celtic goddesses are part of a triad of deities. The Morrigan is often described as having two other closely related sisters, Badb and Macha. In an extension of her tripartite nature, the Morrigan can also be associated with Arianrhod and Blodeuwedd to create another grouping of maiden, mother, and crone.

Terrifying Goddesses: pp. 38, 93, 300 | **The Valkyries Picking Through the Dead:** p. 236

Elves and the Otherworld

The mythical Irish land of the elves was called Tír na nÓg, or the "land of eternal youth." This mystical place was an island that lay beyond the edges of any known maps, to the west of Ireland. Those who lived there were forever young, healthy, and happy. Although it was sometimes compared with the Norse afterlife for warriors, Valhalla, Tír na nÓg was not a place where souls went after death. The island was only inhabited by fairies and elves, also called the sidhe. In some Irish tales they are associated with the Tuatha Dé Danann—a magical people who lived in Ireland before the ancestors of the modern Irish—who were said to have moved to Tír na nÓg. Only a few mortals had even seen the island and a journey to it would often end unhappily. In one popular tale, a man named Oisin was visited by a fairy from Tír na nÓg, whose name was Niamh. She took him back to her island where they lived for three years and had two children. However, when Oisin became homesick for Ireland, he learned that only three years had passed for him in Tír na nÓg, but 300 years had gone by at home. His family and friends were long dead.

Tales of *The Mabinogion*

The Mabinogion is a collection of 12 Welsh folk tales that has become a major contribution to world literature. Some of the tales can be found in documents dating from the 13th century, while others are believed to be even older.

The Mabinogion is divided into three sections. The first part of it is made of four branches, or *mabinogi*: Pwyll, prince of Dyfet; Branwen, daughter of Lyr; Manawydan, son of Lyr; and Math, son of Mathonwy. Loosely connected by a shared character, Pryderi, the tales seem to take place in southwestern Wales. In the first branch, Pryderi's parents, Pwyll and the horse goddess Rhiannon, wed; in the third, Pryderi falls under a spell, but breaks free; in the fourth, Pryderi dies in battle. Although Pryderi is present in the second branch, the story centers on King Bran the Blessed, his sister Branwen, and his half brother Efnisien.

The other two sections of *The Mabinogion* are seven native Welsh legends and three romances, which include the tales of *Culhwch and Olwen*, *The Lady of the Fountain*, and *Enid*. These belong to the Arthurian tradition, which makes them interesting for scholars, but some feel that these two sections should not be included in *The Mabinogion*.

■ *The Mabinogion* is a group of prose stories collected from medieval Welsh manuscripts, first published in modern English in 1849

■ This group of anonymous narratives includes Celtic mythology and Arthurian romance

■ The tales are of quests for love, honor, and revenge, based on mythology and folklore

■ The protagonist of the first section is Pwyll, prince of Dyfet

■ Due to Christianization, in many legends, the gods of the Celtic past had been transformed into kings and heroes

The Marriage of Branwen Angry that he was not consulted in the marriage of his half sister Branwen to King Matholwch of Ireland, Efnisien killed Matholwch's horses. To make peace, Bran gave Matholwch a magic cauldron (**1**). However, the act of violence was not forgotten. Mistreated, Branwen appealed to her brother, King Bran of Britain, for help and he invaded Ireland with his army. Yet Bran was at a disadvantage because the Irish were using the magic cauldron to heal their fallen soldiers. Breaking the cauldron, Bran's army emerged victorious. However, he was killed in the battle. Bran's head was buried in London to prevent invasion from France.

2

Pwyll and Rhiannon One day, Pwyll of Dyfed caught sight of a beautiful woman riding a white horse (**2**). Falling instantly in love, Pwyll chased after her, not realizing she was Rhiannon, the goddess of horses. Pursuing her without success for three days, Pwyll finally just asked Rhiannon to stop. Relenting, she said that she wanted to marry him instead of her fiancé, Gwawl. Thus, Pwyll spent a year trying to trick Gwawl into releasing

Rhiannon from her pledge. Eventually, Pwyll tricked Gwawl into a magical bag, and would not let him out until he gave up Rhiannon. Pwyll and Rhiannon got married and had Pryderi; however, troubles soon followed. While being cared for by Rhiannon's maids, Pyrderi disappeared. To avoid blame, they covered Rhiannon's clothes with blood. As penance, Pwyll made her face humiliations, such as carrying guests into court. Later, Pyrderi returned to his parents and Rhiannon was absolved of guilt.

Manawydan and Llwyd's Wife After Pwyll's death, Rhiannon married Manawydan. The two of them lived with Pyrderi in Dyfed. The land was being plagued by a mysterious mist that made herds and food disappear. One day, Manawydan woke to find his fields empty. Seeing some

mice (**3**), he caught one. Soon, a man named Llwyd came and asked him for the mouse, explaining that it was his wife. Llwyd had been causing problems as revenge against Rhiannon for breaking her pledge to Gwawl, his friend.

3

Culhwch and Olwen With the remarriage of his father, King Cilydd, Culhwch was asked by his new step-

mother to marry her daughter. When he refused, she put a curse on him that he could only marry Olwen, the giant king's daughter. Falling

helplessly in love with Olwen, whom he had never seen, Culhwch searched for her. However, Olwen's father, Ysbaddaden, was also cursed: his death would follow Olwen's marriage. To keep Culhwch from marrying Olwen, Ysbaddaden gave him impossible tasks, such as retrieving a pair of scissors and a comb from the head of Twrch Trwyth, a huge wild boar (**4**). With the help of his cousin King Arthur, Culhwch completed the tasks and finally married Olwen.

4

Cúchulainn

Cúchulainn, formerly known as Sétanta, is one of the greatest heroes in Irish mythology. Cultural connotations of Cúchulainn include association with Irish nationalists—demonstrated by coins depicting Cúchulainn personifying the Easter Rising of 1916. As the subject of many works of art and literature, Cúchulainn is most known as the main character of the Ulster cycle. Here, he is depicted as a fearless warrior, fighting against the people of Connacht for the kingdom of Ulster as a Red Branch knight. In a sentiment comparable to that of the Greek hero Heracles, Cúchulainn felt it was better to be immortal in memory than to live long.

Although there are many versions of Cúchulainn's birth, he was mostly said to be the son of the god Lugh and Deichtine, the king of Ulster's sister. Without a mortal father to raise him, a group of men present at his birth agreed to be his foster fathers. Cúchulainn married Emer; however, it was not easy. She first refused, believing he was not worthy. Once Cúchulainn had proved himself in battle against the warrior-woman, Scathach, he returned to Emer. While she agreed to marry him, her father Forgall did not approve. Cúchulainn had to fight Forgall's men and kill Forgall in order to steal Emer away.

■ The great Irish hero Cúchulainn, was the son of a god and a human princess

■ He is the main figure of the Ulster cycle in the medieval Irish canon

■ He was the best of the Red Branch knights who were loyal to King Conor

■ In war he became a terrifying and monstrous figure, stirred up into a violent frenzy

■ He fought from his horse-drawn chariot

■ He had seven pupils in each eye, seven fingers on each hand, and seven toes on each foot

①

Sétanta Receives His New Name One day Sétanta played a game called hurley with his friends. His skills earned him an invitation to a feast at the house of the blacksmith Culann. Arriving late, Sétanta was attacked by Culann's enormous guard dog In self-defense, he killed the dog (**1**). As Culann was upset, Sétanta offered to guard his house until a new dog was found or reared. From then on, he was known as the hound of Culann: Cúchulainn.

Death of Cúchulainn

When Cúchulainn killed the father of Lugaid mac Con Roi, Lugaid commissioned three magical spears—each prophesied to kill a king—in order to have his revenge. During a battle, the first spear killed Cúchulainn's charioteer Laeg, who was known as the king of charioteers. The second spear killed Cúchulainn's horse, the king of horses. Cúchulainn was struck with the last spear. Mortally wounded, Cúchulainn refused to lie down in defeat. He tied himself to a stone so that he could continue standing until the very end. Although Cúchulainn appeared dead, Lugaid was afraid to approach him until a raven landed on Cúchulainn's shoulder (**3**) and started pecking at his flesh. Lugaid cut off Cúchulainn's head; however, as he did, Cúchulainn's sword fell from his fingers and severed Lugaid's hand.

Affair With Fand

One day, the sea goddess Fand enlisted Cúchulainn's help in a battle. Soon after, they began an affair. However, when the pair were reproached by Emer and a pack of women, Fand returned to her husband, the fairy king Manannán. Using his cloak, he magically made Fand and Cúchulainn forget the whole affair, while Emer took a druid potion to erase any memory of the sad incident.

Cattle Raid of Cooley

Queen Medb of Connacht attacked Ulster in an attempt to steal their famously fertile brown bull (**4**), Donn Cuailnge. As the men of Ulster were debilitated by a curse, Cúchulainn was the only one able to fight. He managed to hold off the army, even fighting off the warrior goddess, the Morrigan. As the Ulster men regained their senses, they joined the fight. Seeing that her men were losing, Medb snuck past the battle and stole the bull. Eventually, Donn Cuailnge managed to escape, but was fatally injured.

Samhain— The Origin of Halloween

The popular holiday Halloween (**1**) can be traced back to the Celtic harvest festival known as Samhain. This festival celebrated the final harvest of the year, marking the end of the fertile time. Preparations were made at Samhain for the cold winter ahead. Bonfires were common. Some of today's neo-Pagans (**3**)

consider Samhain to be the "Pagan New Year," but the ancient Celts did not have that view. Instead, they believed that during Samhain the boundary between this world and the spirit world was open. Spirits were more likely to walk the earth on this day than any other. In order to hide from any wandering ghosts, people dressed in costume to disguise themselves. Food offerings were left on doorsteps for the passing spirits. When Christianity was introduced to the Celtic lands around A.D. 800, the Church created its own holiday on November 1 to honor the saints called All Hallows' Day. Thus, the night before (Samhain night) was called All Hallows' Eve. Little had changed in the celebrations, but the name stuck.

Tradition of Carving Jack-o-Lanterns Carving turnips or gourds and placing a candle inside was a common practice during the festival of Halloween. Only when the holiday came to North America were pumpkins (**2**) used. The original reasons for this practice are not completely clear. The candles and carved faces may have been to scare unwelcome spirits who were wandering the earth at this time. They could also have symbolized the head of the Welsh ruler Bran the Blessed, who requested that his severed head be placed to face France to protect Celtic lands from invaders.

- King Arthur was a mythical king of Britain, an exemplary ruler who unified the country
- He founded the Round Table as a symbol of an ideal society
- His wife was Lady Guinevere
- The most famous knights were Lancelot, Gawain, Ywain, Sir Kay, Erec, Parzival, and Tristan

King Arthur

King Arthur, a legendary ruler of Britain who unified and pacified his land, probably has a historical origin. Above all, he is the symbol for an ideal ruler in an ideal society. Many myths and stories surround him, which include magical occurrences poetically

The sword Excalibur was central to Arthurian myth

treated by several medieval authors. Having ascended the throne as a young man, Arthur held court in Camelot with his wife Guinevere. There he founded his famous Round Table (**1**) with brave knights like his nephew Gawain and Lancelot.

They had magical adventures, fighting foreign knights and ogres. Arthur's adviser was the wizard Merlin. After a long period of peace, Arthur was betrayed by Mordred, who was either his nephew or illegitimate son, and killed in the battle of Camlann.

1

The Sword Excalibur Excalibur was a sword with magical powers. Merlin thrust it in a stone prophesying that only the true king could pull it from there. After many famous knights had tried to pull it out, Arthur, son of King Uther Pendragon, who grew up in hiding, managed it. He became king of Britain. Excalibur helped him to defend his empire and protected him against injuries. In a battle, Arthur destroyed his sword, but it was brought back by the Lady of the Lake (**2**), a water fey also known as as Viviane or Nimue (depending on the specific story) going on to play several pivotal roles in the tales of King Arthur.

Merlin The wizard Merlin (**3**) was born from a mortal woman, but with a demonic incubus for a father. His first escapades began when the sinking tower of the King Vortigern could only be saved by a "fatherless boy," who was most likely Merlin. The young wizard discovered two dragons beneath the tower. It was the magic of Merlin that brought about the conception of King Arthur. Uther Pendragon took a potion made by Merlin to trick a woman, Igraine, into thinking he was her husband. The child born after their night together was Arthur, and Igraine became Uther's wife. Many stories have him either able to change shape, or to simply be in disguise. His other great gift was that of prophecy, and his predictions of the future always came true. In later tales, Merlin is often shown as the adviser to Arthur rather than a magical aide.

Lady Guinevere's Love Affair King Arthur married Guinevere, daughter of the Cameliardian king Leodegrance, in order to politically stabilize his reign. However, the contrary happened. She unfortunately drew the romantic attention of her husband's greatest knight, Lancelot of the Lake (**4**, with King Arthur and Guinevere in film scene). Instantly smitten, Guinevere and Lancelot's love affair almost began when Lancelot brought her to Camelot to marry Arthur. The adulterous relationship shook the authority of Arthur and ultimately led to the end of Arthur's reign.

Quest for the Holy Grail

FETOR

The Holy Grail is an essential part of the stories and romances about King Arthur and his knights. Reflecting obvious Christian themes, in some myths the Grail is said to be the cup Jesus drank from during the Last Supper. The same cup may also have been used by Joseph of Arimathea to catch the blood of Christ during the crucifixion. In other myths the Grail is a bowl containing a consecrated wafer. In every case it is the source of eternal vitality. Initiated by a vision of the Grail at the Round Table of Arthur (pictured) or sometimes a prophecy by the sorcerer

Merlin, the knights began their quest after it. However, only a pure, innocent knight was destined to find it. In some versions of the Grail myth, it is Lancelot's son Galahad who finds the Grail.

Another tale names Percival, also a knight of the Round Table, as the person who finally heals the Fisher King Anfortas, the sick guardian of the Grail, as well as the whole land.

Celtic-Roman Deities

When the Roman Empire spread its area of control throughout Western Europe in the second century B.C., there was a syncretic mixing of the native and Roman cultures. This was particularly the case in Gaul—which consisted of modern France, Belgium, and northern Italy—where the continental Celts settled. The Romans controlled (**3**, Gallic chief Vercingetorix delivering himself to Caesar in 52 B.C.) this area for about 500 years. In this time the political and spiritual power of the Celtic druids began to diminish and a particular Gallo-Roman culture arose. The cultural diffusion that occurred between the Celtic natives and Romans presented itself in two ways. First the pantheon of the indigenous Celtic gods was adapted to Roman counterparts, such as Lenus Mars or Apollo Grannus. Second a Roman god was sometimes paired with a native goddess, as with Mercury and Rosmerta.

The culture of the Celtic-Roman peoples changed again in the fifth and sixth centuries when Christianity spread through the region.

Sucellus Sucellus (**1**) was the Gaul god of the forest and agriculture. He also ruled over fermented and alcoholic drinks. He had a wife named Nantosuelta, but no children. He was worshiped throughout northern Gaul. He was a middle-aged man with a beard and carried a long-handled hammer. Many images have him carrying a barrel. In the Celtic-Roman tradition, he was known as Silvanus Sucellus, a pairing with the Roman god of forests, groves, and wild fields.

Epona One of the few deities to be added to the Roman pantheon was the goddess Epona. Ruling horses (**2**), donkeys, and mules, she was also indirectly associated with fertility. Her widespread popularity was likely because she was worshiped by the imperial cavalry, which carried her cult throughout the Roman Empire and the surrounding lands.

Indian Mythology

Illustration from the Gitagovinda of Krishna and Radha

Indian Mythology

Through the influence of many religions that had their origins and are still practiced in India like Hinduism, Buddhism, Islam, and others, the country's cultural tradition is rich. One of the oldest religions in the world, Hinduism was propagated through the centuries by oral instruction. In order to break down the practices of yoga and the complex notions of Hindu philosophy, this knowledge was transmitted through comprehensive stories. Furthermore, the enormous Hindu pantheon contains deities who represent various aspects of the universe, and thus lend themselves to different parts of daily life.

The development of Indian mythology began with the emergence of India's earliest civilization in the Indus Valley (**1**) around 2500 B.C. The inhabitants of the Indus Valley practiced agriculture, lived in cities, and traded with Mesopotamia. Though they possessed a form of writing, no one has yet been able to

decipher it, leaving much of Indus Valley culture, including its religion and mythology, still a mystery. By 1800 B.C., the Indus Valley civilization had disappeared. Between about 1500 and 600 B.C. a new civilization, called the Vedic society, appeared. Similarities between their language and the classical languages of Greece, Rome, Iran, and Central Asia suggest that the Vedic people may have been invaders who entered India through Afghanistan. They called themselves Aryan ("noble"), which is related to the place-name "Iran," a region whose ancient civilization closely resembled that of Vedic India.

The Vedic people, unlike the city-dwelling farmers of the Indus Valley, were nomadic cattle herders, so they left no permanent structures or artifacts behind. Everything known about them today comes from their orally transmitted sacred tradition, a body of texts collectively known as the Vedas ("knowledge") (**2**, oral instruction of the Vedas). According to tradition, the Vedas were never actually composed and have no author, but have existed since before the beginning of time. Holy men called *rishis* were responsible for "seeing" the Vedas and composing the thousands of hymns that made up the four collections: Rig Veda, Sama Veda, Yajur Veda, and Atharva Veda, which is the youngest.

Though it is difficult to know how reliable they are, the oldest of these texts, the Rig Veda—composed roughly between 1500 and 1000 B.C.—states that Vedic society was divided into four hierarchical classes: *Brahmins* (priests), *Kshatriyas* (kings and high officials), *Vaishyas* (landowners and merchants), and *Shudras* (craftsmen and servants). Slaves were part of the *Dalit* (untouchables). The Brahmins were the highest class because they performed the important rituals of sacrifice that were the center of the Vedic religion. Kings protected the Brahmins and supported them financially. In return, the Brahmins made sacrifices in the name of the kings to bring them wealth, victory, and sons.

The Vedic people worshiped a pantheon of gods, who were the predecessors of the Hindu pantheon (**3**, Indra, king of the gods) so well known today. Many of these Vedic gods were brought with them from their homeland, while some were accumulated when they encountered and assimilated with indigenous tribes as they moved through North India. By the fourth century B.C., the nomadic Vedic tribes were settled in permanent cities and the actual practice of sacrifice was beginning to decline in importance, giving way to a tradition concentrated on the esoteric meaning of sacrifice. This mystical tradition, exemplified in the Upanishads, gave birth to a class of forest-dwelling holy men who left the settlements to spend their lives meditating in the forest. Out of this class of forest-dwellers, new Hindu reform movements like Buddhism and Jainism arose and became a force in North India.

Buddhism stood against the social class order, and thus opposed the authority of the Brahmin class. Instead, Buddhists wanted to define people by their religious knowledge. Buddhism also rejected the idea of an eternal self, or *atman*, which the authors of the Upanishads believed to be the self that was reborn in different bodies, either on earth or in some heaven or hell, through the process of reincarnation. On the other hand, Buddhism postulated liberation, or *nirvana*, through the knowledge that life is suffering and cessation of any sensual pleasures. The Buddha's teachings characteristically centered on one's own responsibility. Originally, the Buddhist tradition did not have any gods. Although Buddhists today honor the Buddha and

Bodhisattvas, the religion never developed as rich a mythology as Hinduism.

While Buddhism spread from India to Sri Lanka, Tibet, Afghanistan, and East Asia, the religion that could now be called Hinduism, as distinct from the Vedic religion, began to develop in response to the Buddhist challenge. During the subsequent period of religious change, the great Indian epic the *Mahabharata* was composed. This epic introduced a new religious idea called *bhakti* ("devotion") that devalued both sacrifice and asceticism in favor of a personal relationship to a high god. Unlike the practice of Vedic sacrifice, which was only open to those who could afford to pay Brahmins to perform the expensive rituals, and the philosophical traditions of the Upanishads, which were only open to those with the education and the capacity to perform austerities, bhakti was a religious movement available to all people willing to devote themselves completely to a deity.

The former Vedic high gods—Indra, Mitra, and Varuna—were displaced by the *trimurti* ("trinity") of Brahma, Vishnu (**4**, center), and Shiva, who symbolize the cycle of beginning, preservation, and destruction of all things, respectively. A multitude of other gods are worshiped in Hinduism, from pan-Indian deities like Ganesha (**5**), known throughout India, to local protective gods like Pota

Raju, the deified sacrificial post worshiped in South India. However, the two gods most closely associated with bhakti worship are Vishnu and Shiva, the worship of whom formed the basis of the two major post-Vedic sects, Vaishnavism and Shaivism, respectively. These two traditions became prominent in India as Buddhism began to decline after the dissolution of the Mauryan Empire. The Gupta and Harsha Empires of the fourth through the seventh centuries A.D. strove for a balance between Hinduism, Buddhism, and Jainism in India. Thus, the power of Brahmins, who had less power under Buddhist rule, began a resurgence under royal patronage. Starting in the third century, cities built around temples dedicated to Shiva and Vishnu became centers of economic and political power. With later dynasties, Hinduism rose again as an "original Indian religion," with its own iconography, rituals, and centers of pilgrimage.

Along with the creator god Brahma, the myths of Vishnu and Shiva make up a large part of the Puranas, a body of texts composed from about A.D. 300 to the time of the arrival of Islam in A.D. 1000. The time of the Puranas coincided with the rise of feudalism in India, the rise of vernacular literature, and an increase in the practice of local lords donating tax-free land to temples and individual Brahmins. Encyclopedic in nature, the Puranas contain descriptions of rituals, philosophy, histories, and stories and legends about the gods, sages, kings, and sacred centers around India.

The mythology of Vishnu developed around the central theme of Vishnu's ability to incarnate himself on earth in order to rescue *dharma* ("cosmic order") when it is threatened. Most often, Vishnu has ten incarnations or *avatars*, the most famous of which are Krishna and Rama, the hero of the epic *Ramayana*. Hindu goddesses, known as Devi, are worshiped alongside the gods. While the gods are usually considered individually, the goddess is one deity in many forms. Some are benevolent like Saraswati, the goddess of wisdom, and Lakshmi, the goddess of fortune, while others are destructive like the black goddess Kali and Durga (**6**), the goddess of battle. Goddess worship, or Shaktism, was especially popular among lower classes. In villages, local goddesses were important figures of devotion. The idea of the goddess as having many forms led to hundreds of small village goddess traditions being subsumed into a larger religious movement.

Aside from the various religious traditions, the prayer ritual of *puja* is performed throughout the Hindu world. A mode of worship practiced in temples, homes, and roadside shrines, believers recite holy Sanskrit verses in front of a picture, statue, book, or some other physical manifestation of the divine. Often, puja involves an offering to the deity that can take the form of food, money, incense, chanting, lights, or the ringing of bells.

Today, Hinduism is the third largest world religion, with over 900 million followers spanning the globe. Mythology acts as a way to educate believers about their gods and break down the often complex religious concepts.

Creation Myths

Creation takes many forms in Hindu myth. Hindu tradition can recognize all stories of creation without fear of contradiction because, in Hindu thought, the universe has no beginning or end, but goes through incessant cycles of creation, destruction, and re-creation. The authors of the Puranas divided each cycle into four descending ages. In the Golden Age, all beings were self-sufficient with no need for food or shelter.

In the Second Age, people got all the sustenance they needed from magic trees that provided whatever they wished for and all men studied the Veda. The gods divided men into priests, kings, producers, and slaves—everyone acted according to his class.

In the Third Age, wars broke out and men were no longer able to understand the entire Veda, so the gods divided it into four books. Finally, in the Dark Age, humans were corrupt and immorality reigned on earth. This age raged until the cosmic dissolution made way for a new creation and a new Golden Age, thus beginning the cycle again.

■ The gods of creation in the Hindu tradition include Vishvakarman, the maker of all things; Prajapati, the Vedic lord of creatures; and Brahma, the Puranic creator god

■ The universe is composed of a continuous cycle of four ages: golden, second, third, and dark

■ The Puranas, post-Vedic Hindu scriptures, detail the history of the universe

■ The main themes of creation stories in Indian mythology are sacrifice, destruction, and renewal

Creation of the World Through Sacrifice— Story of Purusha The giant Purusha (**1**) had 1,000 limbs and 1,000 heads; his body took up the entire universe. To create the worlds, the gods sacrificed and dismembered Purusha. His head became the Brahmin class, his arms became the kings, his thighs became the producers, and his feet became the slaves. The moon was created from his mind, his eye be-came the sun, space came from his navel, and the sky came from his head. All the creatures of the earth and sky came from his melted fat and the gods Indra and Agni were born from his mouth. With the dismemberment of Purusha the gods brought order to the cosmos and created the institution of sacrifice, which would have to be repeated over and over to maintain that order.

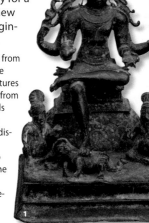

⏩ **Creation Through a Body:** pp. 20, 27, 229, 331, 380

Churning the Ocean Before the creation of humanity, the gods wanted to ensure their dominance over the *asuras* ("demons"). To do this, the gods had to drink *amrita*, the nectar of immortality, which had been lost in the ocean of milk. As the task was great, the gods asked the asuras to help in exchange for some amrita. Using a mountain as a churning rod and a snake as a rope, the gods and demons stood on opposite sides of the ocean, holding ends of the snake. Tugging the snake (**2**), they moved the mountain and churned the ocean. When the amrita rose to the surface, the god Vishnu changed into a woman and distracted the asuras while the gods stole the amrita. The asura Rahu swallowed some of it before a god decapitated him. His immortal head swallows the moon, causing a lunar eclipse.

Hiranyagarbha—The Golden Embryo In Vedic mythology, *Hiranyagarbha* (**3**) refers to the golden embryo (later translated as the golden egg) that comes out of the primal waters and separates the earth and sky, bringing with it all the gods and the sacrifice. For the rishis who composed the Vedas, the golden egg was the uncreated, unmanifest principle that underlies all creation. Sometimes the golden egg is identified with creator gods like Prajapati, Brahma, and Vishvakarman, as well as in later myths with Shiva's dance of creation.

⟨3⟩

Brahma the Creator; Shiva the Destroyer The gods Brahma and Shiva (**4**) represent the Hindu concept of time and the universe. According to this tradition, Brahma created the universe and all living entities within it. Because time is cyclical, one cosmic cycle of four ages, which is made up of 2,160,000,000 human years, lasts for just one day of Brahma's life. Thus, when Brahma goes to sleep at night after the end of his day, the universe is destroyed by Shiva. When Brahma wakes up, he once again creates the world and a new world cycle begins. As his destruction of the world initiates creation, Shiva is also a creator.

Creation Through a Cosmic Egg: pp. 87, 330, 439, 457 | **Gaining Immortality:** p. 127

Indra

Indra (**1**, top-right on his elephant in a scene from the *Ramayana*) appears more times than any other god in the hymns of the Rig Veda. As the king of the gods, Indra was a thunderbolt-wielding storm god. He is still worshiped today in the desert state of Rajasthan during a festival called Inder Puja performed to bring rain during times of drought. Indra's qualities reflect the attributes of a good king: strength, courage, virility, and generosity.

Along with great feats like the slaying of the serpent Vritra and the recovery of the gods' stolen cattle, Indra's myths also detail his weakness for soma, an intoxicating drink. In other stories, Indra is portrayed as a buffoon or even a sinner, most notably when he seduces a priest's wife and is cursed. In the *Mahabharata*, he is the father of the hero Arjuna, and tricks his son's enemy into giving up the armor that made him invincible.

■ Indra was the king of the gods as well as the god of war and thunder

■ He had a hall in Svarga ("heaven") where the righteous dead lived before reincarnation

■ He is portrayed wielding the *vajra*, thunderbolt weapon, or with a bow, a net, or a hook

■ He is often depicted riding Airavata, a four-tusked elephant

Vajrayana—Indra's Diamond Scepter in Buddhism

Indra carries a thunderbolt weapon called the vajra, which also means "diamond." Vajrayana (the "diamond vehicle") refers to the school of ritual-based Buddhism that developed late in the tradition's history in India. Said to supersede both the Hinayana (the "lesser vehicle," a tradition usually called Theravada) and Mahayana ("great vehicle"), Vajrayana Buddhism is practiced today in Nepal and Tibet.

Indra Slays the Serpent Vritra When the great serpent Vritra was holding back the rains within his belly and leaving the world in drought, the gods called on Indra to kill the monster and free the waters. To prepare for the battle, Indra (**2**) drank three bowls of soma and was filled with strength. Then, armed with the thunderbolt weapon made for him by the god Tvastr, he went out to meet the monster. Like Indra, Vritra had magical power over the weather and attacked him with fog and hail. But when Vritra aimed a blow at Indra's mouth, the god became as thin as a hair and dodged the attack. Seeing the serpent's belly exposed, Indra then took his thunderbolt and struck Vritra's stomach, killing the monster and freeing the rains.

Indra and the Stolen Cattle When the demon Vala had stolen the gods' cattle (**3**) and trapped the herd in a cave, the gods called the fierce warrior god Indra to get them back. Accompanied by storm gods called the Maruts, Indra took his thunderbolt weapon, mounted his chariot, and went out in search of the cave. The Maruts tracked the path of the stolen cows and guided Indra to where they were kept. Finally, Indra and his companions came to the mountain in which the cattle were penned. Aiming his weapon at the side of the mountain, he split it open and released the cows.

Figures and Stories Relevant to Indra

Agni and the Khandava Forest, Indra as Protector of the Forest, see p. 293

The *Mahabharata*, Indra's Son Arjuna, see pp. 296–297

Story of Purusha, Indra Was Born From the Mouth of Purusha, p. 288

◗ **Battles Against Serpents:** pp. 51, 233 | **Stolen Cattle:** p. 149

Yama and Agni

The Vedic gods Yama and Agni embody two important aspects of ancient Vedic belief—afterlife and sacrifice, respectively.

One of the wisest deities, Yama was the god of death and the lord of the underworld. He and his twin sister Yami were born to the sun god Vivasvat and his wife Saranya. Yama became the god of death when he was the first man to die and find the path to the underworld. In funeral hymns, Yama is called to lead the deceased to heaven.

Agni, the god of fire, is second only to Indra in the number of hymns addressed to him in the Rig Veda. Although he was said to be present in the sun, in lightning, and in the fire of the hearth, his most important role was that of the sacrificial fire, which transmitted the offerings to the world of the gods. Thus, he acted as a mediator between mortals and the gods. Agni was born out of the water, where he was said later to have returned to hide and had to be coaxed out by the sacrificial priests.

■ In the Buddhist tradition, Yama is a judge of the dead and rules the Buddhist hells

■ In Vedic mythology, Yama found the way to the next world

■ Depicted with green or red skin, he holds a lasso to pull the soul from corpses

■ Agni was the god of fire; found in all flames, he was integral to sacrificial fire rituals

■ He holds an axe, torch, prayer beads, and a flaming spear, and has two heads and three legs

Agni and the Vedic Fire Ceremonies

Sacrifice was the central feature of Vedic religion. It continually restored cosmic order and formed the bond between Brahmins and the kings who often sponsored the rituals. One of the most elaborate of these was the Agnicayana, the "piling up of Agni" in which a giant altar was constructed shaped like an eagle, representing Agni in the form of a bird carrying the offering up to heaven. At sunrise and sunset, Brahmin males offered milk to Agni in a ritual called the Agnihotra, propitiating the god both as the sun and the sacrificial fire (right, Agni with fire).

》 Fire Cult: p. 55

Yama's Hells In the Puranas, Yama rules over a whole realm of hells designed to punish specific crimes. In Tamisram, robbers are repeatedly beaten into unconsciousness (**1**, sinners tortured by Yami's servants). Meat-eaters are sent to Kumbhipakam where they are boiled in oil for as many years as there were hairs on all the animals they ate. Adulterers go to Shalmali where they are made to embrace a figure of red-hot iron while they are flogged. In Ayahpanam, those who have overindulged in liquor are forced to drink molten metal.

Yami and Yama One day Yami decided to procreate and produce humankind. She approached her twin brother Yama (**3**), arguing that the artisan of the gods, Tvastr, had designed them to be the divine couple to procreate humanity. As it was taboo to lie with a relative, Yama resisted and angrily sent her away.

Agni and the Khandava Forest One day, the two heroes Krishna and Arjuna were traveling when they met Agni in the form of a Brahmin. Agni complained to the two men that he was hungry and the only thing that could satisfy him was to consume the entire nearby Khandava forest (**2**). However, he was not able to do this, as long as the storm god Indra protected it. Hearing this, Krishna and Arjuna agreed to help. Agni armed them with a bow and discus from the god Varuna and began to burn down the forest. In heaven, Indra heard the fire and poured down rain to put it out. Arjuna dispelled the rain with his arrows and a battle ensued in which he and Krishna fought off Indra and all the gods. Finally, Indra withdrew and allowed Agni to sate his hunger.

> ### Figures and Stories Relevant to Yama and Agni
>
> **Krishna**, Helped Agni to Devour the Khandava Forest, see pp. 318–319
>
> **Story of Purusha**, Agni Was Born From the Mouth of Purusha, p 288

Varuna and Mitra

■ Varuna was the ruler of the sky and god of the celestial ocean and rains

■ In pre-Vedic times he was chief of the gods

■ He rode on a large crocodile

■ Mitra was the patron of honesty, friendship, and contracts

■ He is probably identical to the Iranian god Mithra

■ Varuna and Mitra are linked, and are associated with the sun

Varuna (**1**), the Vedic ethical god, and Mitra, the god of pacts and friendship, are best known and most often worshiped together as a pair. In the Rig Veda, only ten hymns are addressed to Varuna and one hymn to Mitra, but 23 are dedicated to the pair Mitra-Varuna. It is sometimes argued by scholars that both Varuna and Mitra represent the twin functions of a king: the magician-warrior and the priest-jurist, respectively.

Varuna represents rule through force, obligation, and magical power, as is exemplified in the myth of Varuna's noose. Mitra represents peacetime rule through the oversight and enforcement of social obligations and contracts, as is reflected in the modern Hindi derivative *mitr*, which means "friend."

Unlike Mitra, Varuna also appears on his own in a number of myths and some important rituals, including the varunapraghasa. This Vedic ritual took place at the beginning of the rainy season. During the festivities, the queen or the wife of the sacrificer had to confess her marital infidelities of the last year to Varuna, who absolved her of evil.

▶▶ Mithra: p. 58 | Eastern Cults in Rome: p. 222

Varuna and the Adityas

Varuna was the chief among a class of gods called the Adityas, named so because they were sons of the goddess Aditi, whose name means "eternal." Celestial deities of light (**2**), the Adityas number six, seven, or eight in the early myths, but later are listed as 12 gods to correspond to the 12 months of the solar year. Other important Adityas include Mitra and Daksha, who was father of the goddess Parvati and a major figure in the mythology of the post-Vedic god Shiva.

Rta, the Cosmic Order

Rta, etymologically related to the English word "ritual," denotes the divine law or cosmic order that underlies the universe. It was the conceptual precursor to the later idea of dharma. It holds that the Vedic seers and the Brahmin priests were charged with maintaining the delicate balance of rta on earth through the repetition of their hymns and rituals. In the celestial realm, Varuna and the other Adityas acted as its guardians and protectors. The Rig Veda (right) even refers to Varuna and Mitra as "rta's charioteers."

Varuna's Noose As the god of morality, Varuna had the power to punish those who deserved it. He had a noose, called a pasha, which he used to bind oath-breakers, liars, and sinners. The noose had a dual function, representing the fact that all men were "bound" to obey Varuna's ethical laws, and at the same time symbolizing the threat of punishment for those who transgressed them. Those whom Varuna bound and punished became afflicted with dropsy, a disease that caused the body to retain water and swell up. In some myths, the noose of Varuna takes the form of a snake (**3**), or *naga*.

Figures and Stories Relevant to Varuna and Mitra

Asuras and Demons, Varuna Was an Asura, see pp. 306–307

Holy Animals, Varuna's Crocodile Was a Sacred Mount, see pp. 322–323

⏩ **Universal Principles:** pp. 102, 332, 384, 430

The Mahabharata

The *Mahabharata* (**1**) is a major Sanskrit epic of ancient India. With more than 74,000 verses, it is one of the longest epic poems in the world. The epic details stories such as the life of Krishna (**3**, with a gopi) and the rivalry between two branches of the great Bharata clan: the Kauravas and the Pandavas.

Most imporant of all, the *Mahabharata* contains the *Bhagavad Gita*. Consisting of 700 verses, the *Bhagavad Gita* is a conversation between Krishna, disguised as a charioteer, and the Pandava prince Arjuna on the battlefield of Kurukshetra. Arjuna faced a moral dilemma when he saw members of his family on the opposite side of the battle. Using different analogies, Krishna described the order of the cosmos, the path to knowledge, panentheism, and many other topics. Thus, the *Bhagavad Gita* is known as a comprehensive guide to Hindu philosophies and the principles of yoga. For example, Krishna tells Arjuna about karma yoga, which is essentially performing acts or duties without any concern for results. By eliminating the desire for seeing fruits from action, Arjuna can also eradicate anger and bewilderment from his life.

Victory of the Pandavas The Kauravas, led by Duryodhana, had a bitter rivalry with their cousins, the Pandavas. After losing their kingdom in a dice match, the Pandavas were exiled for 13 years. When they came back to reclaim their kingdom, Duryodhana refused, which led to a war that resulted in the near total destruction of the entire clan. After the war, only the Pandavas (**2**) were left with their advisor and cousin Krishna, who was the human incarnation of Vishnu.

>> **Krishna:** p. 318

Lakshmi and Saraswati

Lakshmi (**1**, seated on a snake with Vishnu) and Saraswati were both wives of the god Vishnu, along with the river goddess Ganga. According to one tale, the wives quarreled so much that Vishnu sent Ganga to live with Shiva, and Lakshmi to Brahma.

Born from the churning of the milk ocean by the gods and demons, Lakshmi was the goddess of prosperity and good fortune. Each time Vishnu incarnated himself on earth in one of his avatars, Lakshmi took a corresponding form as his wife or consort. For example, when Vishnu was Rama, she was his wife Sita.

Saraswati was the goddess of wisdom and the arts, often pictured with a stringed musical instrument called the vina. She was also paired with the god Brahma, either as his wife or his daughter. Today Saraswati is often invoked at the start of an artistic or academic venture.

■ Lakshmi was the goddess of good fortune and prosperity, while Saraswati was the goddess of wisdom, music, and the arts

■ The lotus symbolizes Lakshmi's traits, e.g., luck and honor

■ Saraswati is associated with the color white for knowledge

Lakshmi and the Lotus Flower—Her Eight Forms

As the goddess personifying purity and beauty, Lakshmi is closely associated with the striking lotus flower. She is often depicted in art either carrying or seated within a lotus flower (**2**). In Hinduism, the lotus flower symbolizes long life, honor, and luck. Like a lotus, which has eight petals,

2

Lakshmi has a list of eight forms—the Ashtalakshmi—in which she is depicted. These were acquired so that she could continue to be paired with her husband, Vishnu, with his multiple avatars. Each form corresponds to a different sphere of prosperity. These eight forms are the Lakshmis of material and spiritual wealth (Sridevi), food (Dhanya), patience (Aadhi), livestock (Gaja), offspring (Santana), victory (Dhairya), knowledge (Vidya), and gold (Dhana).

Saraswati Invents the Devanagari Alphabet

Saraswati is associated with wisdom, learning, music, and poetry. She is often identified with Vach, the Vedic goddess of speech. Saraswati is credited with the invention of the sacred language of Sanskrit and of the Devanagari alphabet (**3**, section of the *Sri Bhagavata Puran* in Devanagari script), the writing system in which it (as well as the modern language of Hindi) is written. Sanskrit is

3

not an ordinary language in the Hindu tradition, but is the language of the gods and the language of the holy Vedas.

> ### Figures and Stories Relevant to Lakshmi and Saraswati
>
> **Brahma**, Saraswati's Husband or Father, see pp. 308–309
>
> **Churning the Ocean**, Lakshmi and Saraswati's Birth, see Creation Myths, pp. 288–289
>
> **Rama**, When Vishnu Was Rama, Lakshmi Was His Wife, Sita, see pp. 314–315
>
> **Vishnu**, Husband of Lakshmi and Saraswati, see pp. 312–313

The Saraswati River

Today Hindus consider the Ganges to be the holiest river in India (right, bathers at Sangam, the confluence of the Ganges, Yamuna, and mythical Saraswati rivers). In the Vedic period there was another holy river called the Saraswati, which formed one of the boundaries of Brahmavartta, part of northern India. Like the Ganges (Ganga), the Saraswati River was personified by a goddess. While it is no longer known exactly which river was called the Saraswati or if that river is even still in existence, some people identify it with the Sarasuti, which originates in the foothills of the Himalaya.

≫ Lotus Flower in Egypt—Nefertem: p. 73

■ Kali, the goddess of death, doomsday, and time, **is** a fearful, destructive figure but also a protective mother goddess

■ She has four hands: one holds a sword, another the head of a demon, while the other two hands bless her followers

■ She wears a skirt of severed arms and a necklace of skulls

■ The golden figure of Durga, the warrior goddess, has eight or ten arms, each carrying a weapon, and rides a lion or tiger

■ She embodies *shakti*, feminine creativity and energy

Kali and Durga

The goddesses Kali and Durga are the two most famous of the terrifying forms of Devi, the female aspect of the divine. They were the fiercer forms of Shiva's wife Parvati. Ferocious in battle, sometimes the gods had to calm them down to prevent them from completely destroying the universe.

Although Kali translates as "black goddess," she was also depicted with blue skin. While the more frightful of the two goddesses, Kali was also seen as a benevolent mother deity. As the ruler of time, she devoured everything. Irresistible to both men and gods, she is often depicted as a bare-breasted woman with fangs and a long tongue. Most commonly she is seen straddling the god Shiva who is lying face-up on the ground. Her tongue is sticking out in what is often interpreted as a gesture of shame for putting her feet on her husband.

Golden in color, Durga also represented the Great Mother. Her ten arms symbolized her strength as a warrior goddess, riding either a lion or a tiger into battle. She is often shown fighting the buffalo demon Mahisa. The nine-day Durga Puja is the largest festival in Bengal.

Parvati Fights Daruka There was a demon called Daruka who could only be killed by a woman. Unable to defeat him, the gods called on Shiva's wife Parvati for help. A long time before, when the gods and demons were churning the ocean of milk, a powerful poison called halahala was created and rose to the surface. Shiva swallowed it to protect the gods from its power. As Parvati stopped the poison in his throat, it stayed there, turning it blue-black. Because of this, he was known as Neelkantha, "the one with a blue throat." To prepare to fight the demon, Parvati jumped down Shiva's throat. She combined with the poison to become the black goddess Kali (1). Emerging from Shiva's mouth, she led an attack on Daruka and destroyed him in battle. (1)

» **Terrifying Goddesses:** pp. 38, 93, 265

Kali and the Thieves A band of thieves desired to make a human sacrifice to Kali (**2**). They captured a meditating Brahmin, bound him, and took him to her temple. As a thief raised his knife to strike, the Kali idol came to life and stopped him. She was so enraged at the thieves' plan to kill a Brahmin that she and her retinue decapitated them, and then began to play about with their severed heads. The grateful Brahmin walked away unhurt.

Durga's Battle Against the Demons In the third cosmic age, two demons named Sumbha and Nisumbha had become so powerful that they began to oppress the gods. Sumbha heard about Durga's power and sent a messenger to ask for her hand in marriage. Durga replied that she would only marry one who could beat her in battle. Angry, the two demons attacked Durga, but she defeated them easily (**3**, on the battlefield), restoring control of the universe to the gods.

Kali Kills Raktabija

Another tradition says that Kali was created when the gods could not defeat a terrible demon named Raktabija ("blood-seed"). He could spring clones of himself from every drop of his blood that hit the ground.

The more the gods attacked the demon, the more demons there were to attack and so they withdrew to form a new plan. Each god projected forth his divine energy, or shakti, and all the shaktis combined to form one great warrior goddess, Kali. The gods gave Kali all their weapons and sent her out to meet Raktabija. Kali threw all the clones into her gaping jaws and ate them whole without spilling any blood. Then she cut off the demon's head and held it over her mouth so that she could drink every drop of his blood before it touched the ground. Finally, with his body drained and his head cut off, Raktabija was destroyed.

■ Ganesha was the god of beginnings and obstacles, and the patron of intellectuals

■ He is also known as "lord of the people"

■ He carried an axe, noose, and an elephant goad, which he used to destroy, control, or subdue the obstacles of life

■ He had a potbelly and was very fond of Indian sweets

■ His elephant head signifies the *atman*, or soul, and his human body signifies *maya*, human existence on earth

■ He rode an agile bandicoot rat named Kroncha, symbolizing Ganesha's ability to overcome all obstacles

Figures and Stories Relevant to Ganesha

Holy Animals, Ganesha's Rat Was a Sacred Animal, see pp. 322–323

Kali and Durga, Ganesha's Mother, see pp. 296–297

Shiva, Ganesha's Father, see pp. 320–321

Ganesha

Having a human body with the face of an elephant, Ganesha is perhaps the most distinctive of the Hindu deities. He was the son of Shiva and Parvati, and

Ganesha's mount, or vahana, is a rat

the brother of Karthikeya. Ganesha is usually depicted with a large belly and rides on a rat, which can get in and out of anywhere. His hands hold symbolic objects, and his free hand is often raised in protective blessing, or holds a broken tusk or a plate of sweets.

The worship of Ganesha is also present in Jainism and in Buddhism. A Hindu sect known as the Ganapatyas, which arose during the ninth century in India, honor him as their chief god and the embodiment of supreme reality. Today, Ganesha is often worshiped by students, writers, travelers, and businessmen. He is propitiated at the beginning of new undertakings and is the first god invoked in Hindu ritual contexts.

Writing of the *Mahabharata* The sage Vyasa held the epic (**1**) in his mind's eye. But he was old and feared he might forget. He wanted to compose a great poem that it might endure forever, so he asked Brahma what to do. Following his advice, Vyasa summoned the wise Ganesha and asked him to act as scribe. Ganesha agreed, but stipulated that he would do so only if Vyasa dictated it without pause. Vyasa countered by saying that Ganesha must not write anything before understanding the full meaning of it. This gave Vyasa time to rest during the *Mahabharata's* recounting. So Ganesha snapped off his tusk to use as a pen and began writing.

1

❯❯ **Janus, Roman God of Beginnings:** p. 416

Birth and Decapitation One time, Shiva had gone off wandering, leaving his wife Parvati alone. She wanted to take her bath but had no one to guard the door. Rubbing her arms, she gathered the earth of her own body and shaped it into the figure of a little boy. It came to life and she set him in front of the door with strict orders to not let anyone inside. Soon, Shiva came home to find a boy blocking the way into his own house. Shiva bellowed, "Who are you to block my way?!" "I am Parvati's son and while the goddess is bathing no one may enter." "We have no son! Now stand aside before I get angry! No beggars allowed!" With one sharp look Shiva chopped off his head and threw it away. Parvati came weeping: "You've killed our son!" To comfort her Shiva took the head of an elephant, the first creature he happened to see, and, setting it on the shoulders of their son, restored him to life (**2**).

Buddhi and Siddhi When Ganesha and his brother Karthikeya reached marriageable age, both were eager to secure a bride. So a contest was devised whereby the first to encircle the world would be the first one wed. Without a moment's hesitation, Karthikeya leapt upon his sleek blue peacock and raced off into the sky. Meanwhile, his portly brother Ganesha, rather than mounting his little rat and setting out, simply lumbered over to his parents, Shiva and Parvati (**3**), circled round them with folded hands, and insisted they declare him the victor. Perplexed, they asked him to explain. He said, "Is it not written that he who circumambulates his parents gains the merit of traversing the whole wide world?" Charmed by his clever ruse, they married him to the two daughters of Prajapati (**4**) (the creator of the world). Their names were Buddhi ("wisdom") and Siddhi ("fulfillment") and by them Ganesha had two sons, Kshema ("prosperity") and Laabha ("profit").

Asuras and Demons

■ Asuras ("divine"), the demons of the Indian sky, were opposed to the devas, the gods

■ The idea that asuras were demons developed after the Vedic period

■ They churned the ocean of milk to receive the elixir of immortality with the gods, but were cheated out of tasting it

■ In Iran, the opposed groups were reversed: the devas were demons, and the asuras gods

In the Vedas, asura refers to any divine being—including gods like Varuna—and is closely related to Ahura Mazda, a high god in ancient Iran. In later Hindu mythology, the word applied only to the class of demonic beings who continually opposed the gods. As all gods were *devas* or *suras*, meaning "light," the asuras ("not gods") were associated with darkness. Along with *pisacas* ("ghouls"), *rakshasas* ("goblins"), *vetalas* ("vampires"), *bhoots* ("ghosts"), *kinnaras* ("sprites"), *nagas* ("snakes"), and *gandharvas* ("nymphs"), asuras were the supernatural but not divine beings who inhabited the cosmos.

Asuras were not necessarily evil. The ones who became the most dangerous, like Ravana or Hiranyakashipu, did so by praying, meditating, and sacrificing until their piety and righteousness endowed them with power and invulnerability, which corrupted them. The asuras even had their own high priest, Sukra, who had the power to raise the dead and performed sacrifices for the demon king Bali. The main disagreement between the gods and the asuras was over the nectar of immortality.

> **The Yokai:** p. 372

Figures and Stories Relevant to Asuras and Demons

Churning the Ocean, the Asuras Worked With the Gods, see Creation Myths, pp. 288–289

Varuna and Mitra, Known as Asuras in Vedic Times, see pp. 294–295

Vishnu, Fought With the Demons, see pp. 312–313

Goddess fighting against demon. Many myths describe conflicts between the gods and the asuras

Vamana Wins the Universe Bali, one of the leaders of the demons and the king of Mahabalipuram, ruled over the Triloka ("*tree worlds*"). One day he noticed the earth quaking and his offerings being refused. He asked the priest Sukra what was happening, and Sukra replied that the god Vishnu had been born on the earth as a dwarf named Vamana and the world was trembling under his weight. Bali decided to hold a sacrifice and invite Vamana. When Vamana arrived, Bali offered him a gift. Vamana (**2**) asked for the land he could cover in three steps. Bali agreed and Vamana changed into the cosmic form of Vishnu. He covered the earth and heavens in two steps, winning them back. Not taking the third step, he left Bali the underworld.

Hiranyakashipu and Narasimhan A demon king named Hiranyakashipu had a son named Prahlada, who was a devotee of Vishnu, and would not worship his father. Enraged, the king imprisoned his son.

Prahlada prayed to Vishnu for help, but his father had been granted the boon that he could not be killed by any weapon, not by day or by night, not indoors or outdoors, by neither god, man, nor animal. Vishnu devised a plan to get around the demon's invulnerabilities by taking the form of Narasimhan the man-lion. Vishnu killed Hiranyakashipu (**3**) with his bare hands at dusk in the doorway of a building.

■ Brahma is the creator god of the Hindu pantheon

■ He is part of the Hindu trinity (trimurti) with Vishnu and Shiva

■ He was born from a golden egg (or a lotus flower), created the universe, and gave life to all living things

■ He was associated with the color red and rode on a swan

■ He is depicted with four heads and four arms, which held a scepter (or spoon), a string of beads (or his bow Parivita), a jug of water, and the Vedas

Brahma

As the highest Hindu deity, Brahma was a creator god who formed the material world from the *Brahman,* the divine ground of the universe. He is often identified with the Vedic creator god Prajapati. According to the *Puranas,* a collection of narratives about Hindu gods and heroes, he sired people, gods, demons, and all living things with his daughter Satarupa. When Satarupa ran away, Brahma was paired with the goddess of luck and wisdom, Saraswati. However, in some traditions, Saraswati is also said to be Satarupa. With the sky goddess Aditi, Brahma had his son Daksha, who was the father of Parvati and the father-in-law of Shiva.

Brahma is always depicted with multiple heads, which he grew to watch Satarupa. While he is given an important role as creator, he is seldom worshiped directly. There are only two temples in all of India dedicated to him alone. By making Brahma appear weak, the other two gods of the Hindu trimurti Shiva and Vishnu, were empowered, such as through the myth that Brahma was born from a lotus flower that grew from Vishnu's navel.

The Trimurti

The trimurti, sometimes called the Hindu trinity, refers to the unity of the gods Brahma, Vishnu, and Shiva as the creator, preserver, and destroyer of the universe, respectively. As a matter of course, conceptions of the trimurti vary according to sect, with Vaishnavas exalting Vishnu above the other two and Shaivas holding Shiva to be the highest. While there has never been a Brahma sect to speak of, Brahma plays a role in Buddhism and Jainism. The most well-known depiction of the trimurti is a 20-foot sculpture found in the caves of the island of Elephanta just off the coast of Mumbai.

>> **Triads of Gods:** pp. 206, 264

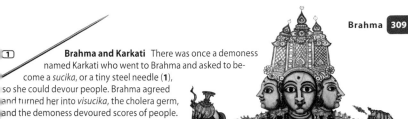

Brahma and Karkati There was once a demoness named Karkati who went to Brahma and asked to become a *sucika*, or a tiny steel needle (**1**), so she could devour people. Brahma agreed and turned her into *visucika*, the cholera germ, and the demoness devoured scores of people. Later, she began to tire of death and meditated until she had attained wisdom. With her newfound enlightenment, Karkati resumed her demonic form and went to a king in the Himalaya where, after answering all the king's questions about the nature of the universe, she was given the job of destroying all the evildoers in the kingdom.

Brahma's Five Heads Originally, Brahma (**2**) had just one head. Before creating the universe, he was lonely and created a feminine form from his body, whom he named Satarupa. Brahma was in love with his daughter and could not take his eyes off of her. Wanting to watch her at all times, Brahma grew five heads, one looking in each direction and one looking upward. Shiva helped Satarupa escape by cutting off one of Brahma's heads. That Brahma was cursed for his improper relationship with his daughter is one of the reasons given for his lack of worship.

Why Brahma Has No Temples One day Brahma and Vishnu went to the Himalaya, the home of Shiva. Along the way, they began to argue about which one of them was the supreme lord of the universe. Suddenly, a giant *lingam* (**3**) ("phallus") of fire appeared in their path. Unable to find its top or bottom, the gods realized that the lingam was Shiva and chanted his name. At this, Shiva appeared as himself and offered each god a wish. Vishnu asked to be Shiva's servant, and Shiva agreed. But when Brahma asked for Shiva to be born as his son, Shiva became angry and cursed Brahma to never be worshiped in temples.

Figures and Stories Relevant to Brahma

Creation Myths, Brahma as Creator God, see pp. 280–281

Saraswati, Brahma's Consort, see pp. 298–299

Shiva, Part of the Trimurti, see pp. 320–321

Vishnu, Part of the Trimurti, see pp. 312–313

The Buddha

Although very little is known about the historical founder of Buddhism, many myths have been developed around his life. The Buddha was a prince named Siddhartha Gautama born into a powerful royal clan of the Shakyas around the fourth or fifth century B.C. Because his father wanted his son to be a king and not a spiritual leader, he kept the boy shut up in the palace away from the outside world. One night, the prince had been carousing and enjoying his harem when he looked around and thought that there must be more to life than chasing pleasure. He snuck out of the palace, where he encountered for the first time an old man, a sick man, a corpse, and a holy man. He decided to find a way out of the cyclic suffering of life. After trying out a few extreme forms of asceticism, he discovered the "middle way" to liberation by rejecting both self-denial and self-indulgence while meditating under a fig tree, which today is known as a Bodhi tree (tree of consciousness). Following his realization, Siddhartha was called the Buddha, the Awakened One, and began to gain followers.

- Vishnu was originally a Vedic sun god

- As part of the trimurti, with Shiva and Brahma, he was perserver of the universe

- He assumed avatars in order to protect the world

- In his four hands he held a conch, a *chakra* (wheel), a club, and a lotus

- His sacred mount was a bird named Garuda

- His followers, the Vaishnavas, form the largest sect in Hinduism

Vishnu

In the Vedas, Vishnu appears as the sun god who walked across the universe in three steps, which symbolized sunrise, noon, and sunset. He later grew more important as one of the three gods that make up the trimurti, along with Brahma and Shiva. While Shiva was the destroyer, Vishnu was the preserver, and

Vishnu's weapon was the Sudarsanacakra

thus was responsible for maintaining cosmic order in the universe. He often accomplished this by assuming various avatars, human or animal incarnations. Vishnu was also regarded as a creator god who dreamt of the universe while reclining on the great snake Ananta Sesha.

Together with his wife Sri-Lakshmi, Vishnu dwelt in the heavenly city of Vaikuntha, which was composed of gold and jewels, and contained giant pools of red and white lotuses. Vishnu's mount was Garuda, a giant half-man, half-bird who was the enemy of all snakes. Once he defeated Indra in a fight over the nectar of immortality.

Battle Against the Demon Hiranyaksha Once a massive, powerful demon named Hiranyaksha dragged the earth down to the bottom of the sea and held it there. As the gods were unable to stop him, they asked Vishnu for help. Vishnu assumed the shape of a great boar and dove to the bottom of the sea where he took on Hiranyaksha. The battle between them (**1**) lasted for a thousand years before Vishnu finally overcame his enemy. Vishnu brought the earth back to the surface on his tusk.

Supporting the Mountain

When the gods and the demons set out to churn the ocean of milk to produce the nectar of immortality, they decided to use the holy mountain Meru as a giant churning rod and the tail of the snake Vasuki as a churning rope. However, they needed something on which to balance the mountain, so the gods asked Vishnu for help. Vishnu took the form of a tortoise (**2**) and dove under the mountain to support it with the shell on his back. The gods successfully churned the ocean and gained immortality.

The Ten Avatars of Vishnu

Vishnu is usually said to have ten avatars (human or animal incarnations on earth). The animal incarnations are Matsya the fish (**3**), who saves Manu from the flood; Kurma the tortoise, who helps to churn the ocean of milk; and Varaha the boar that rescues the Vedas from the bottom of the ocean. The avatars who are neither animal nor human are Narasimha, the man-lion who saves Prahlada from his demonic father Hiranyakashipu, and Vamana, the dwarf who wins back the earth from the demon Bali. His human avatars are Parashurama, the Brahmin warrior who wipes out all the *kshatriya*, a noble warrior class, on the earth 21 times over; Rama, prince of Ayodhya; Krishna, the focus of many bhakti cults; the Buddha; and Kalki, who will come as savior at the end of the cosmic age.

End of the World

According to the Hindu tradition, the present dark age will come to an end when barbarians overthrow the four-tier hierarchy of priests, kings, producers, and servants. They will persecute women, children, and cows. Hypocrisy and unrighteousness will be the dominant characteristics of those in power. No one will read the Vedas, perform rituals, or respect Brahmins. *Mlecchas*, those who do not know the sacred language of Sanskrit, will rule over India and the lifespan will decrease to 23 years. Cities will collapse and people will live in the woods, wearing bark and eating from the ground. In this era of decay, a Brahmin named Kalki will be born. He will be the tenth avatar of Vishnu. Riding on a white horse (**4**), he will restore order in a final battle, bringing the end to the dark age and ushering in a new golden age.

≫ **End of the World:** p. 238

Rama

■ Rama was the seventh avatar of Vishnu and the prince of Ayodhya

■ His heroic life is described in the Indian epic, the *Ramayana*

■ He was married to the princess Sita

■ Rama and Sita symbolize loyalty in marriage and monogamy

■ Rama carried a bow and arrow, and is often shown with his wife Sita, Lakamana, and Hanuman

Rama, the hero of the epic *Ramayana,* is considered the seventh avatar of the god Vishnu and a symbol of chivalry and virtue in the Indian tradition. He was the son of Dasarattha, the king of Ayodhya, and Kausalya. After winning a competition for her hand, Rama married the princess Sita. Years later, he was exiled for 14 years over an intrigue. Although innocent, he accepted his fate and went to the forest. One day Sita, who had followed Rama into exile, was kidnapped by the demon Ravana. Accompanied by Hanuman and his monkey army, Rama defeated Ravana and liberated Sita.

They ruled happily over Ayodhya. However, Rama expelled Sita for being alone in another man's (Ravana's) house. While in exile, Sita gave birth to twins, Lava and Kusha. Chancing upon his sons one day in the forest, Rama took his family to live with him in Ayodhya until they ascended to the sky (**1**).

▶▶ **Heroes Fighting Against Monsters:** pp. 27, 181, 165, 251, 361

Rama Fights the Demons

When Rama was still a boy in his father's kingdom, the sage Vishvamitra visited the court. The sage asked Rama's father Dasaratha to send the boy to his hermitage, Sidhasrama, to drive out the monster Thataka who was troubling him there. Although he could not see how the boy could help, the king sent Rama out with the sage.

With his brother Lakshmana (**2**), Rama followed Vishvamitra back to Sidhasrama. After Rama killed Thataka with his spear, he and Vishvamitra performed a sacrifice. However, Thataka's sons, Mareecha and Subahu, attacked to avenge their mother's death. Rama killed them with his arrows. With Thataka and her sons dead, Vishvamitra's hermitage was peaceful again.

Rama Marries Sita

When King Janaka's beautiful daughter Sita was ready to marry, a contest was held to find a groom. Whoever could string the magical bow of Shiva would win Sita's hand. Suitor after suitor tried to string the bow, but no one could even bend it. Finally Rama, who had heard of Sita's beauty, took hold of the bow and it shattered in his powerful grip. At this, Sita married Rama in an elaborate royal wedding (**3**).

Figures and Stories Relevant to Rama

Asuras and Demons, Rama Battled Against Demons, see pp. 306–307

Battle of Rama and Ravana, Scene From the *Ramayana*, see pp. 316–317

Lakshmi, Lakshmi as Rama's Consort Sita, see Lakshmi and Saraswati, pp. 298–299

Vishnu, Rama as an Avatar of Vishnu, see pp. 312–313

Rama's War Against Ravana

One day while living in the forest, Sita was captured by Ravana, the ten-headed demon ruler of Lanka, who had fallen in love with the princess after hearing about her beauty. In order to recover her, Rama made an alliance with the monkey king Sugriva, who sent his councillor Hanuman (**4**) and his army to accompany Rama to Lanka. In order to help Rama and his monkey army to invade Lanka, Hanuman had to construct a bridge across the ocean. When they reached Ravana's palace, the army defeated his demonic forces and Rama challenged the demon king to single combat in order to reclaim Sita.

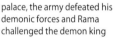

Battle of Rama and Ravana

In an attempt to win back his wife, Sita, Rama went to war against the demon Ravana, who had stolen her. Meeting in battle, Ravana sounded his conch and shot a volley of arrows at Rama. When Rama avoided his shafts and sent forth arrows of his own, Ravana took to the sky and began shooting arrows and magical weapons down on Rama's men. Rama countered all of his attacks and began to shoot off Ravana's limbs. Each time one of his limbs was cut off, it grew back, but after a while Ravana fell down stunned.

Rama withdrew until his foe got up, then resumed his attack. Finally, Rama used his most powerful spell—the Brahma weapon—to kill Ravana, whose soul, because he had once been a great hero, rose up to heaven.

- Krishna, meaning "blue-black," is the eighth avatar of Vishnu

- He is one of the most popular of the Hindu gods

- His dialogue with Arjuna about the main teachings of Hinduism constitutes the *Bhagavad Gita*

- He is depicted as a philosophical prince, or a young cowherd playing a flute

- He was often portrayed with blue-black skin, wearing a crown of peacock feathers and a yellow loincloth; he also appeared as a crawling or dancing child

Krishna

The focus of numerous cults, Krishna is possibly the most popular god in Hinduism. He is an incarnation or avatar of the god Vishnu, but has come to be regarded as a high god in his own right.

Krishna had no specific mount, thus he is seen on various animals

According to the *Mahabharata*, Krishna was a prince in the Yadava clan. After barely escaping being killed by his uncle Kamsa, he was raised by a cowherd couple named Nanda and Yashoda. One day, when Yashoda caught the boy eating dirt, she demanded that he open his mouth. When he did, she saw the entire universe inside and knew his true nature. Krishna's adolescence consisted of youthful pranks and erotic interludes with the *gopi* girls, of which his favorite was Radha. Later, Krishna allied with the Pandavas brothers in the war with the Kauravas. As the chariot driver of one brother, Arjuna, Krishna taught him about cosmic order and wisdom. His teachings, described in the *Bhagavad Gita,* are seen as the most important texts of Hinduism.

Krishna Kills Aghasura

Frightened by a prophecy that Krishna would kill him, Krishna's uncle, Kamsa, tried to kill him. He sent a demon called Aghasura to devour Krishna. Seeing him playing with his friends near the river, Aghasura took the form of a giant serpent and opened his mouth wide. Thinking it was a cave, Krishna and his friends wandered in (**1**) and Aghasura shut his jaws. To escape, Krishna made his body expand until he burst open the demon's stomach.

Krishna and Radha Radha (**2**, with Krishna) became important in Krishna's mythology when she was introduced as his chief consort in the poet Jayadeva's 12th-century *Gitagovinda* ("song of the lord"). Among all of the gopi girls, Radha was Krishna's favorite. Because Radha was married to another man, her relationship with Krishna could not be consummated, making Radha's longing for her lover parallel a Krishna devotee's longing to meet with the god.

2

Krishna and Radha's love was marked by playful fighting and jealous quarrels that had to be mended through the intervention of one of Radha's *sahelis* ("girlfriends"). As the incarnation of Vishnu and Lakshmi, the couple symbolized sexual love and fertility. Sometimes Radha is regarded as an aspect of Krishna's feminine energy. Among the members of the Gaudiya Vaishnava sect, the 16th-century saint Chaitanya is seen as the incarnation of Radha and Krishna fused together in one body.

Figures and Stories Relevant to Krishna

Asuras and Demons, Krishna Battled Against Demons, see pp. 306–307

Holy Animals, Cows as Sacred in Connection With Krishna Gopala, see pp. 322–323

The *Mahabharata*, the *Bhagavad Gita*, pp. 296–297

Vishnu, Krishna as an Avatar of Vishnu, see pp. 312–313

The Rasalila One night, Krishna began to sing under the moon, causing all the women of the village to leave their homes and join him. Yet, when they reached the spot where Krishna had been, he was gone. As they called for him on the banks of the Yamuna River, Krishna reappeared and multiplied himself so that he could dance with all the women at once in a ritual dance (**3**, the rasalila) that lasted all night.

The Holi Festival

Holi, the Festival of Colors, is held in the spring throughout India. Its main feature is the throwing of colors, in which revelers cover each other in brightly dyed powders and water. In Vrindavan, Krishna's boyhood home, and Mathura, the city of his birth, Holi is a major celebration revolving around events in the courtship of Radha and Krishna and involves mock battles between men and women.

■ In the trimurti, Shiva is the destroyer, but elsewhere he is also associated with regeneration

■ He was the patron of Yogis and Brahmins, as well as the protector of the Vedas

■ He appears as a lingam when he represents a reproductive force

■ He is shown with a third eye and several arms, which carry a trident, while riding a white bull

■ His followers, the Shaivas, form one of the three largest denominations in Hinduism

Shiva

Alongside Vishnu, Shiva is one of the two main Hindu gods. In the trimurti, he is the destroyer, a role which, along with his fame as a great hunter, stems from his Vedic predecessor, Rudra. Originally a moon deity, Shiva exhibits female aspects. In later mythology, he possesses a dual nature that is erotic and ascetic; benevolent and terrifying; creative and destructive.

Shiva's wife was Parvati (**1**, coming out to meet Shiva) and he had two sons, the elephant-headed Ganesha and Skanda or Karttikeya, a war god.

Parvati, Shiva's consort, has multiple manifestations

Often depicted on his mount, a bull named Nandi, Shiva wears a cobra instead of a sacred Brahmin thread and dresses in a tiger's or elephant's skin.

In the form of Nataraja ("cosmic dancer"), the inflamed Shiva dances upon the body of the dwarf Apasmara, who represents the ignorance that destroys the world. As Shiva dances, cosmic order resumes; when his dance is over, the world and the cosmic order collapse.

Destruction of Daksha's Sacrifice

When Parvati, daughter of the sage Daksha, married Shiva, her father was displeased by his new son-in-law's strange appearance and disapproved of the marriage. When Daksha held a sacrifice and invited all the gods, he snubbed Shiva by refusing to include him. Parvati learned of her father's disrespect, and went to the sacrifice to confront him. When she arrived, Parvati threw herself into the sacrificial fire and burned to ashes. Hearing this, Shiva became enraged and made two demons from his matted locks. The demons attacked Daksha's sacrifice, burning down the enclosure and beheading Daksha. While the demons raged out of control, the gods begged Shiva to recall them. His anger spent, he complied and replaced Daksha's head with that of a goat (**2**).

The Lingam

After Parvati's death, a grief-stricken Shiva went to the Daru forest. There he met the great sages who lived there with their wives. The sages mistrusted Shiva and when their wives began to lust after the newcomer, they were enraged and cursed Shiva's phallus to fall off. When his phallus hit the earth, it began to quake. The sages were afraid and begged Shiva for his pardon. Forgiving them, Shiva told them to worship his phallus in the form of the lingam (**3**), and he would bestow his grace on them. In temples and shrines, Shiva is worshiped in the form of a lingam that stands on a bowl, called a *yoni*, which symbolizes the vagina. The lingam and yoni are washed and doused with melted butter and other essences to maintain the cosmic unification of male and female. Scholars believe that the cult of the lingam has existed in India since antiquity.

Shiva Beheads Brahma

With the emergence of Vaishnavism and Shaivaism (followers of Vishnu and Shiva, respectively) as the main Hindu sects during the Middle Ages, there was a tendency to ignore the role of Brahma as creator. Some myths name Shiva or Vishnu as the main creator god, depicting Brahma as a "lesser god" who always needs help from more powerful gods. In one such myth, Brahma and Shiva started arguing one day over which of them was greater. Becoming very angry, Shiva cut off one of Brahma's heads with the tip of his pinky nail. When the head fell off, it stuck to Shiva's hand. The Brahmahatya, a fanged, howling demoness surrounded by flames who haunted all those who commit the sin of Brahmin-murder, appeared beside him. With the skull stuck to his hand and the Brahmahatya following him wherever he went, Shiva took on the fearsome form called Kalabhairava (**4**). He set out to wander the earth until he came to the holy city of Varanasi, where his sin was absolved.

Holy Animals

■ A central theme of Hinduism is respect for all life

■ Cows are highly revered in Hinduism; Krishna, also known as Govinda, meaning "one who brings satisfaction to the cows," was a cowherder as a child

■ Many Hindus are vegetarian, but animal sacrifice was part of ancient Vedic ritual practice

■ The gods' mounts had their own symbolic meanings, e.g., Garuda flying is the symbol of the human soul as it rises to heaven

A number of animals are held sacred in Hinduism. The sacredness of cows in India, for example, can be traced to the ancient cow cult of Aryans. The worship of cattle is also connected to the cowherd Krishna, and to Shiva in his role as Pashupati, the lord of beasts. Cattle also hold a special place as the providers of the milk used to make clarified butter for sacrifice and the dung that is used as fuel.

Other important animals and mythological creatures are the mounts of the gods which are not honored in an active cult. These include Vishnu's bird Garuda, Shiva's bull Nandi, Ganesha's rat, Brahma's swan, Indra's elephant, and Durga's tiger. One form of Shiva even rides a dog, usually considered an extremely unclean animal. Monkeys also have a special importance in India because of their connection to the popular monkey god Hanuman.

While orthodox Vishnu worshipers tend to avoid killing animals and practice vegetarianism, the ancient Vedic culture practiced ritual killing, most notably in the famous *ashvamedha*, or horse sacrifice. Modern goddess worshipers still make animal offerings to wild goddesses like Kali.

Figures and Stories Relevant to Holy Animals

Nandi and Shiva When Surabhi, the mother of all cows, began to give birth to legions of snow-white cattle, the milk that came from their udders was so copious that it flowed like a river into Shiva's dwelling, disturbing his meditation. Angry, Shiva opened his third eye and shot fire at the cows, turning their white hides black and brown. The cows were afraid and appealed to the gods for help. To pacify Shiva, the gods presented him with

the great bull Nandi (**1**), the son of Surabhi and Kasyapa, as his mount. Nandi's figurines are found at all Shiva temples as the protector of all animals.

①

» Animals in Myth: pp. 104, 230, 424

②

Garuda and the Snakes

The bird Garuda, Vishnu's mount, had a natural enmity with snakes (**2**, battle between Garuda and the snakes). When he was given permission by Indra to hunt them, the snakes proposed to hold a snake sacrifice to offer Garuda victims on a regular basis. Refusing to go along with it, the snake demon Kaliya challenged Garuda to a battle in the Yamuna River. As the two fought, Garuda splashed water on a sage, who cursed Garuda to die if he ever returned, making the river a safe haven for snakes.

Surabhi's Birth

Surabhi (**3**), worshiped as Kamadhenu ("the wishing cow"), was a celestial animal that had the power to grant her owner anything he desired. Believed to protect humanity from hunger and thirst, Surabhi also guaranteed wealth. There are two stories of her birth. In one, she rose from the ocean of milk while the gods and the demons were churning it to obtain the nectar of immortality. In another, the god Brahma drank too much of the nectar and became sick, vomiting out the celestial cow. Surabhi immediately began to give milk, which collected into the ocean of milk, on the shores of which lived the sages called the Phenapas, who survived by eating sea foam. Surabhi's four daughters, Saurabhi, Hamsika, Subhadra, and Dhenu, serve as guardians of the four directions.

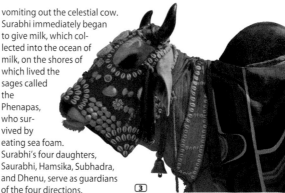

③

Chinese Mythology

In Chinese mythology, dragons are divine and bring good luck

Chinese Mythology

With a history spanning some 6,000 years, China—
along with ancient Egypt, India, and Mesopotamia—
represents one of humanity's earliest high cultures. Like the
others, it gave rise to a rich mythology that served the function of helping to
explain the world. The earliest Chinese myths were passed on orally. Later,
during the classical period around 500 B.C., they were written down in diverse
and sometimes contradictory versions. In 213 B.C., many of these texts were
burned on the order of Emperor Qin Shi Huangdi, who commanded the
destruction of all writings that did not address historical, medical, or
agricultural topics. This order was not rescinded until 191 B.C., and people
then attempted to re-create the lost texts.

In contrast to the mythological systems of other peoples, the traditional
Chinese gods were not viewed as having participated in the creation of the
world. Instead, the universe and the first human, P'an ku, arose from a dark
and formless material through a long process of evolution without the intervention of supernatural forces. The world was seen as being governed by the
principle of yin and yang (**1**): perfect and inseparable pairs of opposites.

According to this tradi-
tion, yin, the feminine
quality, gives form to all
things, while the mascu-
line quality of yang fills
them with spirit.

The earth was con-
ceived as a square
floating in an endless
ocean. It was composed
of five basic elements:

water, fire, metal, earth, and wood. At the center of this world lay China, the "Middle Kingdom" (**2**, the Forbidden City), which was ruled by gods. These gods created China's inhabitants and taught them arts and skills. The first heavenly rulers also provided their subjects with technologies essential to life. Each invention—such as cooking, writing, medicine, the wheel, the fishing net and the plow—was credited to a specific deity. In Chinese mythology, the country's early history is described as a golden age in which people lived in harmony with the gods and each other.

Each of the numerous Chinese deities was assigned a particular area of responsibility: mountains, thunder, drought, fire, rivers, heaven, justice, good fortune, war (**3**, the terracotta army), cooking, the sea, compassion, the moon, wealth, rain, the sun, the stars, water, wind, the taming of monsters, and so forth. The god of heaven was the highest and most powerful deity, ruling over all living things. Evil spirits, monsters, and intelligent animals, such as the phoenix and unicorn, also populate the world of Chinese mythology; elegant dragons flew over the breathtakingly beautiful landscapes of holy mountains.

3

However, although the gods expended great efforts to organize life on earth, it remained vulnerable and incomplete. Whenever yin and yang fell out of balance, natural catastrophes like floods and droughts plagued the people. During these critical times, heroes appeared in the Middle Kingdom, and carried out glorious deeds to save the world from destruction.

Yet human beings also bore their own responsibilities and had to justify their actions. Chinese mythology also includes the concepts of heaven and hell. Paradise was said to occupy an island in the China Sea, where the souls of the righteous dwelt and the gods lived in golden palaces. There, people feasted on the most exquisite rice and drank the finest wines. Illness, pain, and cold were unknown. The traditional Chinese idea of hell was based on Taoist and Buddhist concepts of the next world. According to them, Yanluo Wang, ruler of the underworld, supervised ten subterranean judgment chambers, each with 18 levels. Each chamber focused on a particular variety of sin, which was cruelly punished: sinners were beheaded, hacked into pieces, ground into dust, burned, boiled in oil, and so forth. The Yamas, gods who judged the dead, oversaw these punishments. However, if sinners honestly regretted their evil deeds, they were granted mercy. They could drink the elixir of forgetfulness and be reborn in the world as animals or as poor, sick human beings. Only the worst criminals were refused the right to reincarnation.

China's three great religions—Confucianism, Taoism, and Buddhism—have all engaged themselves with traditional Chinese mythology. The pragmatically oriented Confucian philosophy gave the myths rational interpretations, embedding them in a historical context. Thus, many gods and heroes became imaginary figures of Chinese history, losing their divine auras. Appearing in the guise of emperors and officials, they were honored as models of ideal rulers. For instance, ancient Chinese divinities, such as the sun goddess Xi He and the moon goddess Chang Xi, were transformed into government officials and even changed from female to male. Taoism, on the other hand, stylized genuine historical figures into divinities. The biographies of great leaders were embellished with accounts of their magical powers and mystical transformations. The Taoist pantheon also included some beloved figures from the mythical world who gained new recognition as "immortals" (**4**, Taoist immortal). The heroes of both Taoist and Buddhist mythologies possessed human physical attributes and character traits. They lived among human beings in the world of everyday concerns.

Mythological concepts also influenced China's technological development. Searching for the elixir of immortality—supposedly to be found in a mysterious faraway land of the West—Chinese seafarers constructed a magnetic compass in the fourth century B.C. In the sixth century A.D., paper money replaced the copper coins that people had previously sent with the dead to help them pay for their passage into the next world. Even today, on the traditional holiday of Qingming (**5**), the Chinese burn symbolic offerings of joss paper money at the graves of their ancestors. To ward off evil spirits in the sky, the Chinese invented gunpowder and fireworks in the ninth century.

Creation Myths

According to Chinese mythology, the world is the product of a long evolution. The universe created itself without the assistance of supernatural powers; thus, there was no specific creator. Instead, Taoism is based on the creation of the *Tao* (the "way"), which serves both as a kind of cosmological law and the highest reality.

At the beginning, the initial state of chaos divided itself between the first two original, natural elements: the opposites, yin and yang. These elements became the source for the birth of the material world and all living beings, as well as for the power of creation.

First, chaos shaped itself into a huge egg, which gave birth to P'an ku, the first person. He became the master builder of the universe. After he died, parts of his body became various features of the world, such as mountains, rivers, and plants.

The wisdom of the ancient Chinese people is revealed by the fact that their mythology refers to an important cosmic concept—the expansion of the universe.

■ According to Chinese mythology, chaos formed the original state of the universe

■ In Chinese philosophy, the Tao is the foundation of the world

■ The complete opposites yin and yang were formed from chaos

■ The world's first living being was P'an ku, the ancestral father of humanity

■ He emerged from the cosmic egg and in doing so created heaven and earth

■ His body gave rise to natural phenomena, such as mountains and clouds

■ He is often shown swinging an enormous axe

The Middle Kingdom

The Chinese call their country Zhong-guo (right), which translates as the "Middle Kingdom." This term was first used in 600 B.C. and reflects the worldview of the ancient Chinese people. Based on this notion, China lies at the center of a world surrounded by a boundless ocean. This idea was not exclusively Chinese, as the Romans and the Egyptians also believed that they lived at the center of the world. The name China, as used in European-based languages, comes from the word Qin, which refers to the first Chinese empire established by the emperor Qin Shihuangdii in 221 B.C.

▷▷ **Creation Through a Cosmic Egg:** pp. 87, 289, 439, 457 | **Creation Through a Body:** pp. 20, 27, 229, 288, 380

P'an ku and the Egg Formed From Chaos

At the beginning of time, a murky chaos was found everywhere. One day, an enormous egg arose from the

The Separation of Heaven and Earth

After P'an ku hatched from the egg, he stood between heaven (yin) and earth (yang) and held them apart (**2**). Every day both the sky and the earth grew ten feet larger. But P'an ku was growing too. After

dark, shapeless original mass. Then, after 18,000 years, the inseparable opposites, the feminine yin and the masculine yang, came into balance within the cosmic egg. This balance gave rise to the world's first human being, P'an ku. He was the first person, an ancestor to all of humanity. It is said that after waking from a long sleep, he picked up an axe and, with great effort, freed himself from the egg (**1**). As he broke through the egg, a light, clear substance streamed out of the shell and floated upward, where it transformed itself into the sky. Another substance fell downward, where it solidified to become the earth.

18,000 years he was 90,000 *Li* (36 miles) tall. When he died, his last breath became the wind and the clouds. The sun emerged from his left eye and the moon from his right. The stars were formed from his hair. His body formed five moun-

Figures and Stories Relevant to Creation Myths

The Three Sovereigns, P'an ku's Successors, pp. 334–335

Yin and Yang, Basic Principles of the World, pp. 332–333

tains, which became the sacred mountains of China (**3**). His muscles became fields, as rivers were formed from his blood, and his veins became roads. His skin transformed into flowers and trees, and his bones into jade and pearls.

Yin and Yang

A central element of Chinese thought is the dual principle of yin and yang (**3**). All things and processes in the universe have two aspects that contradict each other, but each can only exist as one pole of an opposition: feminine-masculine, warm-cold, above-below, beginning-end, space-time, light-darkness, east-west, etc. Their dynamic interplay is responsible for the changing movements throughout human history.

Although neither of the opposing poles is morally superior to the other, various philosophical currents have often emphasized one or the other: for example, Taoists favored the soft yin, while Confucianists preferred the masculine, hard yang. The idea that these opposites exist in balance and that change should be accepted was formulated for the first time in the *I Ching* ("Book of Changes").

Masculine-Feminine The masculine yang is white, while the feminine yin is black. However, both yin and yang have a piece of each other at their cores (**1**). The two powers both attract and complement each other. It is this very relationship that make partnership, love, and equality possible.

Fire-Water As fire, yang represents creativity. Yin, as water, evokes transformation. Both original elements (**4**) continually displace each other. During a snowy winter, water dominates and fire dies out. In the spring, water becomes weaker and fire is reborn. In a hot summer, water dies out and fire triumphs. In autumn, water comes to life again and fire fades away.

Sun-Moon Yin is the moon, which embodies weakness. Yang is the sun, which stands for strength. During an eclipse of the sun, these two celestial bodies work together as partners. Neither the feminine, passive energy nor the masculine, active energy of the yang sun dominate the sky at this moment. While the contrast between the sun and the moon is clear, both are found in complete balance (**2**).

▶▶ **Universal Principles:** pp. 102, 295, 384, 430

- The three sovereigns were Fuxi, Nüwa, and Shennong

- Fuxi was the heavenly sovereign and Nüwa was his sister and wife

- They are most often illustrated with human heads and snake bodies

- Fuxi held a panel, a symbol of the earth, while Nüwa's compass symbolized the heavens

- Shennong was the god of agriculture; he also invented the plow and tea

The Three Sovereigns

The first gods were born of yin and yang, and their children were Fuxi, Nüwa, and Shennong. These three sovereigns were given a mission to re-create the world, which

Fuxi taught the first people how to hunt and fish with nets

was in a state of disarray following the death of P'an ku, the first man. They put a great deal of energy into their work. By introducing the arts and useful inventions to the people, as well as teaching them lessons to improve their standards of living, the sovereigns became the founders of Chinese culture. The era of their reigns was heralded as the golden age.

The first sovereign was Fuxi, the heavenly sovereign, and first ancestor of 100 emperors. His marriage to his sister, Nüwa, balanced yin and yang. The third sovereign, Shennong, ruled over the earth and agriculture as the earthly sovereign. Together, the sovereigns were known as the "three august ones."

The Fuxi Temple

Fuxi, the heavenly sovereign and first mythical emperor, was supposedly born in Chengli (known today as Tianshui) in the Gansu province. Therefore his birthplace is known as the cradle of Chinese civilization. In Tianshui, there is a Taoist temple dedicated to Fuxi. The temple was built during the Ming dynasty in 1490 and remodeled in 1597. Fuxi's mausoleum is located in Zhoukou in the Henan province.

Nüwa Creates Animals and People

Nüwa created all domestic animals in six days. On the seventh day, she sculpted the first people out of yellow clay. However, after the goddess had created a hundred people, she grew tired. She took a long, climbing plant, dipped it into the clay, and shook it vigorously (1). As the lumps of clay fell to the ground, they came to life. In this way she created two types of people. The people that Nüwa had sculpted with her hands had strong characters and led successful lives. However, the people created from the lumps of clay were weak and vulnerable. Later, the goddess saved the world and all of her creations from destruction. Upset that he lost his claim to the throne of heaven, the evil water god Gong-gong shook the pillars of heaven, which created a flood that threatened to wipe out all of creation. Nüwa stopped the flood by cutting off the legs of an enormous turtle and using them to support the sky.

Shennong, the Farmer God

Shennong (2) ruled for 120 years. He invented the plow and taught people how to farm. Because this agricultural god discovered tea and 100 medicinal herbs, he is known also as the founder of traditional Chinese medicine. Together with Fuxi he built the *guqin*, a musical instrument similar to the zither used by scholars, poets, and philosophers. Both Chinese and Vietnamese people honor Shennong as their ancestor.

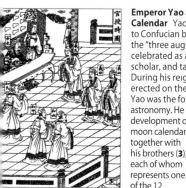

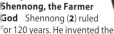

Emperor Yao and the First Calendar

Yao, who, according to Confucian belief, was one of the "three august ones," was celebrated as a philosopher, scholar, and tamer of floods. During his reign, dams were erected on the Yellow River. Yao was the founder of Chinese astronomy. He inspired the development of the moon calendar together with his brothers (3), each of whom represents one of the 12 astrological signs. The calendar (4) helped farmers determine sowing and harvest times.

Figures and Stories Relevant to the Three Sovereigns

P'an ku, First Ancestor of the Sovereigns, see pp. 330–331

Xi He, Her Sons Threatened Emperor Yao's Empire, see pp. 338–339

Yellow Emperor, Another Mythical Sovereign, see pp. 336–337

Teachers of Agriculture: pp. 24, 130 | Great Floods: pp. 28, 32, 335, 401, 411, 445

Yellow Emperor

■ Huangdi, the yellow emperor, was one of the mythical sovereigns of ancient China

■ In Taoism, Huangdi is known as the god of war

■ He invented acupuncture, musical instruments, the compass, and the chariot

The Immortal Huangdi When he was a hundred years old, Huangdi prepared himself to die. As the clock struck his final hour, a dragon appeared and flew him to the heavenly realm of the immortals.

Huangdi, the "yellow emperor," was one of the mythical sovereigns and cultural founders of China. He was credited with numerous inventions and achievements, primarily in the area of medicine. He was credited as having written the *Huangdi Neijing*, the oldest written text on traditional Chinese medicine. He was also often associated with music and with individual instruments. Chinese music was born on the day that Ling Lun, the Chinese god of music, gave the yellow emperor a flute that imitated bird songs. During the Zhou dynasty, the first attempt to date his reign placed it during the third millenium B.C. Like the Zhou, other dynasties traced their ancestry back to Huangdi. Ying Zheng, who was credited with unifying the Chinese Empire, later assumed the title Qin Shihuangdi: the first exalted emperor of Qin.

Huangdi is especially honored by Taoists, who elevated him to the status of an immortal emperor and god of war during the Han dynasty.

Huangdi—God of War According to legend, Huangdi was the protector god of a certain clan, whose totem animal was a bear. This clan was at war with the neighboring clan of the sorcerer Chi You. Huangdi called upon eight other clans to fight this enemy as a common army (**2**). The fighting lasted for days and days. Finally, Chi You breathed a cloud of fog over the battlefield. This emergency prompted Huangdi to invent the compass (**3**). With one attached to each of the warriors' chariots, the combatants were

able to find their way out of the fog. As a result, they were able to defeat their enemy. In the end, the nine allied clans united to become the Chinese people.

Figures and Stories Relevant to the Yellow Emperor

Huangdi—Scholar and Inventor In the *Huangdi Neijing*, which was written as a

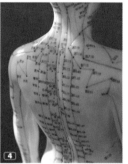

dialogue between the yellow emperor and his ministers, acupuncture plays an important role. Among other things, Huangdi describes the acupuncture points (**4**) and their medical applications. The emperor also invented a two-wheeled chariot with a differential gear, a breakthrough for the period. In the Qin Shihuangdi burial mound near Xian, 89 chariots were found, along with the terracotta army.

The Invention of Silk

Even today, silk is still closely connected with Chinese culture. In ancient times, the material held great economic significance. For this reason, the method of its manufacture was kept strictly secret. It is no surprise that mythological origins were ascribed to this art. Chin His Ling Shih, the wife of the yellow emperor, is supposed to have been the one who introduced the rearing of silkworms and invented the loom.

Divine Rulers: pp. 48, 84, 201, 220, 368

Sun and Moon Deities

■ The moon goddess Chang Xi and the sun goddess Xi He were married to Di Jun, the god of the eastern sky

■ Chang Xi and Xi He embodied the concept of yin and yang

■ Xi He was also known as a calendar goddess

■ Chang Ngo was another moon goddess; she was married to Di Jun's marksman, Yi

■ Xi He is often depicted steering a sun chariot

■ In China, the moon goddesses are still honored with numerous festivals

The god of the eastern sky, Di Jun, had two wives: the moon goddess Chang Xi and the sun goddess Xi He. While Chang Xi had 12 moon daughters, Xi He had ten sun sons. The family lived within an enormous mulberry tree called Fu Song, located in the eastern sea. A second moon goddess named Chang Ngo was married to Yi, Di Jun's best marksman. In reward for his heroic deeds, Yi received the elixir of immortality, but he became arrogant and violent toward Emperor Yao and all other mortals. Seeking to stop her husband, Chang Ngo stole the elixir and took it with her as she fled to the moon, where it was said the lights of her palace could be seen on clear nights during a full moon.

The moon festival celebrated in the eighth month of the moon calendar to mark the harvest can be traced back to this legend. During the celebration, cakes (**1**) are traditionally baked in the form of the moon. In general, the moon goddesses were more beloved than the sun goddesses in China because the moon was believed to help to increase the harvest, whereas the sun was said to threaten the yield.

The Chang Ngo Crater

After the goddess Chang Ngo fled to the moon (right), she lived there in the form of a heavenly toad. She has never been forgotten: a moon crater with a diameter of almost two miles has been named after her. Chang Ngo become internationally famous on October 24, 2007, when China launched a lunar probe named after this beloved goddess: Chang'e-1. This probe went into orbit around the moon on November 5, 2007, and began its investigation of the moon's surface. Among other achievements, this Chinese satellite sent the first pictures of the Chang Ngo crater back to Earth.

Xi He's Sons Xi He (**2**) was also a calendar goddess. As the ancient Chinese week consisted of ten days, the goddess had ten sons, each a sun god. Each was allowed to ascend into the sky only on his day of the week. However, once the boys were up to mischief and appeared all at once in the sky, causing a devastating drought on earth. Emperor Yao prayed to Di Jun, who sent his marksman, Yi, to settle the problem, not expecting that Yi would shoot nine of his sons out of the sky. The one surviving boy became the sole sun in the sky.

Figures and Stories Relevant to Sun and Moon Deities

Emperor Yao, Inventor of the Moon Calendar, see p. 335

Yin and Yang, Principle of Yin and Yang Represented By Chang Xi and Xi He, see pp. 332–333

The Caring Chang Xi As the embodiment of the cold, dark, feminine yin principle, the moon goddess Chang Xi (**3**, annual festival held in honor of the moon goddess in Hong Kong) was calm and collected. She was the mother of 12 moon daughters, whom she sent one by one into the sky so that they could light up the earth at night. Chang Xi herself never slept at night because she anxiously waited for each of her daughters to return. The caring mother received her daughters, bathed them in the eastern sea, and hung them to dry in the mulberry tree called Fu Song.

The Eight Immortals

■ The eight immortals are Zhongli Quan (leader), Li Tieguai (patron of the sick), Han Xiangzi (patron of musicians), Cao Guojiu (patron of dramatists), Lü Dongbin (patron of barbers), Zhang Guolao (patron of the elderly), Lan Caihe (patron of florists), and He Xiangu (the only woman)

In order to obtain immortality, the highest objective in Taoism, the most significant requirement is self-less action. This group of seven men and one woman, who the Chinese honor as the eight immortals, share this quality. They were wise, compassionate, patient, and optimistic in times when most people were irresponsible, avaricious, intolerant, and pessimistic. Because of their qualities, they earned their immortality and obtained extraordinary powers befitting their status, such as the ability to fly or to transform themselves. The eight immortals are extremely popular, not least because eight is a lucky number in China. Unofficially led by Zhongli Quan, a wine-drinking, pot-bellied old man, the eight immortals were said to offer help to those who were suffering and the oppressed.

Only three of the immortals—Zhang Gualao, Zhongli Quan, and Lü Dongbin—are actual historical persons. Although they supposedly lived in different centuries, they all meet in Taoist myths. They were popular artistic subjects, where they were most often depicted sitting together in a boat.

The Eight Conditions

The stories about the eight immortals also include a collection of significant sociological observations compiled over two millennia of Chinese social history. They offer insight into the everyday lives of people living during these earlier times. Here, the eight immortals are said to embody the basic conditions of life, according to respective ying and yang pairs: feminine-masculine, old-young, poor-rich, and upper class-lower class.

⟩⟩ **The Seven Gods of Luck:** p. 364

Crazy Lan Caihe Because he was often wearing beggar's rags, or dressing as a woman when he was tipsy, people always made fun of Lan Caihe. He was known to stand in the street with his basket of flowers, singing (**1**). One day he washed a crippled man's wounds. This man turned out to be the young Laozi, the founder of Taoism. For his compassion, Lan Caihe was granted the gift of immortality.

Lü Dongbin's Magical Sword Lü Dongbin (**3**, with Zhongli Quan) was a scholar and a traveler. He traveled around for 400 years, mingling with the people and preaching. In his hand, he carried a fly whisk. On his back was a magical sword, with which Lü Dong fought dragons and demons. In Taoism these conflicts are interpreted as battles against worldly obsessions and vain, glorious goals.

Figures and Stories Relevant to the Eight Immortals

Yellow Emperor, an Immortal, see pp. 336–337

Yin and Yang, Embodied by the Immortals, see pp. 332–333

Zhang Guolao's Donkey The immortal Zhang Guolao was the patron of the elderly, as he was several hundred years old. He lived on Zhongtiao Mountain, where he immersed himself in his philosophical musings. Now and then Zhang Guolao came out into the real world. During these occasions he would ride his donkey (**2**) over a distance of 1,000 Li a day. After each trip he folded up his donkey as though it were a sheet of paper and stuck it into his pocket. When he needed his donkey again, Zhang Guolao would spray the paper with water, and it would emerge.

Dragon Deities

■ In Chinese, a dragon is called a *lóng*

■ Dragons combined the characteristics of nine animals: the snake, camel, elk, deer, mussel, carp, eagle, tiger, and ox

■ In the Chinese zodiac, the dragon is the most important of the 12 signs

■ The five-clawed dragon has been the imperial family's symbol since the Qin dynasty

■ Dragons were known as having a yang influence; they were majestic, intelligent, and powerful

Dragons symbolize immortality, wisdom, and the might of an emperor in China. According to Chinese mythology, they were deities that bring good fortune, functioning as messengers between the gods and humankind. They were placed third in the divine hierarchy, following heaven and earth.

Only emperors could wear robes with dragons on them

Countless dragons of various sizes inhabited China: enormous dragons that were half a Li (1,056 feet) long, as well as tiny, caterpillar-like dragons. Most were said to have 117 scales—36 with a yin influence and 81 with a yang influence. In Chinese mythology, there are four types of dragons: heavenly dragons that guard the palaces of the gods, winged dragons that control wind and rain, earth dragons that monitor the rivers, treasure dragons protect the earth's resources, and evil black dragons that incite storms and floods.

The dragon's divine status harks back to one of the three sovereigns, Fuxi, whose belly was said to have resembled that of a dragon's.

The Nine Dragons

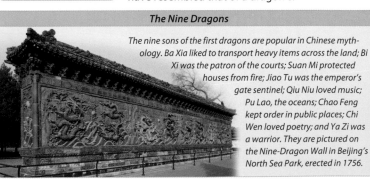

The nine sons of the first dragons are popular in Chinese mythology. Ba Xia liked to transport heavy items across the land; Bi Xi was the patron of the courts; Suan Mi protected houses from fire; Jiao Tu was the emperor's gate sentinel; Qiu Niu loved music; Pu Lao, the oceans; Chao Feng kept order in public places; Chi Wen loved poetry; and Ya Zi was a warrior. They are pictured on the Nine-Dragon Wall in Beijing's North Sea Park, erected in 1756.

≫ Magical Creatures: p. 176

The Four Rivers of China In ancient times, there were no rivers in China. When droughts plagued humanity, the people prayed to the gods for rain. In the eastern part of the country, four dragons lived in a large ocean. They often played in the sky (**1**). One day the god of the mountains lifted the mountains up to the clouds, killing the dragons as they were flying around. As the yellow dragon fell to earth, it transformed itself into the Yellow River. Where the black dragon fell, the Amur began to flow. The long dragon became the Yangtze; the pearl dragon was the Pearl.

> ### Figures and Stories Relevant to Dragon Deities
>
> **Fuxi,** Sovereign With Dragon-Belly, see pp. 334–335
>
> **Huangdi,** a Dragon Brought Him Into the Realm of the Immortals, see pp. 336–337

Kinabalu and the Pearl Up in a mountain cave, the dragon Kinabalu stood guard over a beautiful pearl. When China's emperor ordered his two sons to steal the pearl, they waited until Kinabalu left his post, and flew up to the mountain with paper dragons. Replacing the pearl with a false one, they fled by ship. Seeing that the pearl had been stolen, Kinabalu (**2**) went after the thieves, who killed him with a cannonball.

Chien Tang—The Leader of the Dragons
Ancient Chinese farmers worshiped the dragon deities as rulers of the rain. The dragons' moods determined whether the harvest would be good or not. However, the dragons also ruled the rivers, lakes, and oceans. Each river in China was said to have its own patrons and protectors. The leader of all the river dragons was Chien Tang. He was different from the regular dragons in that he was 900 feet long and had a fiery red mane (**3**). Unlike his fellow dragons, Chien Tang did not have any scales.

Sacred Mountains

The worship of sacred mountains is found in both the Taoist and Buddhist traditions. Mountainous monasteries, temples, and pagodas are popular pilgrimage sites. In Taoism, five sacred mountains are associated with the ancient notion that China forms a square: a mountain rises in each of the four corners and Mount Song (Songshan) towers over the center of the Middle Kingdom. In contrast, Buddhists associate a deity with each of the four sacred

mountains: Mount Jiuhua (Jiuhuashan), Mount Emei (Emeishan), Mount Putuo (Putuoshan), and Mount Wutai (Wutaishan) (pictured). Mount Wutai, the most important, is home to Bodhisattva Manjushri, who helped spread the Buddhist teachings.

Japanese Mythology

This wind god is one of the innumerable Japanese gods, known as kami

Japanese Mythology

Even today, the Japanese still like to call their home country the "land of the gods." The myths and ancient legends of the gods are still deeply rooted in the memories of all Japanese people. For example, everyone learns as a child the stories of the gods Izanami and Izanagi, and of the wild, tempestuous god Susanoo.

The origins of Japanese myths lie in Shinto, Japan's indigenous religion. Up to 84 percent of Japanese people live according to the "way of the gods," the literal translation of the word Shinto. The sun goddess Amaterasu is central to Shinto worship (**1**). She was a daughter of the divine mythological pair Izanagi and Izanami. However, these two not only gave birth to the sun goddess and her brothers and sisters, they were also responsible for bringing all other deities and spirits into being. These spirits, called *kami*, appear in many forms. They are, however, not omnipotent like the Judeo-Christian God, for instance. Instead, they must be understood as higher beings or powers that are responsible for bringing good fortune and happiness, as well as bad luck.

Buddhism, which arrived in Japan in the sixth century, also influenced Japanese mythology. However, this new belief system did not replace Shinto, which was predominant at the time, but instead blended into it. In this way the Shinto deities were simply seen as manifestations of the Buddha and could be honored by believers of both religions. For example, the god Hachiman (**2**) is still worshiped today as both kami and Buddha, and only very few actually know from which religion he came. But because most Japanese people are both Shintoist and Buddhist, this question is no longer relevant.

When Buddhism was first introduced in Japan, the people feared their own Shinto gods' anger. In addition, they were also afraid of becoming a vassal state to China. In order to oppose Buddhism, they simplified the Shinto religion, which lacked a unified doctrine, as well as any form of written documentation. The practice of Shinto varied greatly from region to region. Inspired by the magnificence of Buddhist art, they also began to create artistic depictions of Shinto deities. At the same time, they systematically established shrines as places for Shinto worship. In addition, the court decree to record the Japanese myths in writing must also be seen in light of the measures taken to limit the influence of Buddhism. However, the myths were not recorded just to preserve the ancient stories of heroes and gods. They were also skillfully employed for political purposes.

For example, the myths explain that the gods transferred dominion over the world to Amaterasu's great-grandson, Emperor Jimmu, who is known as the founder of the empire and Japan's first ruler. Therefore the divine ancestry of the Japanese emperors legitimized their authority from that moment on, which had far-reaching consequences. In modern times, the representation of the emperor as the grandson of Amaterasu formed the basis for extreme nationalism in Japan and for the notion that, due to their divine ancestry, the Japanese people were superior to all others. This assumption brought the country into the Second World War. Only in 1946 did the emperor finally abnegate his divine status. Today, the Shinto religion no longer serves political goals and worshiping the gods has again become its central purpose.

Because the Shinto religion is not based on the written word and has no fixed, written commandments, its religious practices are its most important element. At the center of Shinto worship stands shrines, which are the places where practioners pay homage to kami. The most interesting feature of shrines is the *torii* (**3**, Fushimi Inari shrine, Kyoto), a gate constructed of a double cross-beam, which marks the entrance to the sacred space. Often painted bright red, the torii is a visually striking construction that marks the transition

3

between ordinary and sacred space. Characteristically, the entrance to the actual shrine edifice leads
over a bridge. After visitors have crossed the bridge,
they cleanse themselves in a fountain.

The main room of the shrine, which only
priests may enter, contains the "seat" of the
kami, which is usually present in the form of a
stone, a mirror, or a sword. Believers attract
or awaken the deity's attention by tossing
coins into a wooden box, ringing a bell, and
clapping their hands. Then they say a short prayer.
The ritual takes only a few minutes. People can
often be seen performing this ritual at one of
Japan's almost 100,000 shrines, either on the
way to the subway in the morning or on a
brief detour from the daily shopping trip.

Shrines are not always monumental
buildings; sometimes, they are sometimes tiny structures at busy intersections.
Moreover, many families have a shrine at home in the
form of an altar commemorating their ancestors, who are believed to live on
as kami. However, kami are not only found in shrines, but also in trees, stones,
and other locations in nature. These places are usually marked with a *shimenawa*, a rope woven from straw, to indicate their sacred status. On special
occasions, kami are carried through the streets in portable shrines, called
mikoshi, to take part in the festival pageants.

In this way, the ancient myths are reanimated within the context of a living
religion. But they also still play an important role in today's Japanese culture.
Mythology usually provides the subjects for the traditional Noh Theater (**4**,
actress Waki-Jun Mucase performing in a Umewaka Kennokai production of
Aoi No Ue) and even the popular Japanese *manga* ("comics"), which emerged
after the Second World War, avail themselves of this treasure trove.

Izanami and Izanagi

The Shinto religion teaches that Japan was created by the god pair Izanami and Izanagi. From the floating bridge of heaven, Ama-no-Hashidate (**2**), they stirred the ocean with a heavenly spear (**1**) covered in jewels. When they pulled the spear out of the water, the salt crystallized at its tip and the first Japanese island, Onogoro-shima ("self-forming island"), dripped down. The couple stepped down onto the island to perform their wedding ceremony. More islands were formed during this ritual, as well as 800 myriads of deities called kami.

While giving birth to the fire god, Izanami was burned so badly that she died. Her husband made the mistake of following her into the underworld and only just managed to escape. Afterward, Izanagi had to perform cleansing rituals to free himself of the impurities of the underworld. During these rituals, the gods of the sun, the moon, and the storm were created. To this day, cleansing rituals are a central part of Shinto culture. It is customary to wash the mouth and hands before entering a shrine.

■ Izanami and Izanagi were the primordial gods

■ In the Japanese tradition, they are referred to as either husband and wife, or as siblings

■ They created the Japanese islands, as well as many gods called kami; according to the Shinto religion, there are 800 myriads of kami

■ Most artistic depictions of this story show the couple standing on the bridge of heaven, holding a spear

Izanami and Izanagi Have Children   Once the two gods had descended onto the first island, they walked around the spear that was stuck in the soil in opposite directions. When their paths crossed for the first time, Izanami was the first to talk to Izanagi. This was against the rules of the wedding ritual and her first child was a miscarriage, which resulted in the "leech child." It was born without bones, unable to stand upright. This child became the god Ebisu (**3**), one of seven gods of fortune. He was also the patron of fishermen. The couple repeated the ceremony again, this time according to the rules, and many other deities were created until Izanami was fatally injured during the birth of the god of fire. During her ordeal, thousands of new kami emerged from her tears.

3

Izanagi Descends Into the Underworld   Distressed about Izanami's death, Izanagi went to Yomi no Kuni, the "land of darkness" (**4**). Upon his arrival he discovered that Izanami had eaten the food of the underworld, thus she could not leave. Lighting a torch, Izanagi saw his wife's decayed corpse. Feeling

4

dishonored, Izanami chased him to the gate of the underworld. He escaped, blocked the gate with a large rock, and then ritually cleansed himself.

The Kojiki

Along with rituals and ceremonies, the Kojiki ("Records of Ancient Matters," 712 B.C.) (left, the editor O no Yasumaro) tells the history of Japan from creation to the start of imperial power. For a long time, the Kojiki gave authority to the Japanese emperors.

Figures and Stories Relevant to Izanami and Izanagi

Amaterasu, Daughter of Izanagi, see pp. 358–359

Gods of Fortune, Ebisu's Companions, see pp. 364–365

The Wedded Rocks, Symbol of the Original Divine Couple, see pp. 354–355

Primordial Pairs: pp. 74, 114, 446 | **Journeys in the Underworld:** pp. 39, 41, 159, 407

The Wedded Rocks

Two rocks in the Japanese ocean by the coast of Futami are considered to represent the original gods, Izanami and Izanagi, who are believed to have created the Japanese islands. They are known as Meotoiwa, or the "wedded rocks." The two rocks are connected by a rope of rice straw to symbolize the union of the creator pair and the holiness of the site.

A gate with a double crossbar, called a *torii*, is positioned on top of the male rock as another sign of the holiness of these rocks and the deities they represent. Both of these symbols can be found in many Shinto cultural sites. The twisted rope is called a shimenawa, which weighs more than a ton. Due to the wet conditions, it needs to be replaced several times a year. During these occasions, men dressed in traditional work clothes run into the sea at low tide and replace the rope at great effort.

The Kami

■ Japanese gods, called kami, are said to be found in multitudes, with more being created all the time

■ Kami were distinguished as being either celestial (*amatsukami*) or terrestrial (*kunitsukami*)

■ The most important kami such as Amaterasu are worshiped in Shinto shrines

■ With the introduction of Buddhism in Japan, kami were depicted as humans

Kami are the 800 myriads of deities and spirits found in Shinto mythology. These include the kami of nature, tutelary kami, and the spirits of the ancestors, particularly of the Japanese emperors. It is very difficult to determine exactly who or what is accepted as kami. Generally, the kami are depicted in mythology as forces of good and evil, which present themselves as animals, plants, and natural phenomena, as well as humans and diseases. They all had supernatural power. Despite this, they were not necessarily almighty, immortal, or omniscient.

The first kamis were created during the wedding rituals of Izanami and Izanagi. Many new deities are always being created while old ones are forgotten. Some are worshiped by Shinto practitioners today in their own dedicated shrines. Most larger shrine sites, however, honor several different kami simultaneously. In order to honor the kami of natural phenomena, sacred sites or features are usually lined with the shimenawa, a twisted rope made of straw, to indicate their holiness.

Residences of the Kami The most important kami are worshiped in shrines. The holiest object in a shrine is the *shintai*, or "god-body," which is stored in a chamber inside the shrine. It is not an iconic figure of the deity, but rather a symbol of its presence and readiness to be worshiped. The shintai could be a stone, in which the deity's presence was discovered, or an object. Many shintai are mirrors. The residence of a kami is often indicated by ropes made of straw and paper offerings (**1**).

The Sacred Fuji Mountain

Natural phenomena displaying rich beauty were often considered kami, such as certain rock formations, rivers, and trees, as well as wind, thunder, and other natural forces. Mount Fuji (**2**), which is still an active volcano today, is an impressive force of nature. It is currently worshiped by Shintoists, Buddhists and, most of all, by the Japanese ascetics of the mountains, the Yamabushi. Every year, countless pilgrims climb the mountain. Several shrines can be found along the mountain trail. Many of the rock caves in the Aokigahara Forest, located at the foot of the Fuji, are said to be haunted by the *yokai*, or monsters.

2

3

Inari—Kami of Fertility

Inari was one of the most honored Japanese kami. She was the goddess of fertility, rice, and foxes, which acted as her messengers. Inari appears in mythology in a variety of forms, guises, and sexes. As kami of fertility, she is shown in artistic works as a woman (**3**, meeting a warrior), but is depicted as a male when representing the god of rice. Shintoists today visit Inari's many shrines, which are protected by two white foxes that occasionally wear red collars. They are given rice wine, known as *sake*, as offerings.

Honji Suijaku

The term Honji Suijaku ("original state and manifested traces") denotes a belief that emerged in the eighth century that kami were manifestations of Buddhas. This approach allowed both beliefs to co-exist. The most famous kami is Hachiman (left), who is often shown as a Buddha.

- Her full name Amaterasu Omikami means "the great divinity illuminating heaven"

- As a sun goddess, Amaterasu is Japan's most important deity

- She was the first ancestor of the Japanese imperial family

- Amaterasu ruled together with her brother Susanoo in the high celestial plain

- Amaterasu is worshiped today at the Grand Shrine of Ise

- The three imperial regalia of Japan, the mirror, the sword, and the jewels, were gifts from Amaterasu

Amaterasu

As a sun goddess and Izanagi's daughter, Amaterasu is the most important Shinto goddess. She was said to be the first ancestor of the Japanese imperial family. She is still worshiped at the Grand Shrine of Ise, Japan's most important shrine.

Ancient Japanese bronze mirror, a symbol of Amaterasu

At first, together with her younger brother, the storm god Susanoo, Amaterasu assumed rulership of Takama no Hara, the "high celestial plain." However, Susanoo's impetuous acts, such as throwing a flayed horse into Amaterasu's sacred chamber, caused friction between the two. After many quarrels, Susanoo was exiled from heaven and the sun goddess then ruled the land of the kami by herself.

Depictions of Amaterasu often show her as a warm-hearted, good-natured goddess, sitting back to back with her other brother, the moon god Tsukiyomi no Mikoto, with whom she was said to govern the progression of day and night.

The Grand Shrine of Ise

The Grand Shrine of Ise, known as Jingū, is located in Mie prefecture in southeast Japan. As the most sacred Shinto shrine, numerous pilgrims visit it every year. Amaterasu's shintai (a place of residence), a mirror, is kept within the inner shrine. The shrine buildings are ritually torn down and rebuilt every 20 years.

Amaterasu in the Cave The most popular story about Amaterasu is how she barricaded herself in a cave after a fight with her brother, Susanoo, which brought darkness across the world. Only when another goddess, Amenouzume, performed a wild dance in front of the cave did the laughter of the other gods attract Amaterasu's interest, and she pushed the stone slab away from the entrance to the cave. A mirror was quickly placed before her and the goddess, dazzled by her own beauty, stepped out of the cave (**1**). With the sun restored, the mirror became one of the three imperial regalia, emblems of Japanese imperial rule.

Amaterasu—The Sun After Izanagi successfully escaped from the underworld, he washed the dirt and darkness from his eyes in one quick rinse. Suddenly, Amaterasu sprang from his left eye. This is how she was given her role as the bringer of light (**3**). As the Japanese call their country Nihon, meaning "land of the rising sun," it is not surprising that Amaterasu continues to hold such high standing in Japan. The sun's image is represented on the Japanese flag (**2**). The flag's current design was decreed in the 19th century, showing the importance of myths in Japan today.

> ### Figures and Stories Relevant to Amaterasu
>
> **Izanami and Izanagi**, Susanoo's Parents, see pp. 352–353
>
> **Kami**, Amaterasu Was the Most Important Goddess, see pp. 356–357
>
> **Ninigi no Mikoto and Jimmu Tenno**, Amaterasu's Descendants, see pp. 368–369
>
> **Susanoo**, Amaterasu's Brother, see pp. 360–361

Susanoo

The storm god Susanoo had two sides: with his destructive nature, he ravaged the world in anger, allowing rivers to dry out and plants to wither. However, he also brought culture to the people.

For a short time he ruled together with his sister Amaterasu over heaven and earth. Then he complained to his father, from whose nose he was born, that he would rather be with his mother in the underworld than rule the earth. In this way he offended and disappointed his father. However, instead of leaving the high celestial plain, Susanoo provoked his sister to the point that the sun goddess hid herself in a cave. Then he was exiled from heaven forever.

When he arrived on earth, Susanoo went through a positive transformation. He defeated a monster named Yamato no Orochi, who was terrorizing the people. In the beast's tail, he found the Kusanagi, the sword of the imperial regalia. He also taught the people about agriculture and founded a ruling dynasty in Izumo province, where his shrine is now located.

- ■ The trickster Susanoo was the god of the wind and the sea
- ■ He was born when his father Izanagi washed his nose
- ■ After he was banished from heaven, he lived with humanity
- ■ He brought agriculture and many cultural achievements to the people
- ■ He is usually depicted fighting against the eight-headed monster Yamato no Orochi

Tricksters

In mythology, tricksters can often be recognized by their dichotomous characters. They often drift between the gods and humans, sometimes falling into conflict with the gods, after which they enter into a pact with humans. They are said to have passed on useful information about technology, such as the knowledge of fire (as with the Greek character Prometheus) or about agriculture and animal husbandry. In doing so, they laid the foundation for human culture. Susanoo, who was expelled from the community of gods, became a cultural hero after arriving on earth. Tricksters also typically appear in animal form, such as another Japanese trickster, Kitsune, a fox deity. These figures are seen as bringers of luck, but were also said to bring obsession.

Tricksters: pp. 146, 148, 166, 170, 234, 440

Susanoo's Pranks The wild Susanoo (**1**, depicted as an anime character) was infamous for his tricks and pranks, which sometimes had devastating

consequences. After a fight with his sister, he ruined her rice paddies by trampling them and destroying the wells. Another time, after he had removed the hide of a celestial horse, he threw the horse into the sun goddess's sacred chamber. A weaver, who was there making a divine garment for Amaterasu, fell from her loom in horror. As a result she was fatally injured by her weaving shuttle. Because of these episodes, the furious Amaterasu hid herself in a cave and darkness fell upon the world.

Battle Against Yamato no Orochi After being chased out of heaven because of his bad behavior, Susanoo came to earth. Upon his arrival, he met an old married couple, who told him about their troubles with an eight-headed monster (**2**) named Yamato no Orochi. Every year it ate one of their daughters and would soon

come to fetch the youngest. Susanoo promised to kill the monster Yamato no Orochi if he could have their daughter for his bride. He gave the terrible beast eight bowls of poisoned rice wine, intoxicating it, and then he killed it (**3**). In its tail he discovered a sword, which he gave Amaterasu as a way to reconcile with her.

Okuninushi

■ Okuninushi literally means "the great land master"

■ He was the hero of the sagas of the Izumo province, where he was also worshiped as a creator god

■ Later he was incorporated into Japan's national myths

■ He was the god of medicine, magic, and agriculture

■ He is often shown in illustrations together with a white rabbit

Okuninushi is the main character and hero of the ancient sagas of the Izumo province. That these stories originally belonged to an independent myth cycle is revealed by the fact that they include their own creation story. Later, when the province lost some of its political importance, the original Izumo myths were fit into the national myths of Amaterasu. For example, Okuninushi was named the storm god Susanoo's son-in-law. The Izumo shrine, where Okuninushi is worshiped, is still one of the most important Shinto shrines.

Okuninushi had to pass many tests of courage before he could rule the land. He was always fighting against his 80 mischievous brothers, as well as with Susanoo, who refused to let Okuninushi marry his daughter, Suseri-hime. After countless adventures, during which he died twice (**1**) and was brought to life by the gods, Okuninushi finally won Susanoo's favor. With his help, Okuninushi was able to keep his brothers in check and ruled over Izumo.

②

Okuninushi and His Brothers

Once, the 80 brothers of Okuninushi all wanted to marry the beautiful princess Yagamihime. On their way to visit her, they met a rabbit (**2**). The rabbit was in great pain because he had been skinned by a crocodile. Okuninushi was the only one of the brothers who paid any attention to the rabbit, advising him to bathe in clean water and to cover himself with pollen to reconstruct his white fur. For his help, the rabbit, who was actually a god, promised to

Figures and Stories Relevant to Okuninushi

Ninigi no Mikoto, Okuninushi's Rival Over the Rule of the World, see pp. 368–369

Susanoo, Okuninushi's Father-in-Law, see pp. 360–361

win the princess's favor for Okuninushi. This aroused the jealousy and hatred of his brothers, and Okuninushi had to flee from them into the underworld.

Suseri-hime Meeting in the underworld, Okuninushi and Suseri-hime fell in love, but Suseri-hime's father, Susanoo, opposed their relationship. He shot an arrow into an enormous field and ordered Okuninushi to find it (**3**). Then he set the field on fire. With the help of a mouse, Okuninushi survived in a burrow.

③

The Shrine of Izumo

Izumo Taisha is one of the most important shrines in Japan. According to the legends, the first high priest was a son of Amaterasu. Even today, the priests of the shrine trace their lineage back to him. Unique to this shrine are the shimenawa straw ropes that are mounted above the entrance to the main hall. It is said that if a coin thrown from below remains stuck in the rope, the wish of the person who threw it will come true.

The Seven Gods of Luck

The Shichi Fukujin, "seven gods of luck," have been worshiped in Japan since the late Middle Ages. They represented various aspects of good fortune; above all, they were related to material, worldly values. The positive characteristics associated with them, such as thrift and hard work, correspond exactly to the virtues esteemed by urban Japanese culture after around 1600. Of the seven, who are now considered to be kami, probably only two, Daikoku and Ebisu, were originally Shinto deities. All the rest—Jurojin, Benten, Bishamonten, Fukurokuju, and Hotei—have their origins in Buddhism, Hinduism, or Taoism.

Like the eight immortals in Chinese mythology, these seven gods are often depicted sitting in a boat, the Takarabune. It is said that they come to shore in the New Year and distribute their fortuitous cargo, which includes a bottomless wallet, a sacred key, and a lucky coat. Even today, many Japanese people buy pictures of the gods of luck. On New Year's Eve, they place these pictures in drawers or under their pillows.

■ Benten, the only woman among the seven lucky gods, was goddess of the arts

■ The war god Bishamonten wore Chinese armor

■ Daikoku, their leader, was the god of wealth

■ Ebisu, the god of fishermen, held a sea bream under his arm as an emblem

■ Fukurokuju and Jurojin were the gods associated with longevity

■ The friendly Hotei was the god of thrift

Places of Worship for the Seven Gods of Luck

Especially during the first part of the New Year, many people in Japan visit the places where the seven gods of luck are worshiped. In the harbor city of Kamakura, pilgrims are able to visit two Shinto shrines and five Buddhist temples. At each of these sites, one of the seven lucky gods is worshiped.

Daikoku and Hotei (right, statue from the Jochiji temple in Kamakura) are part of a widespread tradition: pilgrims rub the head and shoulders of the Daikoku statue or Hotei's belly with their hands. The goal of this ritual is to obtain some of the prosperity that these gods represent.

⏩ **The Eight Immortals:** p. 340

Bishamonten—The Watchman Originally a god from the Hindu pantheon, Bishamonten arrived in Japan by way of China. He was a war god, always ready to do battle. For this reason, even as a god of fortune, he was always depicted wearing his Chinese armor, complete with a spear. As the most important of the four guardians of the universe and endowed with marvellous hearing, he kept watch over the north. His task was to protect the world from invasions of evil demons (**1**).

The Good-Humored Hotei Hotei was always in a good mood, even though he was fat, deformed, and clumsy. Still, he not only stands for cheerful thrift, but also for philanthropy. For example, it is said that he carried women across rivers. Hotei's character is probably based on a legendary traveling Chinese monk named Budai from the ninth century who carried all of his belongings in a jute bag along with him (**2**). He was considered to be the incarnation of the Bodhisattva Maitreya, the Buddha of the future. In addition, he became the model for the typical Chinese laughing Buddha.

Fukurokuju—The Philosopher The wise Fukurokuju was worshiped as the god of health and longevity. He was most often depicted as an old man with short legs, and his most noticeable feature was his extremely tall forehead (**3**), which, to Taoists, is a sign of intelligence and immortality. He was accompanied by a turtle and a crane, animals that are also symbols of longevity in Japan. This philosopher could survive without eating when he appeared in human form and, as a god, he had the ability to bring the dead back to life. Even though it is often said that Fukurokuju can be traced back to a Chinese philosopher, evidence shows that no such figure actually existed in China. A variety of attributes associated with several Taoist gods are united in Fukurokuju.

Dance of the God Daikoku

Daikoku, leader of the seven gods of luck, stood for material wealth and abundance. Illustrating both aspects perfectly, he was depicted as a stout man, either sitting on a bulging rice sack or standing with it slung over his shoulder. His lucky mallet stood as a symbol of the hard work it takes to become rich. Daikoku is often seen in art together with Ebisu, the god of fishermen. In the 18th century, the "dance of the seven gods of luck" was performed as an interlude in middle-class Kabuki theaters. In this piece, Ebisu and Daikoku danced for the other gods of luck. This tradition was revived in the 20th century and can be seen today at festivals held in honor of Daikoku (Daikoku-sama).

鎮

■ Ninigi, a grandson of Amaterasu, took over Okuninushi's rule

■ He brought the three imperial regalia to earth: a sword, a pearl necklace, and a mirror

■ Jimmu Tenno, Ninigi's grandson, was Japan's first emperor and established the Japanese imperial family

Ninigi no Mikoto and Jimmu Tenno

Because Okuninushi was not able to establish a lasting peace in Izumo province, Amaterasu and the other gods sought out a new ruler for the "middle reed fields." Finally, they decided upon Amaterasu's grandson, Ninigi no Mikoto. Okuninushi accepted their decision and surrendered his rule over the world to his rival on the condition that he be honored as one of the most important gods.

Ninigi arrived on Mount Takachiko (**1**) on the island of Kyushu with three divine treasures. Before long, he married princess Konohana Sakuya Hime. Their grandson, Jimmu Tenno, became Japan's first emperor. He represented a link between mythology and reality. Throughout history, all Japanese emperors traced their line back to him, and in so doing, they claimed to be direct descendants of Amaterasu. The founding of the empire by Jimmu in 660 B.C. is still celebrated in Japan on February 11.

1

▶ **Divine Rulers:** pp.48, 84, 201, 220, 336

The Three Gifts of Amaterasu

When Ninigi descended to earth, he was accompanied by five kami, each a leader of one of the five vocations, who had been sent by Amaterasu. As a sign of his power, Ninigi brought three gifts from the sun goddess with him: the sword Kusanagi (**2**), the mirror Yata (**4**), and the pearl necklace Yasakani (**3**). Each item held mythological significance: the mirror was the very same one that helped to coax Amaterasu out of her hiding place in the cave; the sword was a present from her brother, Susanoo, who had found it in the tail of a monster; and the pearl necklace had triggered the dispute between the two siblings. When Ninigi founded a dynasty, her gifts became the regalia that are still featured at the enthronement ceremony of emperors today.

> **Figures and Stories Relevant to Ninigi and Jimmu Tenno**
>
> Amaterasu, Ninigi's and Jimmu's Ancestor, pp. 358–359
>
> Ancestor Worship, Divine Tenno, pp. 370–371
>
> Okuninushi, Ninigi's Rival for Rule Over the World, pp. 362–363

The Unbroken Line of Emperors

Because 125 direct descendants of the first emperor Jimmu have been recognized, Japan is the oldest hereditary monarchy in the world. Although researchers now believe that Jimmu was a mythical figure, the imperial family still traces its line back to him and also to Amaterasu as a direct ancestor. Even though the emperor officially abnegated his divine status at the end of the war in 1945, many rites exist in which he still carries out his function as a priest.

Jimmu's Crow Jimmu Tenno had a celestial ally: the three-footed crow Yatagarasu (**5**), a kami that could change its form. Amaterasu sent the crow to Jimmu to help him with his military campaign in the east. The crow had earlier proved its worth by choking a beast that was trying to swallow the sun. It helped Tenno by finding paths in seemingly impassable terrain and as a herald. Yatagarasu was also partly responsible for the later unification of Japan. The crow is worshiped in a variety of shrines. Today it has been incorporated into the emblem of the Japan Football Association—an example of the presence of mythological figures in present-day Japan.

Ancestor Worship

As with China or Africa, ancestors play an important role in Japanese religious life. In general, people assume that the dead do not leave the world, but instead remain close to the living, influencing them. For this reason, people make an effort to pay respect to their ancestors. The idea that relatives must show the souls of the dead the way to the other side (to the afterlife) is especially influential in Japan. For example, lanterns are lit during the Buddhist Obon festival (**3**) to accomplish this task.

At the Yasukuni shrine (**1**) those who died in war are specially commemorated. However, visits by high-ranking Japanese politicians are controversial internationally because they could be seen as glorifying particular wars.

The Invention of Traditions
While Shinto was almost forgotten in the centuries after Buddhism appeared, and kami were given hardly any importance in comparison to the Buddha, in the 19th century people started to revive their "own" Japanese religion. This happened in the course of the radical modernization that swept through Japan after its opening to the West in 1868. In order to assert themselves in the face of Western influence, people reintroduced typical Japanese "traditions," which sometimes led to the invention of entirely new traditions. A renewed interest in Shinto accompanied an emphasis on the emperor's succession from Amaterasu, his direct ancestor. Tenno was established as a figure with whom the people could identify, which unified the country. At the same time, the emperor's deification contributed to the readiness of the masses to die for him during the Second World War. Only in 1946 did the emperor finally abnegate his divine status. Today, because he is no longer head of state, he takes on representative tasks and performs ritual acts, such as setting out rice plants (**2**).

>> Ancestor Cult: p. 460

The Yokai

The world of the yokai—ghosts, spirits, and goblins—originated from Japanese popular beliefs. The yokai have inspired a wealth of traditional literature. Ghosts often appear as the main characters of Noh and Kabuki plays, as well as in scary stories or sometimes even unhappy love stories. The various forms of the yokai tradition are also shown through the fine arts (**1**, silk painting by Hokusai). Classifications of ghosts, developed in earlier times, still serve as inspiration for modern films and comic series.

- The yokai are also known as *mononoke*

- They could appear as an animal, a person, or an object; an object that had come to life was known as a *tsukumogami*

- Yokai are extremely popular motifs in literature, paintings, and film

The traditional Japanese belief that spirits exist and roam the world created both a reverence for the ancestors and a fear of their return. If the dead were not properly buried, or if they experienced adversity on their way to the afterlife, they were said to return to earth as restless spirits to bring misfortune to the living.

▶▶ **Asuras and Demons:** p. 306

Oni and Shoki Oni were ugly demons that were not particularly intelligent. In the 13th century they were still considered to be good-natured watchmen who guarded hell. However, as time went on, they succumbed to evil. They became wicked, destructive devils that people tried to avoid. Their greatest adversary was Shoki, the spirit of an unhappy man who had served the Chinese emperor. Upon his death, he discovered his vocation as a conqueror of demons (**2**).

Oiwa the Lantern Spirit In the 17th century, ghost stories were extremely popular and were shown in the performances of the Japanese Kabuki theater. Among other stories, the famous tale *Yotsuya Kaidan* (1825) was performed for the Japanese middle class. In the story, a poor woman named Oiwa was poisoned by her husband and died a horrible death. As unhappy women in love often transformed into spirits, that was what happened to Oiwa. As a ghost disfigured by poison, she haunted her husband from then on, appearing often as a broken lantern (**3**).

Figures and Stories Relevant to the Yokai

Ancestor Worship, Spirits of the Dead, see pp. 370–371

Seven Gods of Luck, Demon Fighter Bishamonten, see pp. 364–365

Kappa *Kappa* (**4**) were bloodsucking beings who loved cucumbers. They appeared in the form of children and had hollow indentations on the top of their heads, which were filled with water. They lived in lakes and pools, thus it was common to throw cucumbers into their habitats to keep a kappa happy. Once, when a kappa attacked a cow that was tied to a tree, the cow ran around the tree trunk, pinching off its tormenter's arm with the rope. A farmer who came along and found the severed arm kept it. He only gave it back to the kappa after he had promised not to bother the people and the animals in that area again.

American Mythology

Indigenous cave paintings in Mexico

American Mythology

Settlement of the Americas has thrived for thousands of years, and has seen a wide range of peoples and civilizations rise and fall. Each developed its own religion or system of spiritual belief, which reflected the history, technology, politics, and aspirations of the people or tribe. Unfortunately, current sources of information are incomplete. We know of some of the major civilizations of Central and South America, such as the Aztecs, the Maya, and the Inca, from accounts of the Spanish conquistadors who made the first European contact, and sometimes from salvaged written records left by the priestly and ruling classes. Important examples are the *Popol Vuh* about the Maya and the extensive encyclopedia about the Aztecs by the missionary Bernardino de Sahagún, both written in the native languages. North American tribes did not generally use written language, thus there are no scrolls or codices. As some tribes did not have much contact with Europeans until the 1800s, their experience differs from the rapid political and cultural conquest of the Aztec, Maya, and Inca by the Spanish conquistadors. The slow paced contact between the American

1

settlers and the North American tribes allowed more time for sources on their beliefs to be written and preserved, most often by missionaries, government workers, or explorers.

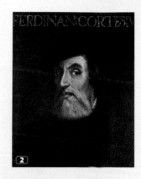

The Aztecs inhabited what is now modern Mexico. Although popularly known as the Aztecs ("people from Azlán"), they called themselves Mexica after one of the ritual names of their sun god, Huitzilopochtli. The first Mexican high culture and forerunners of the Aztecs were the Olmecs, who developed the pantheon, calendar system, and ritual ball game that were taken over by the Aztecs. The center of the Aztec Empire was the city of Tenochtitlán (**1**), built on an island in the middle of Lake Texcoco and site of present-day Mexico City. Settlement began in the 13th century, and from this political base, the Aztec rulers expanded their reigns to include a host of conquered and tributary groups throughout what is now Mexico.

The expansion was accompanied by the integration of foreign and ancient gods. In the end, they worshiped a pantheon of, by some counts, over one hundred gods, goddesses, and spirits, although only a handful of the gods were considered to be dominant or major gods. Cult centers were massive stone temples, set on pyramids with stairs. A priestly class controlled the temples and supervised the performance of yearly and monthly rituals to the major gods, determined by a complex calendar that cycled secular and ritual dates in an interlocking pattern. The priests also performed human sacrifices, which were a complex and profoundly important institution; one that reflected the core Aztec understanding of how their world worked. The gods, at various times, were believed to have shed blood or sacrificed parts of their own bodies for the benefit of humanity. In return, the people offered sacrifices of their own blood and bodies to strengthen the power of the gods in their struggle against the forces of darkness that sought to end the world.

The empire flourished until the 16th century, when the arrival of the Spanish conquistadors (**2**, Hernando Cortés) and the introduction of European diseases to which the local peoples had little immune resistance, conspired to end the Aztec Empire, which was undergoing an internal political upheaval.

Beginning earlier in time—the first large settlements date from the fourth century B.C.—the Maya culture flourished for centuries in the hills of Guatemala and its surrounding flat regions including the Yucatán Peninsula. The Maya were actually several related peoples and developed multiple city-states, which stood in rivalry and trade contact with each other. The Maya civilization peaked in population density and construction of monumental architecture during the Classic period (ca A.D. 250–900) in centers such as Tikal, Chichén Itzá, and Palenque. After this time the Maya centers began to collapse until the arrival of the Spanish drew the Maya to the same fate as the Aztecs.

Maya religion shared many themes in common with Aztec religion, e.g., their sophisticated calendar system, the importance of astronomy, and a pantheon of gods associated with the celestial and agricultural occurrences. Many gods and goddesses were depicted with bird-like or serpent-like features, which was a way to symbolize their divine status. Like the Aztec, the Maya (**3**, priest) practiced human sacrifice, often by drowning young men and women in sacred wells.

In South America, the Inca Empire grew to dominate most of the western side of the continent by the time of first Spanish contact in the 16th century. However, this empire with a well-functioning and egalitarian organization of state and work had humble beginnings in a small city-state of the Killke tribe, centered around the Andes Mountains (**4**, Inca ruins in the Cuzco Valley, Peru). By 1438, a powerful leader named Pachacuti Yupanqui (1438–1471)

conquered the other cultural groups of what is now Peru. He reorganized the Cuzco state into the imperial ruling class of the new Inca Empire. Conquered peoples were subsumed into a federalist system that left their original cultures and beliefs intact, although subjugated to official state religion. In this religion, the Inca emperor was worshiped as a living incarnation of the sun god, Inti. Alongside their large pantheon of personal gods, the Inca also

worshiped Huacas, which were powers located in trees, springs, rocks, and other natural locations.

Equally as diverse as the tribes themselves, North American religions and beliefs reflect a highly sophisticated awareness of human nature and the natural world, as personified by a large array of animal spirits (**5**, buffalo rattle) and celestial deities. Many tribes interpreted a shared group of animal spirits through their own set of traditions, spirits such as Coyote, Bear, and Raven. The North American tribes are also known for developing their famous spiritual traditions of the sweat lodge and the vision quest. Understanding their traditions and beliefs provides a valuable window to a rich source of human experience.

American mythology consists of the gods and stories of an entire continent. The sheer diversity of cultures, from the family bands of Eskimo of the Arctic Circle, to the massive, bureaucratic empire of the Inca in South America, provides those interested in the religions, belief systems, and mythologies of the world with a deep well of human experience to learn from.

Aztec—Creation Myths

According to the Aztec codices, the main sources on the Aztecs (**1**, Templo Mayor, center of cosmology), the primordial world was just water and darkness. The god Ometeotl sprang from the darkness, creating himself from nothingness. Ometeotl, who was both male and female, gave birth to the Four Tezcatlipocas—one god composed of four deities. They were Quetzalcóatl, the White Tezcatlipoca of the East; Xipe Totec, the Red Tezcatlipoca of the West; Huitzilopochtli, the Blue Tezcatlipoca of the South; and the Black Tezcatlipoca of the North, known only as Tezcatlipoca.

The creation of the world was not easy, as every time the Four Tezcatlipocas tried, a gigantic crocodile named Cipactli ate or destroyed whatever they made. The gods became so frustrated they resolved to kill her. The Black Tezcatlipoca dangled his foot in the water. Cipactli took the bait, and while she was chewing off his foot, the brothers grabbed her and ripped her apart. From her corpse they made the world, Tlaloc the rain god, and the first people.

■ Ometeotl, the god of fire, was dually male (Ometecutli) and female (Omecihuatl) and bore the Four Tezcatlipocas

■ The Four Tezcatlipocas created the world and took turns as the ruler of the sun

■ The universe consisted of sky (with 13 levels), earth, and underworld (with nine levels)

■ The Black Tezcatlipoca was depicted with a missing foot and a black and yellow stripe painted across his face

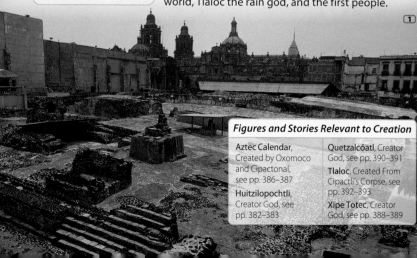

(1)

Figures and Stories Relevant to Creation

2 Oxomoco and Cipactonal

Four aged wise men, less than gods but more than mortals, were named Oxomoco, Cipactonal, Tlaltetecui, and Xochicauaca. They were noted for founding the city of Pánuco and for visiting Tamoanchán, a heavenly paradise for the gods. Oxomoco and Cipactonal (**2**) in particular devised the first Aztec calendar and a system for interpreting prophetic dreams. They also used their skills in divination to lead the first Aztecs to discovering maize.

The White and Black Tez-catlipocas—Rival Suns

The White Tezcatlipoca, Quetzalcóatl, and the Black Tezcatlipoca, known only as Tez-catlipoca (**3**), were brothers and rivals for the office of the sun. Because Tezcatlipoca had lost his foot in the fight with the monster Cipactli, he became the first sun. Quetzalcóatl resented this, and knocked him from the sky with a stone club.

In revenge, Tezcatlipoca made his jaguars eat all of the people in the world. Quetzalcóatl became the new sun and made new people, but Tez-catlipoca was still angry. He turned the new people into monkeys. Quetzalcóatl was so upset he resigned as the sun and blew the monkey-people away with a hurricane. Then Tlaloc became the third sun.

Raising the Land From the Sea Tonacate-cuhtli (**4**), or "he at the center," was a celestial fertility god who represented the male essence of creation. He was thought to live in Omeyocan, the highest level of the heavens, with his wife Tonacacihuatl, the female essence of creation. In some creation stories, he separated the land from the seas while Ometoetl— in the god's dually male (Ometecutli) and female (Omecihuatl) form—created life and people on the land raised by Tonacate-cuhtli.

Creation Through a Body: pp. 20, 27, 229, 288, 331 | **Creation Through Water:** pp. 21, 71

Aztec—Huitzilopochtli

The Aztecs believed that Huitzilopochtli was the most recent god of the sun, after the Black Tezcatlipoca, Quetzalcóatl, and Tlaloc had abandoned that duty in times past. He was considered equal in stature to Tlaloc, Huitzilopochtli's predecessor and the god of rains. As Huitzilopochtli was thought to live in constant battle with the forces of darkness, who sought to sink the world into endless night and destroy humanity. To give the god strength to fight, the Aztecs made sacrifices of human hearts and blood during yearly festivals.

The Aztecs also believed that warriors who died in battle, as well as women who died in childbirth, had their souls sent to serve Huitzilopochtli in his afterworld palace. Huitzilopochtli was thought to shine so brightly with sun rays that the souls of the warriors could only look at him through arrow holes in their shields. Occasionally, Huitzilopochtli sent souls back to the land of the living in the form of hummingbirds. Because of this, as well as the fact that he was born from a ball of feathers, Huitzilopochtli is often shown as a hummingbird, or as a male with a black face wearing hummingbird feathers on his head and legs.

■ A god of the sun and war, Huitzilopochtli was also the patron of Tenochtitlán.

■ He was one of the four gods responsible for creation

■ He was shown as a feathered man holding his magic weapon, a serpent called Xiuhcoatl

Figures and Stories Relevant to Huitzilopochtli

Coatlicue, Huitzilopochtli's Mother, see pp. 384–385

Creation, Huitzilopochtli as Creator God as One of the Four Tezcatlipocas, see pp. 380–381

Quetzalcóatl, Fellow Creator God, see pp. 390–391

The Flag of Mexico

The flag of the United Mexican States, or Mexico, is divided into three vertical bands of green, white, and red. Standing at the flag's center is an emblem of an eagle holding a snake. The eagle stands on a cactus growing out of a rock rising from a lake. This emblem represents the Aztec legend that an eagle holding a snake revealed the divinely ordained location of the Aztec homeland at Lake Texcoco. The rock represents the island in Lake Texcoco where the Aztecs built their capital city of Tenochtitlán.

City/State Founders: pp. 198, 200, 353

Coyolxauhqui and Huitzilopochtli One of Huitzilopochtli's sisters was the goddess Coyolxauhqui. Coyolxauhqui killed their mother, Coatlicue, because she had been impregnated with Huitzilopochtli in a disgraceful way, being struck by a ball of feathers. When Coyolxauhqui cut off Coatlicue's head, Huitzilopochtli leapt from his mother's womb as a full-grown god. He killed his sister then tossed her head into the sky, where it became the moon (**1**).

Founding of Tenochtitlán at Lake Texcoco Long ago, the Aztecs lived in a land called Aztlán. Huitzilopochtli ordered them to leave Aztlán and search for a new home, and renamed them the Mexica. The god then left them under the care of his sister Malinalxochitl, the goddess of snakes and scorpions, who built the city Malinalco for the Mexica's new home. The people grew to hate the goddess and called for Huitzilopochtli to come back. Huitzilopochtli magically made his sister sleep, and while she slept, the Mexica left her. When Malinalxochitl woke up, she sought revenge by giving birth to the god Copil, who attacked Huitzilopochtli. Copil lost the fight and his heart was thrown in the middle of Lake Texcoco. Huitzilopochtli commanded the Mexica to search for Copil's heart and build a city where they found it. The city they built became Tenochtitlán (**2**), the present-day Mexico City.

Aztec—Coatlicue

The goddess Coatlicue was tremendously important to the Aztecs. The representation of her as both fertile mother goddess and goddess of death—she was said to feed on corpses—shows her dual nature as creator and destroyer. As earth goddess, her destructive side is often brought out, because while being the life-giving mother, earth ultimately devours all living things.

Coatlicue's name means "she of the skirt of serpents"

■ Coatlicue was also known as Toci, or "grandmother," and Cihuacóatl, or "lady of the serpent"

■ A mother goddess, she gave birth to the god of war and the sun, Huitzilopochtli, and the 400 gods of the stars

■ She was depicted wearing a skirt made of living snakes and a necklace of human hearts and skulls; she had withered bare breasts, symbolizing the many gods she birthed and nursed

■ Her face was alternately shown as made of two twined serpents, or she was decapitated, with serpents of blood springing from her neck

She also appears as Cihuacóatl, the patron of women who died in childbirth, and the sexually impure and sinful goddess Tlazoltéotl. She was the mother of the sun god Huitzilopochtli—who she conceived with a ball of feathers—as well as his sister Coyolxauhqui, and the 400 gods of the stars.

Coatlicue was shown wearing a skirt of living snakes, which represented the birth of gods from her womb, and her breasts were flaccid from nourishing children. Her hands and feet were clawed for digging graves.

Duality of Birth and Death

The Aztec priesthood (left, priest headdress) had a rich tradition of philosophical thought and debate, comparable to the ancient Greeks. One of the primary concepts of Aztec thought was Teotl, translatable as "oneness in duality," which was ever-flowing and ever-changing energy in motion. Coatlicue represented the part of Teotl in which the earth, which Coatlicue ruled, both gave birth to life and was the home of the dead. Life and death were thus joined in oneness. Coatlicue's own story embodied Teotl: by her death at the hands of her daughter Coyolxauhqui, she gave birth to Huitzilopochtli, god of life-giving sun.

» **Universal Principles:** pp. 102, 295, 332, 430 | **Dualism:** pp. 56, 332

Birth of the Stars Besides Huitzilopochtli and his sister Coyolxauhqui, Coatlicue was the mother of 400 gods, known as the Centzonuitznaua and the Centzonmimixcoa, gods of the southern and northern stars, respectively. The 400 gods hated Coatlicue for becoming pregnant with Huitzilopochtli, and conspired with Coyolxauhqui to murder her. As a result, Huitzilopochtli killed them all, and their dead bodies became stars (**1**, Huitzilopochtli with beheaded Coyolxauhqui).

The Rocky Pilgrimage One day, Emperor Moctezuma I—who ruled from 1440 to 1468—sent 60 magicians on a pilgrimage to pay homage to Coatlicue (**3**) in her home of Aztlán, the place of seven caves, which was the legendary home of the Aztecs. As the magicians reached Aztlán, the ground grew rocky and

hard to travel. The magicians were not able to climb the path to Coatlicue's home under the weight of the gifts they had brought for her. When they met Coatlicue's aged tutor along the way, they eagerly let him carry the gifts for them. When the magicians met Coatlicue, she was crying for her son, Huitzilopochtli, because he was away fighting back the forces of darkness who wanted to kill the sun. Coatlicue was not pleased by the emperor's gifts. She told the magicians that they were fat and lazy, and that they had failed by making the tutor carry the gifts for them. She prophesized that Huitzilopochtli would lose the Aztec cities he ruled in the same order he had gained them, and only then would he come home to his mother. With this, Coatlicue also prophesized the downfall of the Aztec Empire.

The Aztec Calendar

The Aztecs made use of two interlocking calendar systems: a 365-day solar calendar called the Xiuhpohualli and a 260-day ritual calendar called Tonalpohualli. The solar calendar (**1**) worked on a system of 18 months of 20 days, plus five "dead" days at the end of the year. Years were marked by the last day of the 18th month of the ritual calendar. The extra five days at the end of a calendar year were thought to be a dangerous, unlucky time. In contrast to the solar calendar, the ritual calendar used 20 cycles of 13 days each (**2**, a ritual calendar from the Codex Cospi). Every 13-day period, called a *trecena*, was ruled by a different god. The cycle of trecenas determined when festivals and rituals were held. The solar and ritual calendars did not match up at the end of each 365-day year. Instead, they met once every 52 years. A large New Fire Festival was held when both calendars finally cycled back together again.

The 20 Days of the Aztec Calendar The Aztecs named the days of their calendars (**3**, Aztec date stone showing day sign emblems and numerical day markers) by combining a number between one and thirteen—representing the day of the current trecena—and a symbol taken from a list of 20 "day signs." For example, days could be named 11 Rabbit, 3 Lizard, or 9 Jaguar. It would take 260 days for the combination of 20 day signs and 13 numbers to repeat themselves. Years were named after the last day of the 18th month. The solar calendar also gave each month of 20 days its own name, such as Izcalli (first month), Ochpaniztli (12th month), or Tititl (18th month).

Aztec—Xipe Totec

Xipe Totec was originally a tribal god of the indigenous Tlapanec people of the Guerrero Mountains of Mexico. The Aztecs borrowed Xipe Totec and transformed him into one of their most important gods.

Xipe Totec was a god of maize—an important crop to the Aztecs

Xipe Totec controlled the growth of maize together with the rain god Tlaloc (**1**, Xipe Totec on left; Tlaloc on right), and was the patron of goldsmiths. He was also regarded as one of the four high gods—the Four Tezcatlipocas. In that role, he was named the Red Tezcatlipoca of the East, which represented his association with the dawning of the sun. Because he was an important deity to keep happy, Xipe Totec's priests flayed and wore the skin of captives in a festival called Tlacaxipehualiztli. Xipe Totec is often depicted wearing these skins.

■ Xipe Totec was the god of maize and new vegetation, and the patron of goldsmiths

■ He symbolized the death and rebirth of nature

■ He helped create the world, but was also thought to send diseases to humankind

■ Appearing as a man, he flayed himself and shed his skin to give food to humanity

■ In offering to the god, human victims were flayed and their skins removed

■ Without his skin he appears as a golden god, symbolic of maize losing its outer husk

Figures and Stories Relevant to Xipe Totec

Wax Gold Casting The Aztecs, who prized gold jewelry and artwork, made Xipe Totec into the patron god of goldsmithing (**3**). Gold was readily available to the Aztecs, and they most often fashioned it using the lost wax casting technique. In lost wax gold casting, the artist first makes a model out of wax. A mold of hard clay then covers the wax like a shell. The wax is melted away, then molten gold is poured in its place, replacing the wax to make the final work of art. Only nobles were allowed to wear gold jewelry. Within this class, they competed for status by wearing the largest, most complex gold items they could afford. The priests also used gold jewelry (**2**) and statuary as sacrifices to the gods, as gold symbolized maize, the sun, and divine power.

The Four Tezcatlipocas and Birth of Tlaloc Xipe Totec was one of the four divine brothers born of Ometeotl (**4**, as his fire incarnation, Xiuhtecutli), the god of duality, who both impregnated and gave birth to himself. The four brothers were known collectively as the Four Tezcatlipocas: Xipe Totec, Quetzalcóatl, Huitzilopochtli, and the evil god known only as the Black Tezcatlipoca. With his three brothers, Xipe Totec killed the monstrous crocodile Cipactli. Then they created the world and the first people from her broken body. Xipe Totec was also a father to other gods. He helped create Tlaloc, the god of water and drought, and Tlaloc's future wife, Chalchiuhtlicue, the goddess of lakes and rivers. This divine pair was fashioned from the remaining pieces of Cipactli's corpse after the world was made.

The Tlacaxipehualiztli Festival—"The Flaying of Men"

The Tlacaxipehualiztli, or the Flaying of Men, was a festival devoted to Xipe Totec during the 1 Dog–13 Wind period of the Aztec ritual calendar (approximately March in modern calendars). The Aztecs believed that Xipe Totec had once flayed off his own skin to feed their ancestors. The god's self-sacrifice symbolized the way that ripe maize sheds a leafy husk, or skin, to reveal edible corn inside. During the festival, Xipe Totec's priests sacrificed captives by cutting off their skins, dying the skins yellow, then wearing them (right) during rituals. The skins were called "golden clothes," in honor of the golden color of ripe maize.

Aztec—Quetzalcóatl

■ Quetzalcóatl, also known as the White Tezcatlipoca who helped create the world and governs the west as the god of the wind

■ He was associated with Venus, the rising morning star

■ He was often depicted in Aztec mythology as a green snake, the plumed serpent

Quetzalcóatl, also named Kukulcan and Nine Wind, was a major deity and cultural hero to the Aztecs, Maya, and related societies of Central and South America. He is most easily recognized in ceremonial drawings and carvings as a serpent covered in white feathers, by which he was known as the feathered serpent god. In human form, Quetzalcóatl was depicted wearing ritual body paint with a red, bird-like mask, and the Ehecailacozcatl, or the Wind Jewel, which was a symbol of divine breath. He was also shown wearing the Ocelocopolli, a cone-shaped headdress decorated with precious gems, which represented Quetzalcóatl's association with the sun and the planet Venus.

In Aztec and Maya cosmology, Quetzalcóatl was credited with creating the world, naming the lands and seas, discovering maize, domesticating animals, creating fire, and teaching music and dance to the first people of the world. His adherents often called on him to cure blindness, coughs, skin diseases, and infertility.

Moctezuma's Mistake

In 1519, Spanish Conquistador Hernán Cortés beached his ships on the shore of Aztec Moctezuma II's lands. Scholars once believed that the emperor mistook the Spanish invasion for the arrival of Quetzalcóatl, perhaps because myths described Quetzalcóatl as a white conqueror wearing feathers who came from over the sea—just like Cortés and his helmet. Recent studies suggest that this story was probably a political fiction made by Spanish historians writing over 50 years after Cortés defeated Moctezuma.

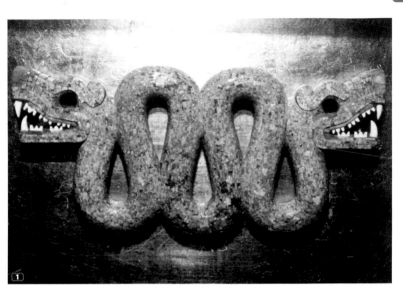

Birth of Quetzalcóatl The Aztecs gave Quetzalcóatl multiple birth stories. In the most common myth, Quetzalcóatl was born to Coatlicue (**1**, double-headed serpent), the earth-mother goddess known as "skirt of serpents." Coatlicue became pregnant when a ball of feathers fell upon her as she swept a temple. By virgin birth, she gave life to Quetzalcóatl, the Feathered Serpent, and his brother Xolotl. In another version, Quetzalcóatl was the son of the god Ometeotl, created when Ometeotl breathed his divine essence upon the earth.

Quetzalcóatl and the Origin of Blood Sacrifice Quetzalcóatl (**2**) created the modern world, the world of the fifth sun, when he and his rival god, Tezcatlipoca, slew the water monster Tlaltecuhtli by grappling her body and splitting her apart. Half of her body transformed into the lands of earth, while the other half became the sky. The monster's divine spirit fell into a rage over the murder; the gods tried to appease her anger, but only the sacrifice of human hearts and blood satisfied her lust for revenge.

Figures and Stories Relevant to Quetzalcóatl

Coatlicue, Quetzalcóatl's Mother, see pp. 384–385

Creation Myths, Quetzalcóatl as Creator God as One of the Four Tezcatlipocas, see pp. 380–381

Cursing of the Aztec Empire, see Coatlicue, p. 385

Aztec—Tlaloc

■ Tlaloc was a god of rain, water, and fertility, and was the third sun god: the Rain Sun

■ He is characteristically similar to the Maya god of rain, Chaac

■ He could send out rain to help the crops or devastate the earth with drought or floods

■ He ruled over a paradise for the souls who died by water called Tlalocan

■ Children were drowned in human sacrifice to Tlaloc

■ He is depicted with goggle eyes and fangs

Tlaloc was one of the more fearsome of the Aztec gods. He is most often seen as a monstrous man with blue skin, prominent fangs, and wide, bulging eyes. His adornments represented his status as a god of rain (**1**), water, drought, and illness.

Tlaloc was believed to carry four magic jugs of water. The water of the first jug, when poured on the ground, caused crops to grow. The second jug's water did the opposite, killing crops and withering whatever it touched. The third jug caused frost and ice, while the water of the fourth jug utterly destroyed anything in its path.

Tlaloc was commonly shown with a net of clouds about his head, a crown of heron feathers, and thunder-making rattles

Priests of Tlaloc were thought to have held particularly violent rituals where they sacrificed children. To honor Tlaloc's control over rain, his priests tore off the children's fingernails and collected their tears of pain in ceremonial bowls. The children were then drowned, so as to send them to live in Tlaloc's afterworld kingdom.

⏵⏵ Maya Rain God—Chaac: pp. 396–397

Tlaloc's Family When the Four Tezcatlipoca gods made the world from the remains of the crocodile Cipactli, they also created Tlaloc to be the god of rain and water. Tlaloc married twice, first to Xochiquetzal (**2**), the goddess of plants, love, and flowers. The marriage ended when the god Black Tezcatlipoca (**3**) kidnapped and seduced her. Tlaloc later married Chalchiuhtlicue, the jade-skirted goddess of lakes and streams. With her, he had Tecciztecatl, the moon-rabbit god.

Tlaloc as Rain Sun As the role of the sun was held by the gods interchangeably, they often fought over this title. When Tlaloc was the sun, he was called the Rain Sun, as he sent rain (**4**, Tlaloc's messenger in a boat pouring rain) and the fields prospered. However, when Tezcatlipoca stole Tlaloc's wife, Xochiquetzal, Tlaloc fell into depression and the rain stopped. The people prayed for more rain, but in a rage, Tlaloc sent a rain of fire that destroyed the world.

The Paradise of Tlalocan

Tlaloc ruled over one of the five layers of the Aztec afterworld, called Tlalocan (**5**) in his honor. Contrary to Tlaloc's reputation as a violent, punitive god, Tlalocan was thought to be a paradise, a beautiful land of mild weather and flowering plants. Because Tlaloc ruled over water and rains, the souls of people who died by drowning or water-carried illnesses were sent to dwell in Tlalocan, as well as the children who were sacrificed to him by way of drowning rituals.

Maya—Creation Myths

■ In Maya mythology, the world was created when the gods shouted "Earth"

■ The gods created all of the land and animals, and last they created people from corn

■ In the Maya universe, a world tree stood in the center of the earth connecting it to the 13 layers of the heavens and the nine layers of the underworld

The Maya creation story is recorded in the *Popol Vuh*, a manuscript written in around 1550, shortly after the first Spanish missionaries reached Guatemala. Here, creation began with a lifeless universe filled with water and shrouded in darkness. The only light in the universe was a pale, glowing light surrounding three serpent gods, who lay under green and blue feathers in the water. These serpent gods were approached one day by three other gods, known collectively as "Heart of Heaven": Caculhá Huracán, Chipi-Caculhá, and Raxa-Caculhá.

The six gods meditated and held council. They knew the world needed to begin. Finally, two of the serpent gods, Tepeu and Gucumatz, decided it was time. They shouted "Earth!" and the world came out of the darkness and water. The mountains rose up from the valleys, and as the waters rolled away, a jungle of trees and vines grew. The gods congratulated each other and finished making the world. They made the mountain spirits, deer, birds, jaguars, and serpents, and their homes. The last aspect of creation proved to be the hardest: creating people. They tried three times before they were satisfied.

Attempts to Make Humanity
The gods first tried to make people from mud. However, when the mud people melted easily, the gods destroyed them and made people from wood. The wood people had no souls and acted like animals. Unhappy, the gods turned them into monkeys. Then the gods made people from corn (**1**). They used corn for the bodies, and corn meal for the arms and legs. Pleasing the gods, the corn people were the ancestors of the Maya.

American Creation Myths: pp. 380, 410, 428

Ceiba—The World Tree

According to the Maya tradition, a magnificent tree stood in the center of the world, connecting the earth to the 13 layers of the heavens and the nine layers of the underworld (**3**). The particular species of tree was usually a ceiba, a South American jungle tree that grows up to 175 feet in height and possesses a remarkably straight trunk. The ceiba world tree was thought to send branches in each of the four compass directions, which the Maya associated with ritual practices. The tree's white flowers were also believed to symbolize the human soul, which was called *sak nik' nal*, or "white flower."

The Ordering of the Universe The Maya believed that the universe was ordered along the four compass (**2**) directions. Each of these directions had a symbolic color: east was red, north was white,

west was black, and south was yellow. In the center of the four compass directions stood the earth, symbolized by the color blue-green. The world was centered on three stones. A tree of life connected the world to the 13 layers of heaven above the tree and nine layers of the underworld, Xibalba, below it. Each cosmic layer was ruled by a different god.

The Venus Calendar

The Maya charted time using a system of calendars developed from various astronomical observations. Particularly important was the Venus calendar. The Maya were accomplished astronomers and were able to chart the movement of the star with enormous accuracy. It is believed that the Venus cycle was important to the Maya as the star was associated with war. The Maya would use their almanac to decide on good times to go into battle and opportune times for coronations. Temples were often aligned with the stars and the symbol of Venus was also used in architecture. Rituals were most likely held on sacred areas dedicated to the star (below, platform of Venus, Chichén Itzá).

Norse World Tree Yggdrasil: p. 240

Maya—Chaac

■ Chaac was the god of agriculture, rain, and fertility

■ Chaac's Aztec counterpart was Tlaloc, the god of rain

■ He made it rain by hitting rain-carrying snakes with his lightning axe

■ Rainmakers from the Maya community could communicate with Chaac and other rain deities

■ He was often depicted as an old man, covered in scales, with a long, twisted nose and fangs.

■ He sometimes carries a shield and his lightning axe

Chaac, the rain, agriculture, and fertility god, was one of the most important and complex gods of the Maya pantheon. Plentiful rains and successful crops were major concerns of the Maya, who settled in an arid region in Mesoamerica. Many rituals like the Cha-Chaac frog ceremony were held to honor him in cites such as Chichén Itzá. The Maya thought he made the rain by hitting the hides of magic rain-bearing snakes with his axe made of lightning.

Chaac's nature was multifold: he was at the same time Chaac, a singular rain god, and four Chaacs, each of whom represented one of the four sacred compass directions by which the Maya ordered their universe. In his four-fold form Chaac was known as Chac Xib Chaac, the Red Chaac of the East; Sac Xib Chaac, the White Chaac of the North; Ek Xib Chaac, the Black Chaac of the West; and Kan Xib Chaac, the Yellow Chaac of the South.

The Aztec god Tlaloc was similar to Chaac. An interesting parallelism also occurred between Chaac's four-in-one nature and the Aztec Four Tezcatlipoca gods, who were likewise associated with the four compass directions and the colors red, white, black, and yellow.

The Cha-Chaac, The Frog Ceremony

The Cha-Chaac, the "Frog Ceremony," is a rain-making ritual devoted to Chaac (right) that was developed by the Maya, which includes four young boys acting as frogs. It is still practiced in varying forms by peasant farmers in the Yucatán today. The ritual takes its name from young boys making frog noises while calling on the god to send rain. Before Spanish colonization, the priests of Chaac sacrificed human victims. Today, farmers offer incense and drink ceremonial corn beer over three days of prayer.

» **Four Tezcatlipocas:** p. 380 | **Tlaloc:** p. 392

Cenotes of the Yucatán

Cenotes (**1**), subterranean wells found throughout the Yucatán, were used as sacrificial pits to Chaac. The Maya believed that the wells were doorways into the god's supernatural kingdom. In tribute to him, they threw gold and drowned young boys in the wells.

Cracking Open the Mountain for Corn

An ancient myth stemming from pre-Maya times demonstrates the importance of Chaac. One day, the ancestors of the Maya were facing starvation because an evil god had stolen all of the food in the land. Directing their prayers to Chaac, the patron god of agriculture, they begged him for food. Hearing the people, Chaac (**2**) took his axe made of lightning and struck a mighty blow upon a mountain. As the mountain split open, the people found enough corn in its center to hold a feast.

Origin of Rain—Adultery With C'agua Sa'que's Wife

C'agua Choc (another name for Chaac, meaning "cloud") was the older brother of C'agua Sa'que, the sun. C'agua Sa'que married C'ana Po, the moon. However, instead of loving C'agua Sa'que, C'ana Po fell in love with Chaac. When C'agua Sa'que learned of the affair, he put gall from male turkeys in C'ana Po and Chaac's food in revenge. This cast a spell that made the two lovers argue about who would get water from the river. C'ana Po became so angry at Chaac that she left and never came back. Heartbroken, Chaac cried, and his tears became rain (**3**).

The Step Pyramids of Pre-Columbian Civilizations

The Aztecs, Maya, and their ancestor civilizations are well known for having built step pyramids. Unlike ancient Egyptian pyramids, these pyramids were not tombs, but were used as platforms for public temples. The name "step pyramid" comes from how the pyramid walls look in cross section. A slope leads up to a flat ledge, itself topped by another slope and a slightly smaller ledge, until the temple's top platform is reached, giving the appearance of a series of gigantic stair steps. The pyramids were generally not made of solid blocks of stone, but from multiple layers of earth and gravel covered with a fitted stone exterior. A single pyramid could require centuries to finish building, and some of the largest could reach gargantuan sizes. The Great Pyramid of Cholula, Mexico, is one of the world's largest man-made monuments, larger by a third than the Great Pyramid of Giza in Egypt.

» The Great Mystery of the Pyramids: p. 68

The best known temple of Chichén Itzá is the Kukulcán pyramid (pictured), or El Castillo (Spanish for "the castle"). The Maya raised Kukulcán between the 11th and 13th centuries A.D. as a temple to the god Kukulcán, a Maya serpent god similar to the Aztec god Quetzalcóatl. The temple's architecture has astronomical features thought to have been religiously important. Each of the pyramid's four stairs has 91 steps. Including the top platform, there are 365 steps in all, equal to the 365 days of the Maya calendar. During the vernal equinox (March) and autumnal equinox (September), seven triangles of light and shadow reflect from the western side of Kukulcán's main stairs, forming the shape of a serpent's body that, as the light changes, winds toward a serpent's head carved at the base of the stairs. The passage of the serpent of sunlight may have represented the ritual appearance of the god Kukulcán himself.

Maya—Huracán

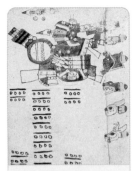

Huracán (**1**) storm god in the Maya Madrid Codex, was the Maya god of wind, fire, and lightning. His name meant "the one-legged," which may have referenced his power to kick or stamp down lightning bolts during storms.

Huracán played a significant role in Maya beliefs, participating heavily in the creation of the world. He was also responsible for the destruction by flood of an early version of humanity that had displeased the gods. In order to reveal the land once more, he repeated "land" until it emerged from the flooded sea. He also appeared in the mythology of the hero twins, Hunahpu and Xbalanque, by asking them to stop the arrogant god Seven Macaw and his son, Cabrakan. Huracán is shown in artistic depictions with a long, snout-like nose, and a small object splitting a mirror placed on his forehead.

■ Huracán, also known as Caculhá Huracán, Tohil, Bolon Tzacab, and K'awil, was the god of wind, fire, and lightning

■ He is shown with one human leg and one leg made from a serpent's body, symbolic of his status as a creation god

Storm Gods As the Pre-Columbian peoples in Central America practiced and depended on agriculture, storms were a great danger as they could destroy entire crops. Both the Maya and the Actecs referred to gods and goddesses (**1**) who controlled storms. The Aztec god Tezcatlipoca shows many similarities to Huracán. Both were storm gods, thus represented destructive, but were also creation gods. They were also both associated with a mirror. While the Nahuatl name of Tezcatlipoca is often translated as "smoking mirror," Huracán has a mirror on his forehad. The mirror-object is typically smoking, representing storms and winds.

Great Floods: pp. 28, 32, 335, 411, 445

Huracán and Hurricane

When the Spanish explorers reached the Caribbean, they adopted the word huracán, *meaning "storm," from the Taíno, a group inhabiting the area. The Taíno word likely derived from the Maya god Huracán's name. As the strong Caribbean storms were not seen in their homeland, it is no surprise that the Spanish acquired a local word to describe them. This new word soon spread. Different anglicized spellings of* huracán *were used until the modern spelling of hurricane was popularized by Shakespeare's use of* hurricano.

Huracán and the Great Flood

At the beginning of the world, the gods first tried making people out of wood. The wood people looked like normal people, but had no souls, which made them act irreverently to the gods. Becoming angry, the gods wanted to punish the wood people. Huracán caused rain to fall ceaselessly, day and night, until the entire world flooded (**2**). The wood people tried to seek shelter from the rains, but could find none. The trees knocked them out of their branches. The caves closed when they approached. Their dogs and household utensils yelled at them and attacked the people for mistreating them; their millstones tried to crush them. Thus, the wood people found no rest until they retreated to the forest where their faces became squashed and they turned into monkeys.

2

The Popol Vuh

The *Popol Vuh* ("book of the mat") is one of the most important records of Maya mythology. It was a kind of history book and bible for the community. It contains the story of how the world was made (**1**, creation), a series of epic stories about the gods, and a history of the ruling family of the Quiché people.

In reality, the *Popul Vuh* known today is only a copy, using European letters, of the original book written in Maya picture symbols (**2**). The copy was recorded in the Quiché language around 1550. The classical Maya lived from about A.D. 250 to 900 and the Quiché were their descendants. The myths were not exactly the same as ancient Maya myths, but scholars believe that there were enough correspondences to make the *Popol Vuh* one of the most accurate sources known for Maya religious beliefs.

Lost in the Archives The earliest known copy of the *Popol Vuh* was found by a Dominican priest, Francisco Ximénez, in the 18th century. He translated his copy into Spanish and added it to the appendix of his book about Guatemalan languages, *Grammar of Three Languages: Kaqchikel, Quiché, and Tzutuhil*. His manuscript was forgotten in the library of the University of San Carlos, Guatemala City, until it was rediscovered in 1854 by Abbé Brasseur de Bourbourg and Karl von Scherzer, who published French and Spanish versions.

Maya—Itzamná

Little knowledge of the Maya high god Itzamná survived Spanish colonization. He is known to have been a creator god who lived in the upper skies, and was thought to be a god of priests and medicine. He gave the Maya cacao trees. Different renditions of Itzamná associated him with Hunab Ku, an invisible high god; Kinich Ahau, the god of the sun; and Yaxcocahmut, a divine, omen-giving bird.

Itzamná was known to play a significant role in the Maya ritual calendar. Out of the four-year ritual cycle, one year was dedicated to him alone. He was also closely linked to certain months in every Maya year: Uo, Zip, and Mac. In the month of Uo, Itzamná was called upon under the name Kinich Ahau Itzamná, or "first priest," while priests sprinkled their holy books with sanctified water. In rituals during the month of Zip, Itzamná was worshiped in his guise as a god of medicine. During the month of Mac, Itzamná was associated with Chaac, the rain god, and was worshiped by old men and women.

■ Itzamná had several incarnations, principally as a celestial ruler and a bird god

■ He gave humankind writing, taught it the calendar, and was a god of medicine

■ Itzamná's sons, the four Bacabs, stood at the four corners of the world and held up the sky

■ Sometimes he appeared as the four Itzamnás who enveloped the world

■ He is symbolized by the snake and the mussel

■ In his bird god form, he is depicted as a hawk or a heron and bears the symbols for day and night on his wings

Divine Rule In a number of books and mural paintings, Itzamná was shown in two principal forms: as a celestial ruler and as a bird god. In his celestial ruler form, Itzamná was dressed as a high priest (**1**), and sat on a heavenly throne, directing farming and hunting activities. In his bird god form, Itzamná was shown as a heron or hawk-like bird, sometimes with the symbols for day and night written on his wings, often

holding a two-headed snake in his beak. Maya kings invoked Itzamná in his bird god form as justification for their right to rule. Kings of Maya cities such as Yaxchilan, Dos Pilas, and Naranjo added Itzamná's name to their own. Temple artwork also showed human figures wearing Itzamná's bird god symbols paying respects to kings, or presenting a king with his ceremonial headband, the Maya version of a crown.

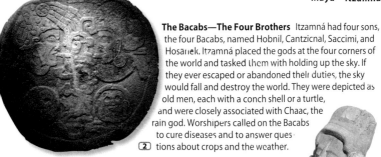

The Bacabs—The Four Brothers Itzamná had four sons, the four Bacabs, named Hobnil, Cantzicnal, Saccimi, and Hosanek. Itzamná placed the gods at the four corners of the world and tasked them with holding up the sky. If they ever escaped or abandoned their duties, the sky would fall and destroy the world. They were depicted as old men, each with a conch shell or a turtle, and were closely associated with Chaac, the rain god. Worshipers called on the Bacabs to cure diseases and to answer questions about crops and the weather.

Marriage to Ix Chel Ix Chel (**3**), also known as Chac Chel, was the jaguar goddess of medicine and midwifery. Her name Chel may have meant "rainbow." She was frequently depicted as an old woman wearing a serpent headdress, sometimes with clawed hands and feet. Her symbol was an overturned water jar, representing rain falling from the clouds. She was sometimes associated with the waning, darkening phase of the moon. Only one myth featuring Ix Chel has survived to modern times. In this myth, Ix Chel was the wife of Itzamná. Together, they had 13 sons. Two of the sons, associated with the howler monkey gods, created the heavens, the earth, and people. Scholars think that Ix Chel's worship may have involved ritual sweat baths, where Maya mothers bathed during pregnancy and after giving birth.

Cocoa

The cocoa seed, source of our modern chocolates, was incredibly important to the Maya and Aztec cultures. Cocoa seeds come from the cacao tree, thought to be native to South America. The Maya are believed to have introduced the cacao tree to Central America, and revered cocoa as one of the founding gifts of civilization granted to them by their high god Itzamná. The use of cocoa later spread to the Aztecs, who made a bittersweet drink from ground cocoa, vanilla pods, peppers, and herbs. This cocoa drink was a favorite of the Aztec emperor Moctezuma II, and over 2,000 pitchers of it were prepared for him and the nobles of his court every day.

■ Hunahpu and Xbalanque were twin brothers who brought Xibalba, the underworld, to an end

■ Associated with the Maya maize god, the heroic pair were not specifically gods, but they displayed supernatural powers

■ Hunahpu, meaning "one blowgunner," was a bird hunter

■ He was known by the black corpse spots on his skin that signified his death and rebirth

■ Xbalanque, meaning "jaguar sun," had jaguar pelt marks on his skin

Maya— Hunahpu and Xbalanque

The hero twins were ball players (pictured)

Hunahpu and Xbalanque were divine twin brothers, sons of Hun Hunahpu, a renowned ball player murdered by the 12 lords of Xibalba, the underworld. Passing through a series of traps and ritual ball games, the twins defeated the Xibalban lords, avenged their father, and brought the entire underworld to an end.

Hunahpu's name translates as "one blowgunner," which referred to his childhood spent hunting birds. He can be identified by the black spots on his skin, which represented how he was killed during the fight against the Xibalban lords, then resurrected by his brother. Xbalanque's name meant "jaguar sun" or "hidden sun." He was known by the jaguar pelt marks on his skin. Both twins were at times symbolized by two stalks of corn, referring to their ritual association with the growth of maize.

Maya Ball Games

Ritual ball games were a central part of Maya ceremonies. Played in each large Maya city, the games were attended by commoners and chieftains alike. The players (left, a ball player), who were mostly captives, were divided into two teams. They played for life or death, as the losing team was sacrificed. The object of the game was to push a rubber ball through the stone-ring on the wall. The players had to do this without touching the ball with their legs or arms—only with their chest, shoulders, or hips. Because the ring was placed high, passing the ball through it was extremely difficult. Thus, whoever managed it often won the game.

➋ **Journeys in the Underworld:** pp. 39, 41, 159, 353,

Pregnancy of Xquic Xquic was the mother of Hunahpu and Xbalanque. She became pregnant with the twins when she was speaking with the skull of their dead father, Hun Hunahpu (**1**). His skull spat on Xquic's hand, which made her pregnant. Because Hun Hunahpu was dead, Xquic had no one to take care of her. She begged Hun Hunahpu's mother to take her into the household, and was taken in, but was not welcomed as a full member of the family. After the twins were

born, their grandmother hated them for crying too much. Their older half brothers, One Howler Monkey and One Artisan, were afraid that the twins would steal all the attention, and tried to kill them. The older brothers threw the babies on an anthill and in a bramble bush, but the twins survived. As the twins grew, the older brothers made them hunt birds for food and do chores, while they played and sang songs. The twins became heroes in spite of this punishing treatment.

Playing Ball in Xibalba
The 12 lords of Xibalba hated Hunahpu and Xbalanque for playing ball too noisily. They summoned the twins to

Xibalba, intending to kill them through a series of traps and rigged ball games (**2**) played with a ball mounted with a razor sharp blade. The twins outwitted every trap using cunning and magic, and

fairly defeated the Xibalbans at ball. They then caused the downfall of the entire underworld through an elaborate disguise. They impersonated miracle workers and tricked the two highest lords of Xibalba into offering themselves as sacrifices, then killed them.

Xibalba—Maya Underworld

Xibalba was an underworld kingdom of the dead, ruled by 12 demons known as the lords of Xibalba. The kingdom itself could only be reached from the mortal world by extreme difficulty: after finding a suitable cave entrance, travelers had to survive passing rivers of scorpions, blood, and pus, then enchanted crossroads that gave misleading directions toward deadly traps. Once in the kingdom, mortals were taken to the palace where the lords of Xibalba resided. The lords forced travelers to spend nights in a series of six magical houses: the dark house, the cold house, the jaguar house, the bat house, the blade house, and the fire house. These houses were named for the traps they contained, and were invariably lethal to anyone who even dared to enter them. The Maya believed that their ancestors and the recently deceased had to suffer living in Xibalba for a time before they were allowed in heaven. Only those who committed suicide, were sacrificed, or were mothers who died in childbirth were exempt and could go straight to the gods.

Inca—Viracocha

Viracocha was the highest and most powerful god in the Inca pantheon. He was god of the sun, storms, fire, and lightning, and the creator of the Inca universe. Viracocha had two children with his wife Mama Qocha ("sea mother"), the sun god Inti and the moon goddess Mama Quilla. Inti and Mama Quilla were said to be the parents of the first Inca ruler, Manco Cápac, and his sister and wife Mama Ocllo. Manco Cápac founded Cuzco, the capital of the Inca Empire, teaching agriculture to the humans and establishing a codex of laws. The following Inca emperors were seen as living incarnations of Inti, and recognized Viracocha as their spiritual father. Although the worship of Inti became the official state cult of the Inca, Viracocha was also honored, but few temples (**1**) were dedicated to him.

Viracocha was often represented as a pale, bearded man with Caucasian features and green eyes. Because of these traits and Viracocha's association with the powers of creation and the sun, scholars have debated a connection to the Aztec god Quetzalcóatl.

■ Viracocha was the supreme god and created the universe

■ He was the god of the sun, lightning, storms, and fire, and father of Inti, the sun god

■ He was worshiped by the pre-Inca people in Peru

■ Represented as a bearded old man, he traveled the earth and taught humanity civilization

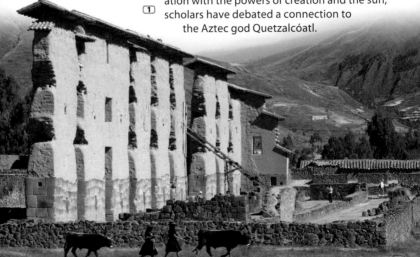

1

2

Destruction of the First World

In the beginning, Viracocha made a world that had no light: no sun, no moon, no stars. He made people live in this dark world, and ordered them to follow his moral teachings. However, they became proud and spiteful. Angered with their disobedience, Viracocha sent 60 days and nights of torrential rain, which flooded (**2**) the world and obliterated its people.

Creation of the New World

When Viracocha destroyed his first world with a flood, he spared three people to be assistants to help him rebuild the world. One of the first things Viracocha did was to create light for the darkened world. The god took his servants to an island in Lake Titicaca, which was believed to be the center of the world. From the island, he ordered the sun, moon, and stars to rise from the water into the sky (**3**). Viracocha had made the moon brighter than the sun, but the sun was jealous. As the sun and moon rose into the sky, the sun tossed ashes over the moon, which dimmed its light to its present level. Later, as Viracocha gave instructions to his three servants for further tasks, one of the servants, Taguapaca, became disobedient. So Viracocha ordered his other two servants to toss Taguapaca into the lake. Screaming curses and insults, Taguapaca was sucked under the waters and disappeared.

3

Wanderings as a Beggar

Once the new world was complete, Viracocha (**4**) decided to explore his lands on foot, to see how well his new people were living and to civilize them. In some accounts, he wore only a plain white robe, or beggar's rags, so that no one would know him. While traveling, the god did not always find a warm welcome. In one town, the people took offense at his appearance, and tried to kill him. Viracocha frightened them off by making fire rain down on a hill. The fire was so hot that it bleached the boulders it touched. Later, Viracocha disappeared after walking across the Pacific Ocean. It was believed that he left the other gods to take care of his creation and only returned during times of trouble.

Quetzalcóatl: p. 390 | **Great Floods:** pp. 28, 32, 335, 401, 445

Inca—Myths of Love and Tragedy

- Inca society was stratified; nobles did not marry or mix with commoners

- The separation of social classes is reflected in the Inca myths of love, which often serve as warnings against social mixing

- A love affair between a shepherd and an Inca ruler's daughter ended with the lovers turned into stones on a mountain

- The goddess Cavillaca threw herself into the sea when the father of her baby turned out to be the lowly god Coniraya

- Mama Coca was killed by her many jealous lovers, and became the goddess of coca

Inca mythology provides interesting glimpses into the social rules for relationships between men and women, in light of Inca class structure. Inca society was noticeably stratified. Commoners formed the largest and lowest level, and were responsible for farming, herding, construction, and the general work needed to keep Inca civilization running. A much smaller class of nobles, centered around the divine kingship of the Inca, controlled the political life of the empire. Above the world of mortals ruled the gods. As one might imagine, men and women (**1**) from different classes of society did not generally marry or mingle. This is reflected in stories of tragic love affairs which invariably ended badly, including for the gods themselves.

Acoya-napa and Chuqui-llantu The shepherd Acoya-napa tended a herd of white llamas (**2**) for the Inca emperor. One day, he met the emperor's daughter, Chuqui-llantu, known as the daughter of the sun. They immediately fell in love. However, they had to keep their affair a secret because of their class differences. If the emperor found out, he would kill them. The shepherd's mother used a spell to turn him into a cloak, which the princess secretly carried with her. He turned back into a man whenever the two lovers were alone. When their romance was discovered by a guard, they escaped by running up a mountain, where they were turned into stone pillars.

Affairs of Mama Coca, the Goddess of the Coca Leaf

In Inca society, the coca plant (**4**), the source of cocaine, was used for many purposes. It was made into medicine, chewed (**3**, man chewing leaves) before long mountain treks to make the journey easier, and formed into decorative artworks. The goddess of the coca leaf was called Mama Coca. She was originally a mortal woman who took on many lovers. When the lovers learned of each other and became jealous, they argued, then turned their anger on the woman. Enraged, they ripped her to pieces, and the first coca plant grew from her blood.

Coniraya and Cavillaca Cavillaca was a virgin goddess of love (**5**, "lovers" said to have been carved by Cavillaca). Very beautiful and innocent in spirit, she was desired by many of the male gods. As hard as they tried to interest her or capture her, none succeeded. Finally, Coniraya, trickster god of the moon and a great magician, took interest in Cavillaca. Taking some of his semen, he fashioned what appeared to be a tasty piece of fruit, and placed it where Cavillaca would find it. Later, the goddess found and ate the fruit, which made her pregnant with a son. To her shame, she did not know who the father was. To find out, she placed her baby in front of a group of the gods. It crawled toward Coniraya, revealing his parentage. Becoming upset because Coniraya was a god of low status, Cavillaca fled to the sea. She threw herself and her baby into the waters, where they turned into rocks.

Inca—Sun Cult

- Sun worship played a central role in the Inca Empire
- Inti was worshiped as the god of the sun
- Inca emperors were intrinsically linked to Inti, and therefore worship of the sun included worship of the emperor
- Observatories, where the light from the sun was measured, were prevalent
- The capital, Cuzco, housed the most important Temple of the Sun
- Inti was symbolized as a golden circle representing the sun with a face in the center

Sun worship was the foundation of Inca culture and religion. The Inca worshiped the sun in the guise of Inti, god of the sun. While Inca rulers styled themselves as "children of the sun," the emperor was also seen as a living incarnation of the god Inti and the sun. Many temples dedicated to the sun were built in the Inca Empire, with the sun temple of Cuzco being the most important sanctuary.

Sun worship also played a role in the establishment and maintenance of the Inca Empire. To show the dominance of the Inca rulers over their many subjects and territories the priesthood established yearly sun worshiping rituals across the empire. These rituals gave sacrifices and worship to the god Inti, and by proxy to his human avatar, the Inca emperor.

Toward the same end, the priests of Inti and the Inca rulers commissioned gigantic solar observatories, designed to measure the light of the rising and setting sun during the winter and summer solstices. The oldest known observatory is located at Chankillo, Peru, and is thought to be at least 2,300 years old.

Festival of Inti Raymi at Cuzco

The Inti Raymi was one of four annual festivals celebrated in the Inca capital of Cuzco. It was dedicated to the worship of Inti and it recounted the origins of the Inca people. The festival was nine days and nights of parades, dancing, animal sacrifices, and ritual drinking. The timing of Inti Raymi coincided with the winter solstice, and marked the start of a new Inca calendar year. Modern re-creations (right) of Inti Raymi have been held at Sacsayhuamán, near Cuzco, since 1944.

Sun Cults: p. 90

The Inca as the "Great Sun"

As the living incarnation of Inti, the Inca emperor was more than a political ruler; he was actually part of the sun worship cult (**1**). He was called the Sapa Inca, meaning "the only Inca," or just Sapa, meaning "the only." The religious counterpart to the Sapa Inca was the Willaq Umu, meaning "priest who tells the story." The Willaq Umu was ascribed the status of a living son of Inti. In practice, the role was often filled by the Sapa Inca's younger brother.

Inti the Sun God Inti (**2**, throne of the sun god at Machu Picchu) was the patron deity of Tawantinsuyu, the Inca Empire. He was the son of Viracocha, the Inca high god, and was married to Mama Pacha, the goddess of the Earth. They had a son, Manco Cápac, and a daughter, Mama Ocllo. According to legend, Inti sent his children to the ancestors of the Inca to teach them how to live and how to establish their empire. He also ordered his children to build the Inca capital city of Cuzco on the site where a golden staff they carried fell to the ground. Inti's symbol in art was a male human face drawn inside a golden circle, representing the sun.

> ### Figures and Stories Relevant to the Sun Cult
>
> **Acoya-napa and Chiqui-llantu**, Chiquillantu Was a Daughter of the Sun, see Inca Myths of Love and Tragedy, p. 412
>
> **The Huacas**, Sun Rituals Were Undertaken on Sacred Huaca Routes, see pp. 416–417
>
> **Viracocha**, Inti the Sun God's Father, see pp. 410–411

Inca—The Huacas

■ *Huaca* is the Inca name for sacred objects and the state of being after death, and is also used in reference to sacred ritual

■ Huaca also refers to spirits and was applied to both living things and geographical places, as well as monuments, from pyramids to small stone shrines

■ As all the world was considered to be alive and sacred, anything of significant note or beauty was considered a huaca

■ A ceremonial route could be a huaca, and was referred to as a *ceque*; such a route in Cuzco was used for sun rituals

Alongside the worship of the gods, the huacas played an important role in the Inca religion. Huacas were people, animals, plants, or objects that were believed to have a special supernatural power. The Inca often identified the huacas by their unusual shapes or exceptional appearance, such as rock formations, doubled corn cobs, and human or animal albinos. Huacas could also be identified by an important political or religious event having happened in a certain location.

However, the term huaca is perhaps most commonly associated with Inca mummies. The Inca nobility typically mummified their deceased ancestors, and placed the mummies in special houses. These houses were huacas, as were the mummies, because they were infused with the power of the ancestral dead.

Huacas associated with geographical places were typically found in the mountains, e.g., difficult mountain passes, clearings on mountain tops, or a particular spot on a mountain believed in local lore to have been touched by the gods.

Huacas and Hidden Gold

When the Spanish conquistadors saw the Inca's rich use of gold, they developed an insatiable desire for it. The Spanish rashly destroyed Inca huaca artifacts and holy sites if they believed gold (**1**) could be found within. One of most destructive episodes fell upon the Huaca del Sol, an adobe temple near Trujillo, Peru. The Spanish diverted a river from its natural bed to wash away the temple walls, but no gold was ever found.

①

» **North America—Sacred Locales:** p. 426 | **Mummification:** pp. 75, 94

Mummification Practices of the Inca

Two different types of Inca mummies (right) were found. In the capital city of Cuzco; the Inca nobility mummified their ancestors and kept them in special houses of the dead. The Spanish conquistadors destroyed them, so the exact process of mummification has been lost. Another type of mummy was children sacrificed on mountain tops. The children were left exposed to the extreme cold and thin air of high altitude, which freeze-dried their bodies almost intact. Because of the divine parentage of the nobility and the sacral destination of the children, these mummies were regarded as huacas.

Huacas and Ceremonial Routes The Inca sometimes ordered larger huacas along specific geographical routes and integrated existing huacas (**2**) into them. These routes served both ceremonial and political purposes. As ceremonial routes, they provided stations of worship along prescribed paths. These paths were sometimes aligned astronomically, such as with the rising and falling of the sun and the various stars associated with planting and harvesting crops. As a political tool, the huaca routes helped join the disparate peoples of the Inca Empire under a single unified system of beliefs.

2

Inca—Machu Picchu

The mysterious Inca city Machu Picchu, built 7,874 feet above sea level in the Andes mountains, is often called "the lost city of the Inca." Hidden high in the mountains, Machu Picchu remained untouched by the Spanish conquerors. The sacred district of the site hosted one of the more remarkable finds at Machu Picchu: the *Intihuatana*, or "hitching post of the sun." Here, during the winter solstice, priests performed a ritual that was supposed to prevent the sun from completely disappearing. Located near the Intihuatana was the main temple, which was dedicated to the sun and its god, Inti. At the summer and winter solstices, the sun shone on the altar through each one of the temple's two trapezoidal windows. Within the temple stood the renowned Room of the Three Windows, which was said to have been where the four sons and four daughters of Inti stepped out into the world in their search for fertile land.

North America—Creation Myths

The creation stories of the North American Indian tribes are diverse, and varied widely depending on the tribe, the geographical region, and the person telling the story. However, several general themes were shared across many stories.

It was not unusual to think of the universe before the beginning of the world as a place of darkness, void, or endless waters. A creator god then acted upon the darkness or the waters to make the sun, the earth, and the animals, or in some cases created another deity to do the work for him or her. Most traditions tell of the creator ordering the world in the same way: heaven, earth, and underworld.

The creator god is sometimes represented as an invisible spirit, a spirit possessing human-like attributes, or an animal spirit. He or she was also often the parent or creator of the lesser spirits of the tribe's beliefs, and responsible for either making people directly, or ordering the lesser spirits to make people on his behalf.

■ Most North American tribes believed in a creator god who created lesser deities

■ The Hopi believed that they had ascended to the modern, fourth world from a series of three prior worlds that had been destroyed

■ The Seminole thought that after the creator spirit had made the animals, he sealed them in a giant shell

■ The Iroquois believed that the earth was made from mud heaped on a turtle's back

Ascending to the Fourth World—The Hopi The Hopi of the Southwest had multiple creation stories. In one version, Tawa, spirit of the sun, created the world from the *tokpella*, or the endless void of space. In another, the world was made by two spirits called Hard Being Woman of the East and Hard Being Woman of the West, while Tawa watched their work. In a third story, Tawa created a heaven and rain spirit named Sotuqnangu (**3**, Hopi Kachina doll, representing the thunder spirit), who created the Spider Grandmother, who then made the world. The Hopi also believed that they lived in the fourth of a series of worlds. Each prior world had been destroyed when the Hopi had fallen into vice and bad habits. Each time, a spirit spared only the virtuous Hopi by bringing them up to the next, new world.

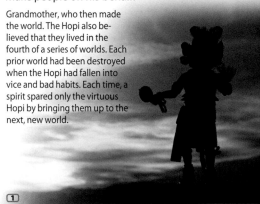

①

The Great Shell on the Mountain—The Seminole The Seminole of Florida and the Southeast believed that in the beginning, the Grandfather Spirit, creator of the world, first made the animals. He sealed them in a giant shell while he finished making the world. When this was done, he put the shell on a mountain and told the animals inside to wait for it to crack open. A long time passed inside the shell, but it never opened. It stayed so long on the mountain that a tree grew by it. The tree grew until one of its roots cracked the shell open. The first animal to leave the shell was the panther, who was followed by the bird, bear, deer, snake, frog, and otter. The animals (**2**) then went to their homes in the new world.

Dreaming Woman of the Sky World—The Iroquois The Iroquois of the Northeast believed that in the beginning, there was no land, only an endless, empty sea. Far above the sea, in the sky, lived the sky world tribe. One woman of the tribe was known for her dreams. One night, she had a nightmare about the magic tree that gave light for the sky world, as there was no sun. At her request, the tribe tried to dig around the tree, but it fell down the hole they dug in the sky. Angered at losing the tree, the tribe pushed the woman down the hole but a hawk caught her. As she had no place to stand, birds and water animals heaped sea-mud on a turtle's back (**3**) until the mud pile grew to become the earth.

North America—Manitou

Aside from countless nature spirits, many North American Indian tribes are thought to have believed in *manitou* (**1**), meaning "deity" in the language of the Ojibwe and Algonquin tribes, inhabitants of the Great Lakes area of the United States and Canada. The term referred to an impersonal spiritual power of exceptional force, which could be found in people, animals, and natural phenomena or features. Meanwhile, the Pawnee in Nebraska honored a great spirit named Tirawa, who was linked with natural phenomena like the sun, moon, and stars.

It was the job of the shamans or medicine men to bridge contact between the living and the spirits of the dead. Shamans employed several methods to receive visions about the future or to learn how to heal a sick person.

When Christian missionaries first encountered the tribes after 1850 and sought to understand their concept of a supreme, high deity, *gitchi manitou*, or "greatest spirit," was coined to make conversion attempts easier by relating gitchi manitou to the Christian God.

■ Some tribes believed in a great spirit, or manitou, an impersonal spiritual power

■ The term manitou derives from the Anishinaabe word for deity

■ The sweat lodge was used as a rite of purification and healing

■ Shamans provoked visions that consulted the spirits

[1]

The Sweat Lodge While the practice of bathing in a sweat lodge (**2**) was widespread throughout North American tribes, it took subtly different forms depending on each tribe's beliefs. Generally, the sweat lodge was a domed hut that was tightly sealed with skins or clay. Stones were heated in a fire, brought inside, then water was tossed over them to fill the lodge with steam. The ceremony had strict rituals and rules, from gathering of special wood to the tending of the fire by special persons. Sweat lodge ceremonies had both aspects of mental purification and physical healing, as well as giving requests and thanks to the ancestors. The ceremony was led by a shaman and began with the evocation of the souls of ancestors and spirits of the tribe.

Vision Quest Ritual Like the sweat lodge, the practice of the vision quest varied greatly by tribe. Generally, a vision quest served one of two purposes: either as a rite of passage for an adolescent boy to become a man, or as part of a neophyte shaman's apprenticeship for learning the tribe's sacred rituals. A vision quest could be accomplished by a variety of means: the aspirant (**4**) might fast for several days, hike or run to

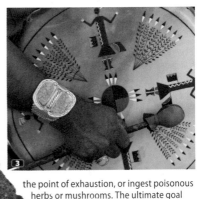

the point of exhaustion, or ingest poisonous herbs or mushrooms. The ultimate goal was to force the aspirant into an altered state of awareness in which he could perceive and converse with his patron spirits. Another way of receiving visions was accomplished through ritualistic infliction of pain, for example, a participant could cut his own body. Shamans also often used hand drum rhythms (**3**) or monotonous singing to enter a trance.

» Shamanism in Africa: p. 436

North America—Totem Poles and Animal Spirits

Totem poles (**1**) are large free-standing tree trunks, carved and painted with the stylized faces and bodies of animals and tribal spirits. Most totem poles were made in the forests of the Pacific Northwest region of the United States and Canada, by the Haida, Tsimshian, and Tlingit tribes. The raising of a new pole was always accompanied by a celebration.

Generally, a totem pole, more correctly referred to as a heraldic column, was raised to honor the family—or a famous member of it—that caused it to be carved. It served the function of marking a family or tribe's territory, as well as warding off evil spirits. The poles often told stories—about an exceptional event or the life of a great chief, for example—which were read from bottom to top. The figures carved on the pole represented the animal heralds of a family. Although the North American Indians believed in animal spirits, they did not believe in totem animals, contrary to the assumptions of earlier scholars.

■ Totem or crest poles were carved to honor famous members of a family and to ward off evil animals

■ Most Indian tribes believed in animal spirits

■ The bear was seen as a chief, or leader of a hunting party

■ The coyote and raven were trickster spirits

■ Iroquois medicine societies were often named after mystic animals like the otter or eagle

Animals in Myth: pp. 104, 230, 322

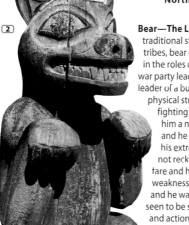

Bear—The Leader

In the traditional stories of many tribes, bear (**2**) was portrayed in the roles of a chieftain, a war party leader, or as the leader of a buffalo hunt. Bear's physical strength and fighting prowess made him a natural leader, and he was known for his extreme courage, if not recklessness, in warfare and hunting. His weakness was his pride, and he was sometimes seen to be slow of thought and action. In totems, the figure of bear was often reserved for the chief, or for prominent, important families. The bear (along with the otter, eagle, and buffalo) gave name to medicine societies formed by the Iroquois. Members of these secret communities shared their healing and magical knowledge.

Coyote and Raven—The Tricksters

In contrast to bear's steadfastness of character, coyote (**4**) and raven (**3**, shaman's rattle) both filled the role of trickster spirits. They were seen to be highly intelligent, sometimes cowardly, sometimes mischievous spirits who cared little for the rules of society that bear epitomized. Coyote, in particular, often used deceit when he came into conflict with bear over who would have the glory and spoils of buffalo hunts.

White Buffalo—The Redeemer

The Lakota tribe believed in an unusual and very interesting animal spirit: the white buffalo, known also as the White Buffalo Calf Woman. The story starts with the Lakota people suffering from famine. The chief sent out two scouts in search of game animals for food. After a long journey, the scouts saw a beautiful woman clothed in white skins. The first scout desired her to be his wife, and ran to embrace her. As he did, a heavy cloud surrounded him. When it lifted, only the scout's bones remained. The second scout was afraid, but the woman calmed him and told him to return home to prepare a feast. She then revealed her name to be White Buffalo Calf Woman. When she came to the feast, she taught the people sacred rituals, and gave them the *chununpa*, or sacred tobacco pipe. The Lakota revered her as a bringer of redemption ever since.

North America—Sacred Locales

■ A place could be sacred because it was inhabited by spirits, because mythic events happened there, or because it was used for rituals

■ Because of their importance, many tribes instituted taboos that prohibited just anyone from entering certain places, thus trying to protect them

■ The Klamath believed that the Crater Lake was created during a battle between two rival chiefs

■ The Lakota Sioux believed the Black Hills mountains to be the center of the universe

Many North American Indian tribes held certain places to be sacred. They saw themselves as the protectors and guards of these places; thus there were strict taboos limiting who visited them. While every tribe had its own understanding of what made a place sacred, and why it is possible to notice widespread similarities between tribes. Sacred places could be remarkable features in the natural landscape, or places that were held sacred because the tribe believed that spirits inhabited or had touched the place. It was common for a tribe to attribute the origin of their ancestors to a sacred place, such as a mountain or a massive hill.

The myths of some tribes refer to spirit animals or deities turning people into stone; thus rocky landmarks could memorialize the event. Battles between legendary chiefs or mythic spirits were sometimes thought to have been so severe that they crushed hills, raised mountains, or created lakes and rivers. Landmarks were also often viewed as the transformed body of a monster, who had been slain by a mythological hero.

The Serpent Mound of Ohio

The Serpent Mound of Ohio is something of an unsolved mystery for archaeologists. The mound itself is physically impressive, running about 1,370 feet long in the shape of a smoothly winding serpent whose tail is coiled three times around. The serpent's open mouth faces a hollow oval, which is mostly described as an egg. Here, layers of burnt wood found suggest that it was a ceremony place. Although there are many theories, it is believed to have been built by the Adena culture or the "Moundbuilders" (from about 1000 B.C. to A.D.1200).

>> **The Inca—The Huacas:** p. 416

The Crater Lake of Oregon The Crater Lake of Mount Mazama, Oregon (**1**), was formed about 5677 B.C. when the volcanic peak of the mountain collapsed, then filled with spring water. The Klamath tribe local to the area believed that their ancestors witnessed the formation of the lake. They attributed the event to an epic battle between Llao and Skell, two mythical chiefs of the Klamath tribe. Their terrible fight ended with the destruction of Llao's home on Mount Mazama, known as the underworld, by Skell, who turned it into the Crater Lake. The tribe held the lake sacred, and in times past, sent young men there on vision quests that involved fasts and highly dangerous climbs down sunken volcanic wells around the lake.

The Black Hills The Black Hills (**2**) are a small mountain range running from Wyoming to South Dakota. The name comes from the Lakota Sioux term Pahá Sápa, literally "black hills," and so named because the trees on the mountains make them look dark. The Lakota believed that the Black Hills were the center of the universe, and thus sacred. However, some controversy about this claim has arisen in times past, because the Lakota came to the area in the 18th century, and displaced other tribes on their arrival. There was a long quarrel about the Black Hills between the United States government and the Lakota tribes that ended up at the U.S. Supreme Court. When the ruling on July 23, 1980, found that the Black Hills had been illegally taken from the Lakota, remuneration was offered. However, the Lakota refused the settlement and continue to fight for their sacred territory.

North America—Lelawala the Maiden of the Mists

A terrible curse fell upon the Ongiara tribe, who lived by the Niagara Falls of New York State: they were dying. The medicine men believed that the tribe had offended Hinum, god of thunder, who made his abode behind the falls. In desperation, they sent a girl to die in the waterfall once a year. It happened that one year, the maiden Lelawala, daughter of the chief, was chosen. The tribe placed Lelawala in a canoe and sent her over the waterfall. But unlike the other girls, she lived. The two sons of Hinum saved her, because both wanted to marry her. Lelawala agreed to marry the son who told her why her tribe was dying. The younger son said that a serpent was poisoning their drinking water. Lelawala's tribe then killed the beast; but Lelawala stayed behind as a spirit of Niagara Falls.

North America—Arctic Myths

The Inuit are the indigenous peoples of the Arctic, occupying areas of Alaska, Canada, and Greenland. Suffering the harsh climate and limited resources of the Arctic Circle has

Sea life, such as walruses, appear in the mythology of the Arctic

led to a mythology surrounding the very animals they relied on to live. Dependent on the hunting of sea animals and the trapping of small birds, the Inuit believed that a raven created the world, which was made of a whale's body.

The Inuit believed in *sila*, a fundamental power that existed in everything from the human soul to the environment. Sometimes it was also thought of as a sky deity. As sila connected everything, all things were seen as essential to each other. This spiritual connection between animals and humans is present in many myths.

■ The Inuit believed that sila, a spiritual power, existed in everything

■ While a raven was thought to be the creator of the world, the supreme being was a sky deity, often identified with sila

■ The maiden Sedna became a sea spirit when her father let her drown in the sea

■ Sedna was tremendously important because the Inuit depended on fishing and whale hunting

■ An *angakkuq* ("shaman") was believed to have power over good and evil spirits

Sedna and Birth of the Whales
Sedna, a beautiful maiden, was once married by her father to a hunter. When it turned out that her husband was actually a raven, Sedna cried so much that her father took her back on his kayak

(**1**). But then the raven attacked them and Sedna fell overboard. The father cut off Sedna's fingers as she clung to the side of the boat. As she sank into the sea, she became a spirit, and her severed fingers became whales and seals.

» **Universal Principles:** pp. 102, 295, 332, 384

The Angakkuq and the Tuurngait

The angakkuq was an Inuit shaman. Among his duties, he was responsible for healing and solving societal problems. An angakkuq was selected based on his natural ability and charisma. It was also said that he was actually selected by the spirits themselves, who gave him a specific power. He served as mediator between humans and the spirits, using tools like drums, chants, and ritual dances. He also had power over the tuurngait, invisible spirits who caused unsuccessful hunting trips, broken weapons and tools, illness, insanity, and general bad luck. Tuurngait (below) were believed to possess people and cause them to commit bad deeds, or become mentally ill. Only the angakkuq had the power to exorcise them. He could also capture tuurngait, and use them as weapons against their own kind.

How Raven Stole the Sun

Long ago, the world was stuck in perpetual darkness. The people had never seen light, until raven (**2**) told them about seeing it in the east. The people begged him to find it for them, so raven flew east until he came to a village. By means of his magic, he learned that the chief of the village kept a golden ball of light in his house. Raven tricked the chief's son into playing with the ball, then stole it and flew back to his own people. When he dropped it by accident, it became the sun.

2

The Man Who Became a Salmon

Anarteq and his sisters liked to hunt reindeer. The sisters would drive the reindeer into a lake. Anarteq would paddle up to the reindeer in a kayak, while they were stuck in the water, and kill the ones he wanted. But during one such hunt, a reindeer overturned Anarteq's kayak. As he sank into the water, he turned into a salmon, and was lost from his family. Years later, Anarteq's father took a hunting party to the same lake. As he paddled his kayak on the lake, the father felt something pulling his paddle. It was Anarteq, in the shape of a salmon. Anarteq clung to the paddle, and as his father pulled

3

him out of the water (**3**), he became a man again. He returned to his family and hunted successfully for many years after.

African Mythology

In rituals honoring their gods or ancestors, African tribes, such as the
Dogon of Mali, perform dances that use masks

African Mythology

Africa is the world's second largest continent. Vast in its expanse, it stretches across the Equator, with the northern half being primarily desert, and the central and southern areas consisting of both savannah plains and very dense rainforest regions. Its climate varies from the tropical to the sub-arctic, as seen on its highest mountain peak, Mount Kilimanjaro (**1**).

Considered by the scientific community to be the birthplace of humankind, it is the only place where evidence of humans from each key stage of evolution has been found. One can see depictions of the progression of man in cave paintings (**2**) found in the Sahara, Tanzania, and South Africa.

Although modern Africa was divided into states during European colonization (the last division occurring after the Second World War), the continent was originally composed of countless ethnic groups that had separate and distinct cultures, as well as various modes of life. While some tribes settled in permanent locations, nomadic life was (and still is) very widespread in Africa.

Cattle-herders and hunter-gatherers moved from one place to another in order to find new hunting grounds or grazing land for their herds. Autonomous city-states, such as Mombasa on the eastern coast, were under the rule of Arabian dynasties. From

around 1000 B.C., a large part of northern Africa was Islamized. As a result, both Sunni Islam and hybrid forms of indigenous religions and Islam were to be found, for instance, with the Hausa people of Nigeria.

A tribe's way of life deeply influenced its religion and mythology, and yet, even through some tribes had similar modes of life, there is no one cultural tradition or mythology to be found in Africa, but rather many thousands. While these are in no way homogeneous, they do share commonalities with one another and with other myths found elsewhere in the world.

Stories of a supreme god, or a creator god who is responsible for the beginning of the universe and of humanity, are found in the myths of numerous tribes. There is an astounding variety of stories about the creation of the world, encompassing everything from the idea of the cosmic egg to twin dual gendered forces whose union gives birth to civilization, as with Mawu-Lisa, the creator twins of the Fon religion. The creator god, most often associated with the sky and heaven, is described as paying little to no attention to the world after he created it and as having little contact with humans; therefore, he is seldom called upon.

Some tribes believe in a variety of gods, most often created by the supreme god, who play a central role in their daily lives. People call on them and ask for their assistance and guidance. These gods are most commonly asssociated with forces of nature or other specific functions: for example, the Yoruba tribe

of Nigeria call on various powerful deities, which they call *orishas,* that represent elements found in nature, such as Shango, god of lightning and thunder, and Olokun, god of the ocean.

For other tribes, the creator god is considered to be the original ancestor of that tribe, from which the first human couple, and thus the tribe, stems. Actually, the practice of ancestor worship is common throughout Africa. It is thought that ancestors have mystical powers and great authority, and therefore have a direct influence over the lives and well-being of their living kinsmen. They are contacted through a shaman (**3**), a mediator, and elaborate rituals and ceremonies are carried out to pay them respect. The spirits of ancestors are generally thought to be good spirits who help their decendants; however, they must be constantly appeased in order not to evoke their anger.

Engrained deeply in African religion is the belief that not only people, but everything within nature contains spirits or souls. Whether it be trees, rivers, lakes, animals, the sun, moon, or stars, they all carry a significance and power that is venerated. This practice of worshiping nature is commonly referred to as animism.

Humor, intrigue, deceit, and wisdom color the landscape of African mythology, and nothing encapsulates this better than the figure of the trickster. Appearing most often in animal form, the trickster delights in wreaking havoc upon man (**4**), such as one of the most well-known tricksters, Ananse the spider of the Akan peoples. Yet, there is often a lesson in these stories, and so the trickster can also

4

be a culture hero. These stories were so popular that forms of those told in Africa traveled with the slave trade to the Americas and Caribbean, appearing in tales as Brer Rabbit and Aunt Nancy. Various religious beliefs and practices, primarily from the west coast of Africa, were introduced to these areas, mixing with local indigenous religions and Christian beliefs to form new religions like Voodoo, Umbanda, and Candomblé.

Passed down through generations, the myths and beliefs of Africa have been preserved as the result of a rich oral and musical tradition. From the creation of the universe, to the legends of ancestors, one can find examples of the importance of myth in the elaborate epic recitals, drum poetry, reenactments, ceremonies (**5**, like this annual Zulu reed dance), and ritual mime performances held throughout the continent. From the beginning of time, Africa has been at the core of discovery, history, culture, ingenuity, and lore. Diverse in landscape and diverse in its inhabitants, Africa is a land with one of the most varied and imaginative mythologies in the world.

5

Creation Myths

Africa is the cradle of humankind. It would be appropriate then that the creation myths, or stories of origin, found throughout African storytelling are a vital part of its history and culture. Among the different people of Africa, one can find a broad variety of accounts of how the universe, humanity, and life came into being.

■ Most African traditions hold that a creator god created the universe, humankind, as well as other gods

■ One popular idea of creation was that life was created from a cosmic egg

■ The Bambara tribe of Mali believe that life originated from a root sound

■ The Mbuti of the Congo became mortal after eating the forbidden fruit

The belief in a creator god, or a creation force, is very common. Often, he has a female consort. In addition to creating the universe and mankind, he also creates other gods and spirits.

Skull believed to be the earliest member of the human family

For the Dogon and the Mande people, it is the myth of the cosmic egg that explains creation. The creation myth of the Mbuti people may also sound familiar, in that when the supreme being created a paradise in which humanity would dwell, he issued a prohibition that they not eat of the fruit of the tahu tree. This rule was broken, and humanity was forced to experience the vicissitudes of mortal life.

The First Mortal—The Fang
Nzame, Mebere, and Nkwa were one god

⓵

with three aspects. Nzame was the transcendent aspect, and Mebere and Nkwa were the male and female aspects. Nzame created the universe. After Nzame had finished, Mebere and Nkwa suggested that the earth have a ruler. First they appointed three animals to rule jointly: the elephant for its wisdom, the leopard (**1**) for its power, and the

monkey for its suppleness. When this did not work, they created a being in their own image to rule—Fam. But he became arrogant and disrespectful toward Nzame. In his anger, Nzame destroyed the earth he had created, yet Fam survived as he had been promised eternal life. Nzame, Mebere and Nkwa created the plants and animals anew, and made another man in the image of the gods, this time a mortal one, Sekume, who with his wife Mbongwe became the ancestor of the Fang.

Cosmic Eggs—The Dogon
The Dogon people of
Mali say that the

creator, Amma, made an egg
(**2**) in four sections, each of
which contained the earth, air,
fire, and water. When the
elements began to act
upon one another, a series
of seven explosions
followed. As a result, life
was created. Amma also
planted a seed in herself that
produced twins. One of the
twins, Yurugu, rebelled and
broke out. Amma scattered the
parts of the second twin,
Nommo (**3**), throughout

the world because she wanted
to restore order.
Afterward, she
brought the
parts back
together, and
once again gave
Nommo life.
Nommo went
on to create
the four spirits
that would
become the
ancestors of
the Dogons.

**The Search for
Land—The
Igbo** In the be-
ginning of time, the
creator goddess, Ale, created a hornbill bird (**4**), Ogbughu. Ogbughu became
distraught after the death
of his mother because he
could not find a place to
bury her. So he buried her

in his head, and as a
result, hornbills have
a growth on their
heads. As Ogbughu
was flying, he saw a
man and a woman
coupling down
below in the
water. As a
result of their
motion, land

began to appear
out of the water.
It was decided
then that this
land was where
life would be
buried, and
that all that
comes from the
earth must re-
turn to it.

**The Sound of Creation—The
Bambara** The universe was
created from a single point of
sound that could not be
heard called Yo, the root
sound. Yo created the
heavens, the earth, and all living things. Human
consciousness came from Yo and the creator
spirits Faro, Teliko, and Pemba. Faro, the spirit of
water, created the seven heavens to correspond
with the seven parts of the earth, and fertilized
them all with rain. Teliko, the spirit of air, created a
set of twins, the precursors of people. Pemba, the
principle of creation, descended on earth as a
seed of the balanza tree (**4**) and created Musokoroni, who became his wife. Musokoroni created
plants and animals. Pemba ultimately betrayed
her, and she transmitted the impurity brought on
by his betrayal to everything she touched,
causing disorder and chaos to set in.

▷▷ **Creation Through a Cosmic Egg:** pp. 87, 289, 330, 457

Tricksters

The trickster is a mythical figure who often combines cunning and deceit with wisdom. The trickster delights in provoking conflict and undermining order, often with humor; however, most tales involving tricksters also have a moral dimension and often point out human realities and faults.

In some myths, the trickster is responsible for introducing fire, agriculture, tools, and even death to humans. With facets that include invention and discovery, the trickster becomes in part another mythical archetype: the culture hero.

Tricksters are found throughout African tales and are most commonly, although not always, animals. For the Akan people in West Africa, the trickster is a spider. The Yoruba of Nigeria have a trickster tortoise, and in central and eastern Africa, the Bantu tribes' trickster presents himself as a hare. The stories of the mythical trickster as an animal have traveled all the way to the Americas and the Caribbean in the form of modern folk tales of Brer Rabbit and Ananse the spider, otherwise known as Aunty Nancy.

■ The trickster is both shrewd and devious, and gets great joy from creating chaos

■ Tricksters are most commonly animals

■ The trickster can also be a culture hero

■ African trickster tales have traveled to the Americas and the Caribbean

Legba—The Fon Legba was the youngest child of Mawu, the creator god. Although a trickster, he was not only important for his rule over divination, but also as a mediator between humankind and Mawu. Once, Mawu and Legba (**1**) lived close to the earth, but Legba was always being scolded for causing trouble. As Legba did not like to be reprimanded, he went to a village and persuaded an old woman to throw her dirty bathwater toward the heavens at Mawu. Mawu became so aggravated that he began to move further and further away from earth, until he eventually ended up far within the heavens. However, as Legba was left behind, his duty became to report on human happenings to Mawu, and this is how it came to be that there are temples in every village in Legba's honor rather than his father's.

Moni-Mambu—The Bakongo
One day the trickster Moni-Mambu came upon a village where the women were harvesting peanuts (**2**). After greeting them, Moni-Mambu was offered some peanut stew,

and told that he should go to the hut and eat the stew with the children. Moni-Mambu went and ate the peanut stew, and afterward, he ate the children. When the women returned to the hut, they were

horrified at what Moni-Mambu had done. But he said he had only done as he was told, and that was to eat the stew with the children. The women could not disagree, and so let Moni-Mambu go.

Huveane—The Bantu
The boy Huveane was out hunting with his father when he pointed to some cool water hidden up high in the rocks. He knocked pegs into the rocks, and helped his father climb up. When his father reached the top, Huveane took out the pegs so he could not come down, ran

home, ate the meal in the pot (**3**), and filled the pot with animal dung. The villagers believed him to be evil, and, as his parents reluctantly agreed, though he should be punished. But, Huveane managed to overcome all their attempts, and continued to plague his family with practical jokes.

Ananse—The Akan The spider, Ananse (**4**), is said to have brought about disease. Ananse asked Nyame, the supreme being, for sheep and in return promised him a beautiful maiden. Instead, when he arrived in the village, Ananse kept all of the women for himself. When Nyame heard this, he had

all the women brought to him, except one sickly woman, who told Ananse to wash her with water from a gourd. She instantly turned into a beauty. Upon the news, Nyame had (**4**)

all of the women come and dance for him while Ananse played the gourd. Ananse's wife objected, knowing the gourd contained diseased water. Ananse tried to force her to dance, striking the gourd, which split and sent disease into the world.

Tricksters: pp. 146, 148, 166, 170, 234, 360

Cultural Heroes

Like in many cultures throughout the world, the cultural hero in African lore is a mythological figure who brings monumental change to his people, through invention and discovery. This figure's contributions were instrumental in the tribe's ability to both survive, progress, and flourish.

For many tribes, the cultural hero is an original ancestor, a king, or hero. Gifts brought by these heroes were often the knowledge needed to farm, hunt, and build. The Dogon tribe, for example, received the knowledge of ironmaking from their cultural hero, allowing them to make tools with which to tame the landscape. The mythical figure of the trickster and the cultural hero are often combined into one figure, such as the trickster spider Ananse of the Akan peoples.

■ A cultural hero brings to a group of people the skills necessary for survival

■ A tribe's cultural hero is often the first ancestor, an important king, or a hero

■ The cultural hero is frequently combined with the trickster into one figure

Mask of Chi Wara, cultural hero of the Bamana tribe

Tsoede—Hero of the Nupe One day, the son of the *Atta* ("king") went hunting in a land not his own, and fell in love with the daughter of the chief there. He stayed with her and she became pregnant, but because the son's father died, he had to return home to take over the throne. As a token, he left her a charm and a ring to give to their unborn child. After the woman gave birth to a baby boy, she

named him Tsoede (**1**). Many years later, Tsoede went to the land of his father, now the Atta, who recognized his son instantly because of the charm and ring he wore. Tsoede's father mysteriously became ill, and when a diviner said that only a fruit from a high oil palm would cure the king, Tsoede succeeded in

plucking it. Tsoede was favored by his father because of this achievement, filling his half brothers with rage. As the years went on, and the Atta could feel his death coming, he advised Tsoede to flee from his half brothers. He assisted him in his flight, giving him riches, including a great bronze canoe and iron chains full of magical powers. Tsoede continued on, conquering Nku and making himself ruler of all Nupe, sharing with the people there the trade of blacksmithing, bronze casting, and canoe building.

» **Bringers of Culture:** pp. 24, 32, 41, 166

Lonkundo—Hero of the Mongo-Nkundo Lonkundo the hunter (**2**) taught his people, the Mongo-Nkundo of the Congo, the skills of trapping and tracking forest beasts. His father, Mokele, was born miraculously. The wives of Wai were all pregnant, but the pregnancy of one of them was so prolonged that she was scorned. An old woman took the egg out of the womb of this wife, and a handsome boy, Mokele, hatched. When he hatched, the world was in darkness and so Mokele stole the sun and

brought it back to his community. He married Bolumbu and Lonkundo was born to them. When his parents died, Lonkundo learned how to hunt from his father's spirit, who appeared to him in a dream. His father told him to go to the local well and look for the track of a wild animal and once he had found it, he should make a trap from raffia fibers and twigs and set it for the beast. Lonkundo also dreamed that he captured the sun, but it was not the sun, it was Ilankaka, the sun goddess, who became his wife.

Chi Wara—Hero of the Bamana As a result of the union between the sky goddess Mousso Koroni and an earth spirit, the mythical half animal, half human figure of Chi Wara was born. Chi Wara's lower body was similar to that of an aardvark, whose sharp claws scratched the earth, tilling the soil so that crops could be planted. His upper half was that of an antelope, with an almost human face, whose tall thin antlers looked like growing millet (**4**). When Chi Wara came to the earth, he taught the

Bamana how to sow and plant the land. In celebration of this gift, the Bamana rejoice at dances (**3**) held during the harvesting season.

The Hero Blacksmith of the Dogon According to the Dogon of Mali, one of their eight ancestors rode down from heaven on a rainbow in a ship the shape of a granary. He brought with him a hammer and anvil (**5**). With his knowledge of using the forge and iron tools, he taught the Dogon people how to make tools. The hammer he brought contained seeds with which he also taught the Dogon how to clear and plant fields of crops. As a people who rely heavily on agriculture, **5** this was important.

Hephaestus—Blacksmith God: p. 150

Myths of the Zulu and the Maasai

The Zulu of South Africa and the Maasai of East Africa are pastoral and semi-nomadic tribes who are also often exalted for their skills as warriors. The myths of these two groups often refer to the elements to which they owe their survival and prosperity—the earth and cattle.

Among the Zulu, Umvelinqangi is the supreme god who descended from the heavens and created reeds on which grew the creator of humanity, Unkulunkulu ("the ancient one"). From the other reeds, Unkulunkulu broke off people and animals, and created mountains, rivers, and landscapes. He taught the Zulu how to hunt, make fire, and grow food.

According to the Maasai, En-kai is the creator of the world, and is said to have lowered a strip of hide from the heavens, sending cattle down as a gift to his people on earth. Jealous hunters from an opposing tribe cut the strip, severing heaven from earth. Believing they were directly chosen to inherit all the world's cattle, the Maasai became known the world over as warriors when fighting to defend their cattle, or take the cattle from another tribe.

■ The myths of the Zulu and the Maasai in South and East Africa often revolve around their lives as cattle herders

■ Umvelinqangi was the highest creator god of the Zulu

■ The Zulu were said to have been created by the god Unkulunkulu, also known as "the wise one"

■ The creator rain god En-kai, also known as Ngai, gave the Maasai ownership of all the cows in the world

■ When En-kai cast a disastrous flood upon the world, he saved Tumbainot and his family

Zulu—The Mortality of Man The world was created by Unkulunkulu when he split multicolored reeds (**2**). At first, he thought that people should live forever, and asked a chameleon named Unwabu (**1**) to spread the news among humanity that they would be immortal. However, because Unwabu moved slowly, and took every opportunity to rest and eat, Unkulunkulu changed his mind and sent a lizard, Intulo, in his place. As Intulo was faster than

Unwabu, the news of their mortality reached humanity first and was accepted as the only option. Thus, humans became, and remained, mortal.

Zulu—Hlakanyana The trickster Hlakanyana could speak before he was born, calling impatiently to his mother to give birth to him. He emerged from his mother's womb with the face of an old man and remarkable abilities. One day he went to a cattle enclosure (**3**), where strips of meat were being roasted, and offered to carry the men's food to their huts. Smearing blood on the mats of each hut, he took all the meat and told the men that dogs had eaten it. Afterward, Hlakanyana went on with his pranks, traveling the world.

Maasai—Liberation of Women During a time of warfare and theft, it was not safe to let cattle out to graze. During such a time, one family's cattle became so deprived of food that the brother and sister took them into the bush. Upon establishing camp, the boy told his sister to stay behind while he went to watch the cattle. One day, suspicious after seeing strange footprints around their camp, the boy pretended to leave, but stayed behind in order to spy on his sister. He soon saw men from an enemy tribe come to the camp, and overheard as his sister and the men made plans to steal the cattle while he was out doing the daily milking. Knowing their plan, the next day he armed himself and went on with milking as usual, but when the men arrived, he killed them. It is said that because of his sister's actions, women (**4**) were allowed to come and go as they pleased, as this was easier than attempting to control them.

Maasai—The Great Flood Once, when the Maasai were not being mindful of En-kai, the god resolved to destroy humankind. However, he decided to tell a man named Tumbainot to build an ark of wood and board it with his family and various animals to save them from the flood that he planned to release that would drown the earth. With the flood started, everyone within Tumbainot's ark was kept safe. However, provisions soon became scarce. When the rain stopped, Tumbainot released a dove, which soon returned because it found no place to rest. Next, he released a vulture (**5**) with an arrow attached to its tail feathers. When the vulture returned without the arrow, he knew the flood was receding.

Great Floods: pp. 28, 32, 335, 401, 411

Myths of the Yoruba and Fon

The myths of the Yoruba in Nigeria and of the Fon of Benin share similar traits. One of the central characteristics of their mythologies is the duality of divinity, as seen with dual-gendered gods.

In Yoruban mythology, the supreme god, Oldumare, is described in different traditions as being male, female, or both. Other gods, the orishas, represent several aspects of Oldumare. The most important orishas were the trickster Eshu and the thunder god Shango.

According to the mythology of the Fon, Nana-Buluku, the dual-gendered creator, gave birth to the twins Mawu and Lisa. Both held opposite functions: Mawu represented the female aspect and held dominion over the earth, the west, the moon, and the night; Lisa represented the male aspect and watched over the sky, the east, the sun, and the day.

The myths of the Yoruba and the Fon have traveled through migration, and continue to take on new forms in the U.S., Cuba, Brazil, and Haiti. One of the most famous examples is the creolized Voodoo religion.

■ A common link between the mythologies of the Yoruba and Fon is the principle of duality

■ Oldumare, the creator god of the Yoruba, had both male and female aspects

■ Olorun ruled over almost 400 orisha, with attributes and functions that varied

■ The Fon culture is one of the originators of the Voodoo cult

■ Voodoo includes the worship of many gods and ancestors

Fon—Mawu and Lisa The twins (**1**) Mawu and Lisa created humans on the first day. On each of the following days, they made the earth habitable, gave people the gifts of sight, speech, and awareness, and gave them technology. In the creation of the earth, they were helped by their servant, Aido-Hwedo, a serpent, who carried Mawu and Lisa in his mouth. The earth's surfaces and its curves were created by the servant's movement. After the earth was created, Aido-Hwedo coiled himself into a circle underneath the earth to hold it in place. **①**

▶ **Primordial Pairs:** pp. 74, 114, 352 | **Voodoo Goddess Maman Brigitte:** p. 262

Yoruba—Birth of the Orishas It is said among the Yoruba that as the primordial being Orisa-nla was in his garden, his servant Atunda rebelled and sent a massive boulder [**2**] rolling, smashing Orisa-nla into fragments. These became the hundreds of orishas of whom a handful are principal mythic figures. Some of the orishas are personifications of natural forces, such as Yansan, orisha of wind, or Shango (**2**), orisha of thunder and lightning. Some are personifications of love and beauty, such as Oya, orisha of fertility.

Yoruba—Oshun and the Creation of the World Oshun was the goddess of rivers, and the manifestation of fertility. One day a male orisha attempted to subjugate Oshun because she was female. Angered, she removed *ase*, her divine energy, from the world, making subsequent efforts at creation fruitless. It was not until she had given birth to a son, Eshu (**3**), that creation was again possible. Eshu became the conduit of ase, as well as a trickster god. His wreaking havoc on the world and the other orishas became the subject of multiple myths.

Fon—The Oracle of Fa Both the Yoruba and the Fon developed sophisticated systems of divination (the interpretation of omens and fate). Fa is the Fon god of divination and also the sacred word that Mawu-Lisa created for each person that described their fate and fortune. She sent Legba, her messenger, to teach people the method of divination. Fa lived on a palm tree (**4**) in the sky and could see all that went on in the world. Every morning, Legba climbed the tree to open Fa's 16 eyes with the nuts of divination. Fa put one palm nut in Legba's hand if he wanted two eyes open and two if he wanted one eye open. When the palm nuts were used correctly, they opened the eyes of Fa and the doors of the future.

▶▶ **Divination and Prophecy:** pp. 120, 134, 207, 217

Animism

An animistic worldview forms an important part of African religion and mythology. Animism derives from the word *anima*, which means "soul." Accordingly, animistic cultures assume that the world is populated not only with humans and animals, but also with numerous spirits, souls, and demons who affect the world of the living. The afterlife and "real" life are not separate entities, but rather have close contact with and influence on each other. The most important spirit groups include nature spirits and the spirits of ancestors.

The nature spirits live in trees (**4**), springs, rivers, and mountains; therefore all of nature is understood to have a soul. Sacrifices are offered to the spirits in order to compensate for human intervention in nature.

Ancestor spirits are called upon to provide protection in a manner similar to gods, and they are also consulted about everyday situations such as planting and harvesting, conflicts, and family affairs. Their presence is represented by

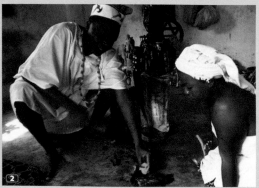

fetishes, masks (**1**), or totems. A connection to the ancestors is established by offering a sacrifice or by magic, among other methods. Sorcerers or healers carry out the rituals (**2**).

Fetishes A supernatural power can dwell within any object. Such carriers of power—e.g., plants, figurines (**3**), stones, or pieces of wood or metal— are called fetishes. They serve as intermediaries between the gods and humans and are said to bring good luck and ward off evil spirits.

4

Australian and Oceanic Mythology

The mythology of the Australian Aborigines includes heroic creatures who lived during the Dreamtime

Australian and Oceanic Mythology

Until white explorers and colonial powers arrived in the 18th century, the cultures of both the tribal societies of the Pacific islands and the Aboriginal peoples of Australia had remained isolated and their traditional way of life had been preserved. Because they had no cultural tradition of writing (except for the inhabitants of Easter Island, known to them as Rapa Nui), transferring the knowledge of myths through songs and stories played an important role in the cultures of the clans, and continues to today. The white newcomers responded in very different ways to these cultures: while the people of Oceania were romanticized during the Enlightenment and beyond as "contented savages" and enjoyed a certain amount of protection, the Australian Aborigines and the bellicose Maori of New Zealand were known as "barbaric savages" and have been oppressed even into recent times.

The islands of Oceania are divided into the areas of Polynesia, Melanesia, and Micronesia. The Maori of New Zealand, as well as the inhabitants of Hawaii and Easter Island (Rapa Nui), belong to the Polynesian culture group. It is likely that the islands were settled starting in 1500 B.C. by several waves of people arriving from the west (e.g., Taiwan and the Philippines) by ship. The original farmers were overcome by the later arrival of their better equipped aristocratic peers, the *ariki*. These new settlers set up a strict hierarchical social order in which higher social status was ensured if a person could trace his or her ancestry back to the original aristocrats, who were worshiped as cultural heroes. In this way, the ariki took on the functions of chiefs, large landowners, and priests. Many of the island peoples and particularly the Maori demonstrate this social status with the intensive tattooing of their faces and bodies (**1**).

The social hierarchy also had an effect on the myths and the worlds of the gods (**3**). Most often, creator deities were found at the top hierarchies of the gods. The gods in the middle were often associated with natural phenomena, such as the moon or sun, or cultural phenomena, such as war or childbirth. The ancestor spirits were found at the lowest level. In addition to their social order, Polynesian myths also reflected other central themes related to their everyday lives. Shipbuilding and navigating

between islands and along the dangerous coasts surrounded by razor-sharp reefs are often featured in the myths of Oceania. The Maori and some Polynesian clans explain their overseas origins in a myth about their forefathers traveling by canoe from the mythical land of Hawaiki. The Polynesians actually did build long canoes that could navigate the open sea and could hold up to 200 people (**2**).

The concepts of *mana* and taboo (from the Polynesian word *tapu*, meaning

"sacred," "forbidden," or "untouchable") permeate the mythological and religious worlds of the people of Oceania. Mana refers to a spiritual life energy of astonishing power. It can manifest itself in extraordinary natural phenomena, in human accomplishments, or in objects that are of special significance for a clan or a family. Mana is also a power related to individuals, which is already in, or is available to, any person, object, or event. It also refers to the powers associated with respected specialists in a society, such as aristocrats, priests, boat builders, and navigators, and can be inherited. For this reason, adoptions play an important role among families of aristocrats and priests: through adoption, gifted young people share in the mana of the adopter, placing themselves in their lines of power.

Taboos can apply to people, animals, foods, locations, and, above all, anything that has to do with death or corpses. Taboos are usually associated with a certain time period as well. A ban is placed on taboo items and they may not be touched. Taboos, which are found in every society, regulate how people should interact with events and phenomena which are seen as threatening, which is especially important in societies without a written code of law. Most often taboos support the social hierarchy, in that for certain people (of higher social status) or specialists, they apply only in limited ways or not at all.

For a long time, the Aboriginal peoples of Australia, who live as nomadic

hunters (**4**) and gatherers, were considered by Europeans to exemplify the
notion of the "primitive savage." They
could identify neither a social organization based on a chief nor a clan
hierarchy. It was only later that they
were able to understand the truly
complex rules for living and for
marriage in the clans.

The clans and tribes live in certain
territories, and according to their belief system, they do not own this land,
but instead they are taking care of it
and using it in the name of their
ancestors and the beings from the
distant mythical past. The close connection to their ancestors and creator
beings from the Dreamtime is charac-

teristic. The myths about those beings who once shaped the world and who
left their traces all over are still present today and still determine the aboriginal
self-concept and the worldview. Many particular landscapes, such as the
famous red, shimmering sandstone rock Uluru, or Ayers Rock, are sacred to
them. Using the Dreamlines that run through the land, they walk the paths
made by the Dreamtime beings. Because singing often accompanies these
journeys, the paths are also called Songlines. But the Dreamtime beings were
not just responsible for forming the natural world. As cultural heroes they also
gave people rules and laws, which regulate how people live among one
another. The validity of these laws is recognized to this day.

Not many of the myths of the Aboriginal people of Australia have been
written down, but they live on in songs and stories, and not least in the cliff
drawings (**5**) that are said to have come from the Dreamtime beings themselves, as well as in the modern work of Aboriginal artists.

Oceania—Creation Myths

The creation myths of Oceanic island populations are very diverse and every region usually has its own. They tell about the creation of the land (**1**) and also the divine structure of society. The main characters are the creator gods, as well as numerous demigods that provided humanity with advancements, such as better boat-building techniques and navigational skills.

The leading tribal chiefs, or ariki, were landowners and considered direct descendants of the tribal founders. They were high-ranked in society and they had a spiritual power called mana. Many societies of the Polynesian islands considered Tangaroa as the highest ranked creator god and the first ancestor of the ariki. Other island societies and the Maori of New Zealand honored only one creator god known as Io, Iho, or Kiho. The gods of the Maori were said to have originated from the union of the divine first ancestors, Rangi and Papa, father sky and mother earth.

■ Oceanic creation myths have the islands originating from the ocean

■ All Oceanic societies have creator gods and demigods, including Maui and Tiki

■ Rangi and Papa were the first ancestors

■ Societal order was considered to be god-given

■ Tangaroa was a creation god and god of the sea

①

Tangaroa Hatches From the World Egg The creator god Tangaroa (**3**) was the god of the sea and father of fish, marine animals, and reptiles; therefore, he was the father of the basis of life for the Oceanic people. It was especially important to make sure he was happy before making any sea journeys. The sky and the earth emerged at his birth when he hatched from the world egg (**2**). After breaking the egg, its top edge turned into the sky while the bottom edge turned into the earth. Tangaroa was chased into the sea by his brother, the storm god Tawhirimatea. Tangaroa's relationship with his other brother Tane was tense as Tane was the god of land and vegetation. Therefore, the two brothers were opposing gods of sea and land, which was reflected in their relationship.

Traveling to Hawaiki Many Polynesian tribal chiefs are considered to be descendants from the mythical original land Hawaiki. In particular, the Maori of New Zealand consider Hawaiki as their native land from which they traveled to the islands by canoe (**4**) to populate them. Hawaiki is considered equivalent to the underworld, as the deceased are believed to go there. The starting point of this journey is Cape Reinga (**1**).

Tiki—The First Person Tiki (**5**) was the son of the gods Rangi and Papa. Initially, he was alone. When he saw his own mirror image in a pond, he jumped into the water. He was so disappointed that he filled in the pond, which then gave birth to a woman. One day she was excited by an eel and this excitement was passed on to Tiki. This incident led to the first act of procreation.

Cultural Hero Maui The most popular Oceanic hero is Maui. On Hawaii, he is considered a demigod and trickster. One day, he decided to slow down the path of the sun because the days were too short. He climbed a mountain and caught the sun with a lariat made of his sister's hair. The sun asked for her freedom and promised to keep the days long during the summer; they would only stay shortly (**6**) during winter.

▶▶ **Creation Through a Cosmic Egg:** pp. 87, 289, 330, 439

■ In the strict hierarchy of Polynesian gods, creation gods like Tangaroa were at the top

■ Tane was the god of the forests and birds, who created light and life

■ Tu was the god of war; Rongo, the god of peace

■ Hina was the moon goddess; Laka, the goddess of beauty; Pele, the Hawaiian goddess of volcanoes

Divine Society The dreadful god of war, Tu, wanted to kill his parents, Rangi and Papa, to allow light and life into the world. However, his brother Tane chased them away instead. Unhappy about this, Tu punished his brother. He caught Tane's children, the birds (**1**), in traps and cages. He also went after his brothers Rongo, god of agriculture, and Haumia-tiketike, god of wild plants. Only one brother was too powerful for Tu, Tawhirimatea, the god of storms, thunder, and lightning.

Oceania—The Gods of Polynesia

The strictly hierarchical society of Polynesia was reflected in its gods. The most important gods were the creation gods, who were said to be the ancestors of the kings and tribal chief families, followed by several other gods. The four major male gods were Tangaroa (Kanaloa), the sea god; Tane (Kane), the god of the forests and birds and creator of sunlight and life; Tu (Ku), the god of war; and Rongo (Lono), the god of peace, fertility, and agriculture, who descended onto the earth from a rainbow.

Female deities included the moon goddess Hina. As the major female goddess, she is often considered on the same level as the mother of earth, Papa. Other goddesses were Laka, the goddess of beauty and dance, and Pele, honored in Hawaii as goddess of (active) volcanoes. The lowest ranked gods were guardian and ancestral spirits, or *aitu*.

①

>> **Fighting Between the Gods:** pp. 26, 117, 118, 238, 245

Moai—Mysterious Ancestors of Easter Island More than a thousand *moai* (**2**), wooden statues, were constructed between A.D. 400 and 1200. They are thought to represent tribal leaders and famous ancestors. They were considered to be mediators between humans and gods. The moais were part of ceremonial sites where rituals and ceremonies were carried out.

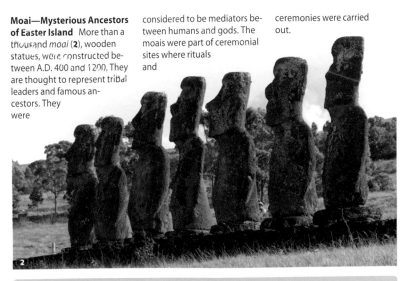

Cargo Cults

Cargo cults originated mainly in Melanesia during the 19th and early 20th centuries. They are based on myths about heroes of earlier times who would return as "white gods" on ships and bring plentiful food for the humans. Cargo ships of the white people arriving at the shores of Melanesia were associated with these heroes. Some tribes were misled by eschatological prophets to destroy their food and animals because they believed that food was going to be abundant from then on. This mass movement was accompanied by civil unrest.

Hina and Tuna, the God of Eels One day Hina, goddess of the moon, went to fetch some water from a swamp. While there, Tuna, the god of eels, swam into her calabash and raped her. Afterward, Hina told her husband, Maui, about the incident. Seeking revenge, he caught the god of eels and cut him into pieces. Today's existing eel (**3**) species were said to have evolved from these pieces of the god's body.

Ancestor Cult

The traditional Oceanic worldview does not strictly separate the now and the hereafter, or material reality and the supernatural spiritual world. Ancestors (**1**) played an important role as guardian spirits; their advice and help was always requested, and they were honored in various ceremonies (**3**) so that they did not get irritated. All individuals needed to confirm the line of power from their ancestors because the mana, or spiritual power, of every object and person was passed on by the ancestors. Tribal leaders especially received their powerful mana from their ancestors. Mana was only retained if the ancestors were treated as if they were living members of the family. After death, a person was not said to have left the world, but rather had merely ascended to a higher level of existence. Even today in some regions, social status and hierarchies are largely determined by ancestral lines.

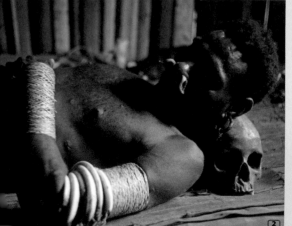

Melanesian Skull Cults
Several Melanesian peoples worship within skull cults. Because the spiritual power is thought to be embedded in the human head, skulls are revered. The skulls of ancestors are frequently washed and painted or their eyes are decorated with shells. Then they are positioned at a place of honor in the household of the descendants (**2**). The headhunting tradition seen in some peoples is based on the mana belief: when a headhunter captures a skull, for example from a hostile warrior, he acquires his mana and can use it to his advantage by honoring it in certain ways.

>> Ancestor Worship: p. 370

3

Australia—Dreamtime

- The world was created by powerful creatures of the Dreamtime

- Dreamtime creatures left traces behind called the Dreamlines

- The rainbow snake is a famous Dreamtime creature

Australian creation myths are characterized by the belief that all organisms are related to each other, which results in their close connection to the living world. The Aboriginal pantheon does not include personalized gods, but rather creatures that lived on earth in a mythical primeval time, the Dreamtime.

The supernatural creatures of the Dreamtime created the empty world, followed by landscapes (**1**, the Olgas), lakes and rivers, plants, humans, and animals. As cultural heroes, they brought advances such as the power over fire, weapons, and hunting skills, as well as clan orders and wedding regulations to humanity.

Even today Dreamtime myths are still partly passed on within tribes and clans by word of mouth. The worldview and philosophy of Aboriginal life is characterized by these myths and the Aborigines continue to feel a connection to the creatures of the Dreamtime.

Dreamlines Although the creatures of the Dreamtime left the earth after creating the world and passing it on to humanity to care for, they did leave traces behind. They were believed to have traveled the earth on paths known today as Dreamlines (**2**, artistic illustration). To this day, Dreamlines exist in certain locations.

Because they are sacred, these locations are still associated with taboos. If the taboos are upheld, then these sacred landmarks can help to empower and protect people. Many Dreamlines are described in the cult songs, known as Songlines, that tell the adventures of the Dreamtime creatures creating the world and its features.

Dreamtime Creatures

Dreamtime creatures were depicted on cave walls (**3**), rocks, animal skins, and bark as part animal, part human creatures. According to the myths, they were passing through the land and shaped it during battles (**4**), alliances, and adventures. Then they passed it on to humans. The Aborigines considered themselves not as owners, but rather as users and administrators of

the land, serving the Dreamtime creatures and their ancestors.

The Rainbow Snake Many myths of the Aborigines tell stories about the rainbow snake (**5**) Yurlunggur (or Wollunqua).

Due to its power over one of Australia's most valuable resources, water, it is considered one of the most important

Dreamtime creatures. During the Dreamtime, it rose from the water and is considered a symbol of fertility. It is the only Dreamtime creature that did not leave the earth. In South Australia, where the rainbow snake is called Akaru, the snake was said to live in waterholes, guarding them. When the snake was not comfortable in its waterhole, it would stretch out to give itself more room and, as a result, water flooded the land. Whoever wanted to get water from the hole had to warn the snake first to avoid being swallowed.

Australia—Tracing the Ancestors

■ Ancestors—humans, animals, and mixed creatures—were said to pass on their spiritual power (maban) to their descendants

■ Maban was part of natural phenomena, but it was also present in objects, or tjurungas

■ Many tribes had their own ancestral totem animals

The Aborigines continue to feel very close to their ancestors. As the Dreamtime creatures were also their ancestors, the Europeans often used to refer to the Aborigines as a "people without history." Some Aboriginal clans trace their ancestors back to certain animals (**1**, show at the opening ceremony of the 2000 Olympic Games). They left their spiritual power at certain sacred locations for their descendants.

Tribal members usually called themselves by the ancestral totem animal of their clan, for example, as kangaroo-man or bird-woman. The ancestors and the ancestral animal were honored during ritual ceremonies where protective powers were transferred to the entire clan. Some clans also considered certain plants or cultural objects as their totem ancestors.

1

The Wandjina The Wandjina, or Wondjina (**2**), were ancestral creation beings. At one time, these cloud and rain spirits ascended from the sea and went into ponds and waterholes. They are shown on petroglyphs as humans with exaggerated eyes and nose, but without a mouth. The Wandjina were said to have caused a great flood by opening their mouths after they became unhappy with humanity. According to legend, the Wandjina painted their own images on rock walls.

Ancestral Gifts The ancestors left their descendants with objects containing maban, known as *tjurungas* (**3**). They were sacred stones, pieces of wood, paintings, or even songs. Individual persons, tribes, and clans kept them and passed them on to the next generation of the male line.

Corroborees

Clans connect with their ancestors and the Dreamtime creatures by performing dances, rhythmic music, and songs in a predetermined order. Such ceremonies are called corroborees, and they usually happen within an individual clan. Because of the sacred matter of these ceremonies, strangers are not allowed to take part nor are they allowed to watch. The performances usually show scenes from the Dreamtime, animal scenes, and, occasionally, everyday situations are reenacted.

The Moon and the Dugong One myth of the Dreamtime tells the story of two siblings, a brother called Moon and a sister called Dugong. While they were digging for edible roots, the sister Dugong was bitten by a leech and went into the sea to alleviate the pain. Before going into the sea, she turned into a large marine animal (**4**), now known as a dugong. Moon did not want to stay behind by himself, so he joined her. Dugong's bones were found later, but Moon did not die. His bones turned into the shells of the sea. He was later revived after eating the bulbs of lilies and lotus plants.

Uluru

Uluru is located in the desert of central Australia and was formerly called Ayers Rock. In 1985, the rock was returned to the local Anangu people. The rock is a sacred place for the Anangu people, thus climbing is forbidden. The Aborigines explain its unique shape with Dreamtime myths. In one myth, the red lizard Tjati got his boomerang stuck in the rock. When Tjati tried to pull it out, he left key-shaped cavities behind on the northwest side of the rock.

Appendix

Deities and their main pages listed by primary functions

Maat, goddess of truth, p. 103

Agni god of fire, p. 292

Chaac, god of rain, p. 396

Hestia, virgin goddess, p. 153

Index

Bold-faced page numbers indicate the main pages of the entry. *Italicized*
entries indicate literary and musical titles.

Library of Congress Cataloging-in-Publication Data available upon request.

ISBN: 978-1-4262-0373-2

Printed in China

Authors:
Matthew Bullen (American Mythology: pp. 374–431)
Brian Collins (Indian Mythology: pp. 280–323)
Noreen Doyle (Egyptian Mythology: pp. 60–105)
Markus Hattstein (Ancient Near Eastern Mythology: pp. 54–59;
    Australian and Oceanic Mythology: pp. 450–467)
Rebecca Mak (Japanese Mythology: pp. 346 373)
Nana Oforiatta-Ayim (African Mythology: pp. 432–447)
Terri Paajanen (Norse and Celtic Mythology: pp. 224–279)
Igor Trutanow (Chinese Mythology: pp. 324–345)
Andrew W. White (Greek and Roman Mythology: pp. 106–223)
Prof. Annette Zgoll (Ancient Near Eastern Mythology: pp. 14–53)

Academic Consultant: Markus Hattstein

Staff at Peter Delius Verlag:
Editor in Chief: Juliane von Laffert
Editors: Michele Greer, Marianne Kraske, Fabian von Laffert, Olivia De Santos, Sven Schulte
Translators: Julia Esrom, Elizabeth Hine, Patricia Linderman, Paula Trucks-Pape, Frédéric Vagneron
Picture Editor: Bettina Moll
Layout Assistant: Angela Aumann
Graphic Design: Burga Fillery

The publishers would like to express their gratitude to akg-images Berlin/London/Paris, Alamy Stock
Photography, Bildagentur Huber, Bildarchiv Preussischer Kulturbesitz, Bridgestone Museum of Art,
Corbis, dpa Deutsche Presse-Agentur, Getty Images, Godong, iStockphoto, kpa photo archive,
Maxppp, Project Gutenberg, Shutterstock, The Bridgeman Art Library, The Library of Congress,
United Archives and Robert Aichinger, Marshall Astor, Tim Chisholm and Vanessa Smith, T. Chu,
Julia Curi, Disdero, Jonathan Ellgen, Eric Gaba, Ginolerhino, Guss, Ow Gwriansow, James Gordon,
Hardnfast, Hovic, Hrana Janto, Jungpionier, Anna Krenz, Ken and Nyetta, Dr. Stefan Meierhofer,
Marie-Lan Nguyen, Jürgen Liepe, Oosoom, E. Patton, Axel Rouvin, Shizao, Tagishsimon,
Tarourashima, tsc traveler, Bernd Uhlig, Vassil, Wonders, Xalva, Annie Zheng for the permission of
image reproduction in this book. For detailed credits, links and picture captions please visit our
website www.theKnowledgePage.com

**National Geographic
Essential Visual History of World Mythology**

Published by the National Geographic Society
John M. Fahey, Jr., President and Chief Executive Officer
Gilbert M. Grosvenor, Chairman of the Board
Tim T. Kelly, President, Global Media Group
John Q. Griffin, President, Publishing
Nina D. Hoffman, Executive Vice President; President, Book Publishing Group

Kevin Mulroy, Senior Vice President and Publisher
Marianne R. Koszorus, Director of Design
Barbara Brownell Grogan, Executive Editor
Carl Mehler, Director of Maps
Judith Klein, Project Manager
Jennifer A. Thornton, Managing Editor
R. Gary Colbert, Production Director

Founded in 1888, the National Geographic Society is one of the largest nonprofit scientific and educational organizations in the world. It reaches more than 285 million people worldwide each month through its official journal, *National Geographic*, and its four other magazines; the National Geographic Channel; television documentaries; radio programs; films; books; videos and DVDs; maps; and inter-active media. National Geographic has funded more than 8,000 scientific research projects and supports an education program combating geographic illiteracy.

For more information, please call
1-800-NGS LINE (647-5463)
or write to the following address:

National Geographic Society
1145 17th Street N.W.
Washington, D.C. 20036-4688 U.S.A.

Visit us online at www.nationalgeographic.com/books

For information about special discounts for bulk purchases,
please contact National Geographic Books Special Sales: ngspecsales@ngs.org
For rights or permissions inquiries, please contact National
Geographic Books Subsidiary Rights: ngbookrights@ngs.org